Summing Up

A Professional Memoir

SUMMING UP

A PROFESSIONAL MEMOIR

BERTRAM FIELDS

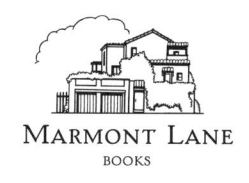

MARMONT LANE
BOOKS

Marmont Lane
BOOKS

Summing Up: A Professional Memoir

Copyright © 2020 by Bertram Fields. All rights reserved. No part of this book may be used or reproduced in any matter whatsoever without written permission except in the case of brief quotations embodied in critical articles and reviews.

For information address Marmont Lane Books
139 South Beverly Drive Suite 318
Beverly Hills, CA USA 90212

www.marmontlane.com

First Edition

Publisher: Bobby Woods/Marmont Lane Books

Design: ♡✕☕=⚡

Cover Portrait: Stephen Douglas

Printed in PRC.

ISBN 13: 978-0-9998527-5-0
Library of Congress Control Number: 2019931447

ALSO BY BERTRAM FIELDS

Royal Blood: Richard III and the Mystery of the Princes

Players: The Mysterious Identity of William Shakespeare

Destiny: A Novel Of Napoleon & Josephine

Shylock: His Own Story

Gloriana: Exploring The Reign Of Elizabeth I

AS D. KINCAID

The Sunset Bomber

The Lawyer's Tale

For

BARBARA

Summing Up

A Professional Memoir

BERTRAM FIELDS

MARMONT LANE
BOOKS

"It is not the critic who counts; not the man who points out how the strong man stumbles, or where the doer of deeds could have done them better. The credit belongs to the man who is actually in the arena, whose face is marred by dust and sweat and blood; who strives valiantly; who errs, who comes short again and again, because there is no effort without error and shortcoming; but who does actually strive to do the deeds; who knows great enthusiasms, the great devotions; who spends himself in a worthy cause; who at the best knows in the end the triumph of high achievement, and who at the worst, if he fails, at least fails while daring greatly, so that his place shall never be with those cold and timid souls who neither know victory nor defeat."

— Theodore Roosevelt

Contents

1	Some Brief Background	15
2	My First Case	21
3	My First Mentor	27
4	The Dirt Case	31
5	Divorce LA Style	35
6	A Close Call	38
7	Two Different Worlds	41
8	A Unique Period	44
9	A Suspect	46
10	Learning Some Tricks	51
11	A Unique Bonus	56
12	The Tipping Point	58
13	Judicial Dicta	62
14	Selling A Lawsuit	67
15	Investments	69
16	Jonathan Livingston Seagull	76
17	Insider Information	82
18	My Worst Moment	84
19	Treaty Obligations	87
20	"Just The Facts, Ma'am"	93
21	Green Underwear	98
22	A Near Miss	101
23	A Good Decision	103
24	The Secret Case	104
25	Beatlemania	106
26	A Lack Of Diversity	112
27	"Tropicana Six"	115
28	The Missing Film	118
29	Consumer Litigation	124
30	Post-Production	127
31	An Extraordinary Opponent	130
32	Recruiting	133
33	I Screw Up	136
34	Saying The Unmentionable	138
35	A Dramatic Life	140
36	How Times Change	147
37	Local Counsel	150
38	"Calling The Kettle Black"	154

SUMMING UP: A PROFESSIONAL MEMOIR

39	FOREIGN ADVENTURES.................156
40	A ROYAL TRAGEDY......................164
41	NEGOTIATION...........................166
42	THE "AD"................................176
43	REMEMBERING A CODE SECTION...178
44	THE LEAST HAPPY FELLA..............179
45	FOREIGN AFFAIRS.......................183
46	A HOLLYWOOD MEETING...........187
47	MY FRIEND, MARIO....................192
48	GOOD PEOPLE AT A BAD TIME.....201
49	AN ENCOUNTER WITH GENIUS.....206
50	WHAT'S A "SEQUEL"?..................213
51	A MAJOR THREAT......................216
52	THE LIAR IN CHIEF....................220
53	MAKING MOVIES.......................223
54	WERE YOU WRONG THEN OR ARE YOU WRONG NOW?.........227
55	"DISNEY WARS".........................238
56	VOIR DIRE...............................249
57	"WALTZING MATILDA"................256
58	HAPPY BIRTHDAY......................259
59	WRITING BOOKS.......................261
60	JACK.....................................267
61	ADMINISTRATIVE LAW?...............271
62	TEACHING..............................294
63	SLY DEALINGS..........................295
64	A CHAIN OF EVENTS..................298
65	ANTHONY...............................302
66	"CIVIL EXTORTION"...................305
67	EXTRAORDINARY PEOPLE...........310
68	"DE-CLIENTING".......................315
69	THE POWER LIST.......................320
70	GREED...................................321
71	MARKETING?...........................323
72	TRUST MATTERS.......................324
73	"OLD GLORY".........................329
74	SUMMING UP..........................331
	ACKNOWLEDGEMENTS................333
	ABOUT THE AUTHOR..................335
	INDEX....................................336
	ILLUSTRATIONS ....I-XXIV

BERTRAM FIELDS

1

SOME BRIEF BACKGROUND

I'M A LAWYER. Much of my practice has involved litigation; but it has also included negotiations of all kinds and other transactional work. I've loved it. All of it.

My late wife, Lydia, used to say that, to me, practicing law was the greatest of games, that I loved it like someone addicted to chess or bridge, only it was much more complex and, for me, much more fun.

I recognize that it's no game, that people's lives, fortunes and reputations are at stake. The responsibility is enormous. Still, I can't help loving the challenge and the process.

This is not an autobiography. It's about cases and events of my law practice. Still, some brief background seems appropriate. I was born in Los Angeles, the son of a surgeon and a ballet dancer. Each day at dawn my father left home to operate. My mother took care of me, wrote poetry and danced. I saw her dance at the Hollywood Bowl.

And, some Saturdays, I'd go with him to the hospital, playing marbles on the floor of the doctor's lounge, while he made his "rounds."

Dad was a charming, highly emotional rogue. A dedicated and skilled doctor, he was also a card player, a gambler and a ladies' man. Mom was a brilliant loner. She loved him and stuck with him, even though her family questioned her sanity.

I attended local schools until Pearl Harbor, when America went to war. My father, far too old to be drafted, told us, with tears in his eyes, that he owed everything to America; and—goddamnit—he was going to defend it. He accepted a commission as a captain in what was then called the Army Air Corps.

We followed Dad from base to base. Our longest stay was in Carlsbad, New Mexico. I attended the local high school, played football (think *Friday Night Lights*) and discovered girls (think serious frustration).

Sadly for me, Dad was transferred to Las Vegas Army Airfield. Believing "Sin City" was no place for an adventurous teenager, they sent me to Los Angeles to live in a boarding house for UCLA students. That's where I spent my last year of high school—on my own at sixteen. I earned money for dates caddying at a local golf course. I ironed my own clothes, made my own decisions and tried to make the best of things.

Dad was finally discharged and my folks returned to LA, where he began rebuilding the medical practice he had left behind to enter the service. I moved back in with them; but, somehow, the relationships had been altered.

At this point, college took over. I went to UCLA, filled with ideas of social justice. I ran for President of the freshman class on a campaign to end racial discrimination in Westwood, where serious discrimination still occurred. The other six candidates campaigned on promises of "a great Freshman Ball" and "free beer." Not surprisingly, I finished seventh. But I'd fallen in love with campus politics (John Ehrlichman and Bob Haldeman—later of Watergate fame—were classmates and key deal makers). I partied a lot and studied some, but not very much.

Somehow, I got sufficient grades and test scores to get into Harvard Law School, where my life was profoundly changed. Exposed to a distinguished and inspiring faculty, as well as classmates who had been at the top of their college classes all over the country, I learned to think—really think—for the first time.

And what a time it was to be at Harvard. I could walk ten minutes from the Law School and attend a music lecture by Aaron Copland or a lecture on poetry by Archibald MacLeish. And the women! Radcliffe still existed, its campus a few blocks from Harvard Yard. It was filled with brilliant young women far better educated than I. They would tease me about my ignorance, my sponge-like eagerness to learn and my quaint "Western accent."

As my first law school year was ending, I had no idea how I was doing. Could I flunk out? Some very bright people had. Well, I thought, if that happened, I'd find something else to do with my life—maybe work on a freighter or just bum around Europe.

It didn't happen. I made the *Harvard Law Review* and graduated magna cum laude. I was offered a job teaching at Stanford Law School; and I spent that summer at Stanford preparing my course, playing volleyball and sporadically studying for the bar exam, which I took in San Francisco that summer.

But, we were in the middle of the Korean War. One day, my father called to say that my final grades had arrived from Harvard, and that I got six "A's". I said "Dad, I only took five courses." He laughed and said the 6th "A" was from my draft board. I'd been classified "1A." I was about to be drafted. What a time for humor.

The Dean of Stanford Law School offered to intercede with my draft board, seeking a deferment to allow me to teach. But, I remembered my Dad's decision after Pearl Harbor. I owed this country, just as he did. I told the Dean "no thanks." Having just passed the California bar, I drove to Hamilton Air Force Base north of San Francisco and was sworn in as a First Lieutenant in the U.S. Air Force. AO2251564. You never forget your serial number.

I was in Air Force JAG; and, for two years, I tried court martials virtually every day. It was superb training, and I loved it. Once, when I was stationed at RAF Station Brize Norton in England, the American Base Commander ordered me court martialed. My crime? "Over-zealous defense of a guilty airman," which he labeled "conduct unbecoming an officer." He neglected to mention that my client, the "airman" in question, had been found "not guilty" after a vigorously contested court martial. Still, I was terrified. Friends said that, if the military powers wanted to "get" you, they "got" you. Could they really convict me for successfully defending a client, albeit a military client? If so, could they send me to Leavenworth while I appealed?

Fortunately, the Base Commander's order had to be approved at Eighth Air Force Headquarters at High Wycombe near London. The Senior Judge Advocate there issued an order countersigned by the Commander of the Eighth Air Force, making it quite clear that successfully defending an airman in a court martial was not a crime. All charges against Lt. Fields were dismissed. I was a free man—not popular with the Base Commander, but free.

On my return to a stateside air base, I was assigned to drafting appellate opinions at Fifteenth Air Force Headquarters. When my two years in the Air Force were almost up, I was offered the chance to move to Madrid to be the point man for the Air Force in negotiating leases for new air base sites throughout Europe. My proposed new commanding officer had already selected a lovely villa for me on a hillside overlooking Madrid. All I had to do was to sign on for an additional three years.

It was a fantastic opportunity. But I was married, my wife was pregnant and I had already accepted a job with an LA law firm. Perhaps foolishly, I turned the Air Force down. Sometimes I wonder what my life would have been had I accepted the Air Force deal and stayed on in Europe. Probably, I'd still be there.

Many years later, I was offered another opportunity to change professions, this time to become the head of production at a major studio. It was a fascinating proposal for a dramatic change in my life. This time, I considered it seriously, but, once again, I decided to stay with the law.

It's always intriguing to contemplate the road not traveled. But I can't complain. I probably made the right choice. My law practice has kept me alert and intrigued for over 60 years. Yes, there's been tragedy. Lydia, my wife of 25 years, died tragically of cancer in 1986. But, five years later, I married Barbara; and we remain very happily together. My son, Jim, has an extraordinary level of intelligence, a unique sense of humor and an unwavering moral compass. My grandchildren are a delight. All things considered, it's been a very good life.

2

My First Case

After leaving the Air Force in 1955, I began the practice of law in LA. Because of the many court martials I had tried, I considered myself a trial lawyer. I'd take on anything—and I did.

My first case was one I can't name, for reasons that will become obvious. It was a criminal case, and my client (I'll call him "Mr. S"), although a Beverly Hills resident, was accused of sexually stroking an undercover policeman in the men's room of a porn movie house on Main Street in downtown LA—what used to be called "Skid Row." Somewhat different from the assignments my Harvard classmates were getting at Cravath in New York and Covington & Burling in D.C.? Yes it was; but that's what I wanted.

I began by having Mr. S take a polygraph test—I thought that a positive result might persuade the City Attorney to drop the case. Unfortunately, Mr. S failed the test. Still, he insisted that he was innocent—that the test was wrong. Undeterred, I pushed on.

I went downtown to the City Attorney's office, hoping to look at their file—something defense counsel could do as a matter of right in military prosecutions. But there seemed to be no such right in prosecutions by the City Attorney. And, everyone I spoke to there said, "you gotta talk to Rothman."

Finally, I met "Rothman," then the City Attorney's chief prosecutor. He was a tall, skinny freckle-faced young man who shook my hand heartily and said, "Sure, kid, you can see the file." "Kid"? I thought he might be two years older than I. But he did let me see the file. It wasn't promising.

Soon, we were engaged in a real jury trial—my first. The People vs. Mr. S. My opponent wasn't "Rothman"—it wasn't that important a case, and it seemed a slam dunk for the prosecution.

After opening statements, the arresting officer took the stand. He testified, as you would expect, supplying each element of the crime. My client, he said, had stroked his penis and propositioned him in the men's room, as they stood next to each other at the urinals. He seemed sure of himself and, unfortunately, believable. The jury was attentive to his testimony, most of them taking careful notes.

I figured that his cross-examination was my only chance. In looking at the file, I'd noticed that the cop had been on Robbery Detail at the time, but that, after the arrest, he'd been reassigned to the Vice Squad. Strange.

I tried what I call a "no lose" question. Either answer might help.

"In fact, officer, after you made this arrest, you were demoted—demoted from the Robbery Detail to the Vice Squad—isn't that true?"

"That's not true, counselor. That's a promotion! We all wanted to be on Vice. I got that transfer because of my good work."

"You got it because of this arrest, right?"

"It didn't hurt."

Okay I thought, that gives me an argument. He needed to make a Vice arrest to get that transfer. There's the motive to lie. But I knew I shouldn't push it. Instead, I tried another "no lose" question.

"Well, officer, isn't it true that my client just brushed against you—sort of by accident?" A "yes" would be great. But a "no" might lead him to exaggerate.

"No counsel, that's not true at all; and I think you know it."

He was angry. Good. I saw a chance.

"Come on, officer, if it was more than just brushing by you, just how long do you claim he stroked you?" My voice oozed disbelief.

The cop didn't hesitate. He fired back. "At least 45 seconds, counselor, at least 45 seconds."

One thing I'd learned in trying all those court martials, you make a good point, move on—don't try to underline it or you may lose it. I just said "your witness" and sat down.

The prosecutor, caught off guard, said "no questions" in a tone indicating he didn't need any. He rested the government's case.

I'd told the jury in my opening statement that Mr. S would testify, rather than take the Fifth Amendment. But I decided to make his testimony as brief as possible. He explained to the jury that, on the night in question, he was feeling tense and nervous. To relax, he went for a long drive. He ended up on Main Street, and, when he saw a theatre still open at midnight, he decided to take in a movie.

He testified that, after a time, he went to the men's room and was standing at the urinal when a man at the next urinal asked, "Film get you worked up?" Not wanting to be rude, Mr. S replied, "Sure." The man left and Mr. S returned to his seat. A few minutes later, he was arrested by the man who had been at the urinal and another man. Both wore civilian clothes, but both were policemen. I asked, "Did you touch that man in any way—any way at all?" I got a firm "No." That was it. I rested our case; and there was no rebuttal by the prosecution.

In closing argument, I walked up to the jury box. "You've got a choice. You can believe the officer or you can believe Mr. S. One of them is telling the truth. The other is not.

"Remember, unless you believe 'beyond a reasonable doubt' that it's the officer who's telling the truth, you must find Mr. S not guilty.

"You might ask, 'Why would the officer make up a story like this?' He's told us why. He wanted to get off the very dangerous robbery detail and get on the much safer Vice Squad. As he told you himself, it was a big promotion. So he was determined to make a Vice arrest. Probably he thought Mr. S was some sort of deviant even being in that kind of movie house at midnight. So he felt justified in arresting him, even without any evidence.

"But one thing tells you for sure who's telling us the truth. If you're wearing a watch, please hold it up and look at it." Standing right at the rail in front of the jury box, I took off my watch and held it up in my left hand.

"Here's an officer of the law trained to give accurate estimates of time and distance. And what does he tell us? He's standing at the next urinal and he claims my client began to stroke him. Remember just one stroke was enough to constitute the crime. After one stroke Mr. S could have been arrested. And remember this officer of the law told you he was stroked for 45 seconds. He said it twice, '45 seconds!'

"Let's say I'm the officer and this rail is my client's private parts. Let's repeat the so-called crime." I started stroking the front rail of the jury box with my right hand—moving it back and forth across the wooden rail.

After maybe ten strokes I said, "Okay, that's five seconds. One stroke was enough to constitute the crime. But does he arrest my client? No. According to him, he stands there and keeps getting stroked."

I continued to stroke the rail back and forth, back and forth.

"Okay that's 10 seconds. Here they are—this officer of the law—just standing there getting stroked by my client. What are they talking about? The score of last night's Dodger game?"

I continued stroking. By the time I got to 20 seconds, the entire jury was roaring with laughter.

The jury retired to the jury room to elect a foreperson and deliberate. In less than half an hour, they sent out word that they'd already reached a verdict.

Next came a moment I've lived through over and over again. But this was the first time in civilian life. The jury filed in and took their seats. At the Judge's direction, they handed him their verdict form. After reading it, he handed it to the clerk, who returned it to the jury, directing that the verdict be read. The foreman looked up at the Judge and said, "We the jury find the defendant not guilty."

Wow! I'd won my first trial. It was a very good feeling. I wanted to repeat it—as often as I could.

"Rothman," the deputy city attorney who graciously let me see the file, turned out to be Frank Rothman, who became a brilliant trial lawyer and, over the years, was, at different times, an opponent, co-counsel, a hostile witness and, through it all, a friend.

3

My First Mentor

When I was still at Harvard, I was recruited by Gang Tyre & Brown, an excellent Los Angeles law firm headed by Martin Gang, a distinguished lawyer and Harvard graduate. When I was ready to leave the Air Force, the Gang firm made me a firm offer. But so did David Tannenbaum, then a legendary California lawyer, whose extraordinary practice included representing the head of every major film studio.

I liked Martin Gang very much, as well as his partner, Mickey Rudin, a highly skilled lawyer who, like me, had been an editor of the *Harvard Law Review* and had been the Gang partner who first recruited me by telephone on a snowy night when I was still at Harvard.

The problem was that more than one person advised me confidentially that Martin Gang's health wasn't good, so he probably wouldn't practice much longer. David Tannenbaum, by contrast, was a big, healthy guy likely to continue his successful practice for many, many years.

It was close, but I accepted the Tannenbaum offer. The advice I'd been given proved more than just inaccurate. Three years later, David Tannenbaum died suddenly of a cerebral hemorrhage. Contrary to my "inside information," Martin Gang continued in the active and successful practice of law for the next forty years.

But, I did get one marvelous benefit from my choice of firms. My mentor in the firm was a magnificent older lawyer named Louis Swarts. "Louie," as he pronounced it, was a graduate of the Harvard class of 1901. He had founded the firm with David Tannenbaum, but, by this time, he was practicing pretty much half time.

Louie was a tall man with a hawk-like face and splendid white hair. He had been a young trial lawyer in New York; and, although he loved California, he refused to abandon the tenets of classic New York attire. When spring arrived, Louie inevitably wore his seersucker suit and straw "boater" hat—even in the rain. After September first, no matter how hot the LA weather, the seersucker and boater were tucked away and Louie was in his three-piece flannel suits.

Louie had a towering reputation in his day, having been the founder of the Copyright Society and the representative of such luminaries as Jeanette MacDonald and Jerome Kern. But, much of that was in the past. Kern had died and, although Jeanette MacDonald remained a client, her career was at its end.

When Jeanette was the biggest star in Hollywood, she had a contractual dispute with MGM, then the most important studio. In an attempt to resolve the problem, Louie Swarts attended a meeting with L.B. Mayer, then the legendary head of MGM. They didn't like each other, and soon they both grew angry. Louie put on his hat and told L.B. he'd never speak to him again. Mayer replied that was fine with him.

In a rage, Louie reached for the giant brass handle on Mayer's office door. But the handle came off in Louie's hand, and the door remained closed and locked. Mayer used his phone to call MGM maintenance. But before they arrived and could get the door open, Louie Swarts and L. B. Mayer were locked in the room together not speaking to each other for over an hour, Louie pacing the floor while Mayer smoked cigar after cigar in angry silence.

In one of our first conversations, Louie asked me what I thought was the best restaurant in the Boston area. Without hesitation, I responded "Locke-Ober"—a splendid, classical restaurant that, sadly, is no longer there.

"Well, my dear"—Louie called everyone he liked "my dear"—"I am barred from that splendid establishment."

"You're barred from Locke-Ober?"

"Yes, my dear. It's a long story. When I was at Harvard, I was intrigued with a young woman who performed at the 'Old Howard' in Scollay Square. The 'Old Howard' was a famous burlesque house—now long gone.

"Well," Louie continued, "one evening I had obtained a post-performance engagement with this young lady; and we were served a late dinner in one of the private rooms that were then available upstairs at Locke-Ober—rooms furnished not only with a table and chairs, but also with a commodious sofa.

"We enjoyed a splendid dinner, including a roast of beef and an excellent bottle of wine. And, my purpose going beyond the meal, I glanced over at the sofa and began to remove the young lady's garments.

"Well, my dear, things went well enough until I encountered a rubberized garment that clung to her body like a second skin. I didn't know it at the time, but it was what we now call a 'girdle.'

"Much as I tried, I was simply unable to remove this garment. Thinking to cut the Gordian Knot, like Alexander the Great, I reached for the large carving knife we had used for the roast. My plan was to cut the garment away, freeing the young lady's lovely body.

"Unfortunately, the lady misperceived my intentions and began to scream for help. Quickly, there came a pounding on the door and two large, stern looking men entered. They quickly helped the lady into her dress and, hearing her complaint, turned to me with an angry expression, demanding that I leave the premises and never again return to Locke-Ober.

"And so, my dear, I have never again visited that splendid establishment."

Obviously, after 50 years had passed, Louie could have dined at Locke-Ober with no problem. But he never did. That was like him. A promise was a promise.

Louie had many wonderful stories and, in between telling them, he taught me a lot about being a lawyer. He was an extraordinary man and I remember him with great fondness.

4

The Dirt Case

Another early trial was one in which the client had to be talked into turning it over to someone as young and inexperienced as I. It wasn't easy. David Tannenbaum had to guarantee the client I wouldn't lose. Then, of course, he told me of his guarantee and made it clear that losing was not an option.

Our client was a major construction company, and our opponent was an earth contractor, a company that supplied earth to fill depressed areas where homes were to be built. In this instance, our client had a giant hole to fill many yards long, wide and very deep.

The issue arose after our opponent's trucks had filled the massive hole with dirt. They claimed this took a number of truckloads that were twice what our client estimated they needed; and they claimed they could produce signed "trip tickets" for every load. Our client didn't believe it and had sent them half the money they demanded. Now they sued for the rest.

The trial was before a middle-aged Judge in Inglewood, California. My concern over David's assurance to the client was magnified tenfold when, in an early recess, my opponent and the Judge openly discussed their golf game for the coming weekend.

I momentarily contemplated asking the Judge to recuse himself, but decided against it. Instead, I plunged ahead, doing my best to avoid disaster. The first two witnesses from our opponent testified to fairly innocuous matters; and I followed a rule I'd learned in numerous court martials: if a witness doesn't hurt your case, your best bet is generally not to cross-examine—better to say "no questions," telegraphing to the jury that the testimony was meaningless—a waste of their time. I followed this rule, giving a bored "no questions" when they'd each concluded their direct examinations.

Late that afternoon after court, David Tannenbaum asked me to come into his office. It seemed that our client's foreman had been in court that morning and had reported to the client that, "This green kid's going to lose our case for sure. He didn't even know to cross-examine their witnesses."

I explained the situation to David; and he passed the explanation on to the client with his recommendation to be patient and his repeated assurances (at my expense) that we'd certainly win.

Two days of trial followed, with fierce attacks over the validity of our opponent's "trip tickets," the possibility that half the truck loads had been delivered elsewhere—something I suggested, but couldn't prove. We had the testimony of our project manager and our foreman providing a radically different estimate of the number of trucks that had delivered the dirt and the amount of dirt that had been delivered.

At this point, the case could go either way. But, as we neared the end, I hit on an idea that might turn the tide. I had established the size and capacity of the trucks our opponent had used and the fact that each truck was filled to capacity. But that didn't tell us how much dirt was delivered in how many trucks; the fundamental issues still remained.

As the case was nearing its close, I called my final and hopefully decisive witness—one I had lined up just two days before, having had an idea I believed could win the case. A gray-haired gentleman entered the courtroom with the cuffs of his trousers rolled up and his shoes covered with dirt. He was carrying a long steel rod with engraved numbers. He took the stand and explained that he was a professor of geology at Cal Tech and had just come from measuring the depth, width and length of the hole with the long rod he displayed. He had pushed the rod through the fill until he struck bottom in at least 64 locations, satisfying himself that the bottom of the hole was level and as to its depth from the surface. He then explained that, given these measurements of the hole, there was a maximum amount of dirt that could possibly have been placed in it and that given the agreed capacity of our opponent's trucks, only half of the truckloads of dirt claimed by our opponent could possibly have been delivered to our client's hole. The claim that twice the number of truckloads had been delivered—as our opponents argued—was physically impossible. Half the number claimed was all the dirt the hole could possibly take.

Opposing counsel tried to cross-examine the professor; but he got nowhere. We rested our cases, and both sides looked to the Judge. I anticipated that he would take the matter under submission and send us his written decision in a few days. I still feared his golfing relationship with my opponent.

I was wrong—dead wrong. Without missing a beat, the Judge announced that his decision was ready. He pronounced judgment in our favor, totally denying our opponent's claim.

Our client was delighted; but, given David's reckless promise, he was not really surprised. And I—I was mostly relieved.

5

Divorce LA Style

One morning, David Tannenbaum called me into his office to tell me that, while we were not his regular lawyers, we were going to be brought in as co-counsel for Edward G. Robinson, then a huge film star, in his high profile "divorce." That's what we called it in those days—now it's called "dissolution," I can't tell you why.

The problem was that "Eddie," as David called him, had all his money tied up in his fabulous art collection—then probably the most valuable private collection in the world. Eddie wanted to sell, but Gladys, his wife of many years, refused to sell a single painting.

David and Mendel Silberberg, senior partner of the firm that regularly represented Eddie, had an idea. If the paintings could be taken off the walls where Gladys was accustomed to seeing them and removed from the house, she would ultimately relent and allow them to be sold.

The court had issued a temporary restraining order preventing Eddie Robinson from <u>selling</u> any of the paintings; but there was no order against his <u>lending</u> them. So, David and Mendel had worked out a clandestine deal with Rick Brown, then the Director of the LA County

Museum of Art (LACMA). While Gladys was away in Palm Springs, Eddie would lend the entire collection to LACMA, so that, when she returned, she'd find bare walls, and, after her initial rage, she'd finally relent and agree to a sale.

How did that relate to me? Here's how. I was to be at the Robinson home at midnight to meet Arthur Groman, then a young lawyer from the Silberberg firm. We were to supervise the loading of the entire Robinson collection into a fleet of LACMA trucks.

So, at midnight, Art Groman and I embarked on an amazing adventure. First, we examined the collection. Fantastic! Cézanne's *The Black Clock*, perhaps his masterpiece, Van Gogh's *La Père Tanguy*, Tahitian paintings by Gauguin, Degas' dancers, and assorted Picassos, Renoirs, Pissarros and works by every great painter of the era. It was incredible.

And so, for the next three hours, Art Groman and I, with a team from LACMA, physically carried these fantastic works out to the LACMA trucks, where curators from the museum were carefully wrapping and stacking them. I personally carried Degas' wonderful bronze ballet dancer out to the trucks. Then, I went back for Cézanne's *The Black Clock*.

When Gladys Robinson returned the next day, she flew into an understandable rage. Her lawyer immediately sought to hold us all in contempt. But the judge correctly ruled that Eddie had been restrained from "selling" the collection, not from lending it, and this was clearly a loan to LACMA, not a sale.

David and Mendel Silberberg had been right. After a time, Gladys relented, the case was settled and the entire collection was sold to Stavros Niarchos, the Greek ship owner, for what, at the time, was a record price.

I had a final dinner with Eddie Robinson, who after a few drinks, told me tearfully to think of Gladys not as she was now, but as the slim, lovely girl he'd once been in love with. I was moved. A week later, Eddie was back with his new love, ensconced in New York's Stanhope Hotel, just across the street from the Metropolitan Museum.

Arthur Groman went on to become one of America's leading lawyers. Like Frank Rothman, Art and I were opponents and friends for many years. Both are now dead; and I miss them.

6

A Close Call

When David Tannenbaum died, one of the clients I inherited was Mike Todd, a hugely successful New York producer who had married Elizabeth Taylor and had just produced the spectacular *Around the World in 80 Days*, which set box office records and won the Academy Award for Best Picture.

I represented Mike on various things; and, when we were meeting one afternoon, he told me he was flying to New York the next day for some meetings—could I come along. Mike had his own plane and it sounded exciting and, of course, I was flattered. But I had a court hearing the next day and, regretfully, had to decline.

The following day, driving home, I heard a news bulletin on my car radio. Mike's plane had crashed somewhere in the mountains. There were no survivors. I was sorry for Mike and his kids. But I was rocked by my own close call. But for a court hearing, that would have been "it."

I went on to represent Mike's son in presenting a new motion picture process financed by his father and called "Smell-O-Vision." A strange "professor" had invented a bizarre machine consisting of numerous pipes and valves that would blow "actual smells" into pipes laid under the theater seats. The pipes had holes from which the smells would flow into the audience. Mike Jr. and his assistants supervised the installation of this complex machine in the Carthay Circle Theatre for the premiere of *Scent of Mystery*, the first "Smell-O-Vision" film.

It was a gala crowd that gathered that night for the premiere. Would the industry be changed by the introduction of smell as it had been by the introduction of sound? While I had never discussed it with Mike, he had apparently thought so, and Mike, Jr. was doing his best to make it happen.

The night of the premiere finally arrived. The distinguished audience was finally seated and the performance began. In an early scene, the hero was getting a shoe shine. There was a loud "hiss" and, from pipes under every seat, came the unmistakable smell of shoe polish. Okay, not a bad start.

Then the hero went to his girl's apartment and handed her a huge bouquet of roses. The pipes hissed again and, again, the audience sniffed. What was that? It was sort of like roses, but mixed with shoe polish. What the professor hadn't worked out was how to clear one smell before the next smell was released. The roses were there. But so was the shoe polish.

Throughout the film, for those few who stayed, there were murmured queries of "What's that?" "I think it's garlic." "No it's gasoline." "Maybe garlic flavored gasoline."

The next day, one newspaper reported that "Smell-O-Vision lived up to its name—it stunk." It was the end of a bold experiment. I felt sorry for Mike Jr., who was a good young guy, trying his best to carry on his famous father's idea.

In the course of representing Mike, I met his famously beautiful wife, Elizabeth Taylor. Some time after Mike's death, I heard that Elizabeth was planning to marry Eddie Fisher. Having been Mike's lawyer and feeling somewhat protective of his family, I called Elizabeth to suggest that she ask Fisher to sign a prenuptial agreement that would protect her and Mike's family from any claim Fisher might make to what had been Mike's assets, in which Elizabeth now had a significant share, as well as to Elizabeth's own future earnings, which would otherwise be community property. Elizabeth was enraged. How dare I suggest that "Mr. Fisher" would ever make such a claim! She hung up, and it was years before we spoke again. Of course, when they divorced, "Mr. Fisher" made just such a claim. Elizabeth didn't call to say "Wow, were you right!" But I never thought she would.

7

Two Different Worlds

My firm represented an enormously wealthy New York financier who was engaged in a monumental battle with his children over the terms of a trust.

At this point, I was still considered too young and with an insufficient reputation to argue this important a case; and we retained Walter Ely, a uniquely talented trial lawyer, who later became a Justice of the Federal Court of Appeals for the Ninth Circuit.

The New York lawyer for our client was the notorious Roy Cohn, who'd represented Senator Joe McCarthy in the legendary Army-McCarthy hearings. Cohn was not formally counsel of record in our case. But he'd be flying out to attend the hearing.

Walter Ely, for whom I developed great respect and fondness, never cared much for doing research, so that became my job. I delved into the intricacies of trust law and came up with what I considered a strategy that I felt would win the case for our client. I then prepared a detailed memorandum, setting out the legal authorities and the strategy that I was sure would do the job.

But I had one other assignment. I was to meet Roy Cohn at the airport when he arrived from New York. I was in the back seat of the limo when the driver returned with our famous co-counsel and his pigskin luggage. I introduced myself and, as the car pulled away from the airport, I removed my memorandum from my briefcase and launched into an excited explanation of my legal theory, of which I was very proud.

Cohn simply raised his hand. "Listen, kid," he said in a gruff New York voice, "we don't need that. Here's the thing. How do we get to the judge?"

"How do we *what*?"

"Get to the judge, for Christ's sake! Don't you speak English?"

Stunned, I said, "If you mean what I think Mr. Cohn, we don't."

"Yeah sure, kid. Anyway spare me the memo. I'll deal with this."

The rest of our drive was made in silence.

A few days later, Walter Ely, who had read my memorandum, won the case, not so much with my arcane theories of trust law, but by telling the court, in an emotional tone, "This great man, in the sunset of his life, should not be tyrannized by his ungrateful relatives."

I never found out if Roy Cohn had really tried to "get to the judge." I heard a rumor that he'd actually paid some money to someone, who, in reality, had no way of "getting to the judge," but was glad to take Cohn's money. I do know one thing. If he'd ever suggested such a move to Walter, he'd have been thrown out of the office—and I mean physically.

Years later, I had a New York case involving a client of Cohn's. This time, he couldn't have been more cordial and cooperative. Either he'd mellowed with the passing years or he thought I now had sufficient importance to warrant courteous treatment. I'm sure he'd forgotten that I was the kid in the car so many years before.

8

A Unique Period

THE THINGS I'VE WRITTEN ABOUT in this time frame occurred in a rather singular period in the city's cultural history. My late wife Lydia and I lived in an apartment high in the hills overlooking the Sunset Strip. Each night I'd come home at 8 or 9 o'clock to a pitcher of martinis, and we'd get blasted, listening to music and looking out at the million-lighted city.

Down below me, the Strip seethed with hippies, runaways and druggies. It was time to "turn on, tune in and drop out"; and what seemed to be a grungy, lost generation peopled the area.

A few of them appeared from time to time in court. A federal judge threw out a case when the plaintiff's lawyer showed up to argue a motion in filthy jeans and a T-shirt. No one even commented any more about lawyers appearing in court with long hair, scruffy beards and earrings.

One day, I had a pretrial conference with a lawyer I'll call Sam. While we were waiting for our case to be called, I handed Sam my pretrial statement. This was a case involving a motion picture contract and disputed rights in the film. My statement was captioned with the names of our clients, mine, a small film company, and Sam's, a screenwriter.

Sam smiled—I thought somewhat vaguely—and handed me his pretrial statement. It was captioned The Acme Trucking Company vs. Gardner.

That was nuts! "Sam," I said, "you've brought a statement about the wrong case."

He gave me a sly smile. "No problem," he said. Taking out his pen, he crossed out the Acme Trucking caption and, in a somewhat shaky hand, wrote in the name of the correct plaintiff.

"But Sam," I said, "your statement is all about a trucking accident. Our case is about film rights."

"No problem," he repeated. "I'll explain to the Judge. Anyway, these pretrials don't mean shit."

But Sam was wrong. The Judge was kind enough not to enter an immediate judgment against Sam's client. But he sent him home with a stern lecture and continued the pretrial conference to a later date, warning Sam that the next time there would be "consequences."

Sam got lucky that time. The next time, not so much. A few months later, I heard that Sam was arrested for smoking pot in the Courthouse hallway. Yes—in the Courthouse hallway outside of twenty courtrooms with a Deputy Sheriff sitting inside every one.

I never saw him again. I hope he's alive and "clean." But I doubt it.

9

A Suspect

ONE OF THE FIRST MAJOR CLIENTS I got on my own was Mike Garrison, a brilliant and talented feature film and television producer. He'd produced two very successful films, as well as the hit TV series *The Wild, Wild West*. Mike was on his way to the top. I handled contract negotiations for him, as well as a dispute with a network, and I was proud of being his lawyer.

Mike had also become a close friend. He had just bought and moved into a beautiful and expensive new home in the hills above Sunset Boulevard. One night at dinner, Mike announced that he was about to leave on a trip to Europe. He gave me a key to the house, lest any problems arise.

The next morning, I got a shocking call from the LA Police. Mike had apparently fallen down the stairs of his new house and had suffered severe and probably fatal head injuries. Could I come up to the house as soon as possible?

I asked where he was hospitalized and went there first. But Mike was in a coma and obviously near death. He died that night.

After leaving the hospital, I drove to Mike's house and encountered a scary situation. The first thing I saw was a chalk outline of Mike's body at the foot of the marble staircase that had been such an important architectural feature of his new entryway. Then, I was confronted by a homicide detective, and was quickly surprised.

"Where were you last night between midnight and three AM?"

"At home asleep," I said, grasping the idea that I could be a suspect in what could be a murder case.

"Can anyone verify that?"

"Sure, my wife can."

"Anyone else?"

"No, who else would know I was home asleep?"

The detective made a note in his pad. If I had been advising a client in that situation, I would have told him to stop the conversation right there and get a lawyer. Of course, being a lawyer and being "the client" myself, I didn't.

"You had a key to this house, right?"

"Yes."

"When did you last use that key?"

"I never used it. He just gave it to me last night."

"And you were the executor of his will, isn't that so?"

"I didn't even know he had a will. We never discussed it."

"You're his lawyer. He's a rich guy, and you never discussed his will? Is that what you're saying?"

"That's right. I'm not an estate planner; and he's a young guy. It just never came up."

"You're saying you didn't expect to get a big executor's fee if he died?"

"That's correct," I replied. Then I decided to be somewhat more aggressive.

"Listen, Lieutenant, Mike was my most important client. I could have earned major fees—<u>if</u> he was alive. If he was dead I got nothing."

"You're saying you didn't know you're his executor?"

"Am I? If so, I didn't know. I didn't even know he had a will. Did he?"

"We don't know yet. I thought you'd know."

"Sorry, I don't. Now I'd like to get to my office, if that's okay?"

"It's okay, but you're not planning to leave town any time soon, are you?"

"No, but are you saying I'm a suspect?"

"Right now, anyone who knew Mr. Garrison is a suspect."

I left, somewhat shaken, but hoping I didn't show it. It turned out that Mike had no will. The police never contacted me again, and they never solved the crime. If there was a crime, which I doubt.

Probably Mike, who drank heavily, was simply drunk, slipped and fell down the stairs, hitting his head on the unforgiving marble. The irony is that he was having those stairs carpeted the next week.

I had to make arrangements for Mike's casket and burial. It was a surreal experience. I began speaking to a representative of the mortuary. "I know that Mr. Garrison would have wanted the simplest coffin you have. He was like that. Let's look at those."

"Certainly. This over here is our least expensive model. Very nice—if you don't mind seepage."

"Seepage?"

"Yes, you see, in some situations, it happens with these caskets."

I didn't know what "seepage" was, and I didn't want to know. The man went on to tell me that, since Mr. Garrison was a very large man, we'd probably need a customized casket.

"Oh, he wasn't that big, and he wouldn't have wanted the extra expense."

"Right. Well, if necessary, we could fold Mr. Garrison."

"Fold him?" I said, choking.

"Yes, to fit the standard size. Not a problem."

And it went on from there. I was offered a dark suit with one unusual feature.

"This suit has no back."

"Well, you see, he'll be lying on his back. You won't see the back of the suit."

When I was offered a back rest for Mike's coffin, I'd had it. I finally said "No."

I "produced" Mike's funeral at Forest Lawn, playing the records he loved and giving a short talk about what a brilliant and funny man he was.

And that was the last of my friend and client, except for some fine memories. After he died, I found out that Mike had false teeth. For some reason, the hospital gave them to me. I buried them in the garden of our home in France. He'd always wanted to visit us there, but had never made it. Now, in a sense, he had.

10

Learning Some Tricks

In the early days of my practice, I would have taken any case that walked in the door. But many of my earlier cases were divorces. In those days, before the enactment of the "no fault" divorce law, we had battles over adultery, cruelty and desertion. Divorce cases were mini-wars, the adversaries were not just to be defeated. They were to be destroyed. Why? The division of community property, the award of "alimony" (the term then used) and, realistically, even child custody, turned on the outcome of the trial. An example was Dr. Petter Lindstrom's famous case against Ingrid Bergman, who lost custody of her children because of her affair on the Island of Stromboli with Roberto Rossellini, her Italian director.

I represented a talented and successful director in a bitter divorce case against his wife, an attractive, much younger woman, represented by one of the country's most famous and skilled lawyers, Arthur Crowley.

Arthur contended that my client was secretly gay. Of course, the word wasn't yet coined, so Crowley's word was "queer" when talking to me, and "effeminate" when addressing Judge Allen Lynch, who refused to admit expert opinion testimony on the subject.

My client had assured me that Crowley's claim wasn't true. Still, in those years, a conservative judge might feel hostility toward a man who was even alleged to be gay. And, while Judge Lynch seemed unreceptive to Crowley's argument, I worried that his simply making the claim might affect the Court's decision.

Crowley called a witness who had attended a party at the couple's home. Essentially, his testimony was that my client was drinking heavily—not too damaging. Crowley asked the witness about their conversations. After he testified to a brief and relatively unimportant conversation, the man said, almost as an afterthought, that my client "said some other things too, but that was the main part." Then, strangely, Crowley seemed disturbed and the witness looked embarrassed. "No," Crowley said, "don't get into that. You've answered the question."

"Wow," I thought, making a note to get the rest of the conversation Crowley seemed so anxious to hide. When Arthur ended his direct examination, I raced to the podium. "All right," I said, "tell us the rest of your conversation that night."

Now Crowley leapt to his feet. "Objection your honor! Outside the scope of direct examination." He seemed desperate.

Sensing I had something really devastating, I responded that the witness couldn't give us half of a conversation and conceal the other half. Judge Lynch agreed. He allowed the question.

Now the witness seemed nervous, as if reluctant to testify to the rest of the conversation, making me even more sure that I was onto a case winner.

"Okay sir, tell us what else was said."

"Well, I didn't want to get into this; but your client said he found me very attractive and maybe we could 'get together' some time."

Bang! I realized I'd been suckered into a trap by Crowley. He'd coached the witness to throw out the line that more was said and to appear reluctant to talk about it. Meanwhile, Crowley would act like the omitted part would hurt his client, so I'd be desperate to get it into evidence. Then, when I forced the witness to tell it, the damaging stuff that might otherwise have been excluded would get into evidence and, worse, it would seem highly credible, because the witness had tried his best not to bring it out.

It was a clever trap, a lesson I learned that day, and a device I've used since then.

The case was starting to look really bad. But, fortunately, the day before the trial, I'd driven into old Hollywood, taking a chance on interviewing the wife's mother. I'd considered it unlikely that I'd get anything worthwhile from her, and I was surprised she'd even see me. But, trying court martials, I'd learned not to rely on investigator's reports and to go out in the field myself to interview every potential witness. So, I thought I'd give it a try. And what I got was gold. Before I left, I handed the mother a subpoena.

When it came time to put on our case, the mother testified that, on repeated occasions, her daughter had told her she was in love with a good looking young man, that she'd been sleeping with him for some time and was going to divorce my client to marry him.

I could tell Crowley was stunned. So was the Judge. This was case-dispositive testimony from the plaintiff's own mother. Because the wife was plainly guilty of adultery, under the rules that then applied she could get neither alimony nor any of the community property. Turning to the witness, the Judge said, "Madam, do you realize what you're doing to your own daughter?"

"I do and I'm sorry. But Mr. Fields told me I had to tell the truth."

When the mother was excused, we rested our case. Judge Lynch announced a recess and returned to his chambers.

Then, Crowley taught me another trick. He went to the front of the courtroom, stood just outside the door to the Judge's chambers and shouted at the top of his voice seemingly at me, but in reality for the Judge's ears.

"That was the most outrageous, lying testimony I've ever heard!"

The bailiff rose and motioned Crowley away from the Judge's door. But the damage was done. Obviously, the Judge must have heard.

Would it affect his decision? It didn't. Given the evidence of adultery, Judge Lynch granted the divorce and the community property to my client. There was no alimony, and his wife had to pay her own fees. It was a huge win for my guy, and a very close call.

A week later, when I was pulling my car in front of a restaurant with my late wife, Lydia, I saw Arthur Crowley getting into the car in front of ours. He stopped, turned around and walked purposefully over to our car—not to my side, but to Lydia's. He motioned for her to roll down her window, which she did.

"I just wanted to tell you what an outstanding lawyer your husband is. He's going to be great. I mean it, he'll be one of the great ones."

He just turned and walked back to his car.

Many years later, when I heard that Arthur had died, I wrote his widow, telling her about that evening, what he'd said and how much it meant to a green, young lawyer, especially from someone who already was "one of the great ones."

11

A Unique Bonus

YOU MAY RECALL an old short story called "The Juggler of Our Lady" by Anatole France. It's about the monks of a monastery who take in a snow-covered stranger on Christmas Eve. He's wearing shabby, patched clothing and is near freezing. He tells them he's a traveling juggler, who's out of work.

They give him supper, and then he watches as one monk after another places a gift before the altar of the Virgin Mary in the monastery chapel. One monk places a beautiful painting before the altar, another a marvelously carved crucifix. These were remarkable gifts made by the monks with great care during the year.

Finally, all the splendid gifts had been placed before the altar, and the monks had retired. But one monk went from room to room extinguishing the many candles. When he came to the door of the chapel, he was stunned. There alone before the altar of the Virgin was the traveler. He was juggling before the statue of the Virgin. It was the only gift he could give.

You may wonder what that story has to do with my legal career. Well it does—sort of. Many years ago I represented Sir Cedric Hardwicke in a trial. Sir Cedric was a once famous British actor, who was getting on in years. Despite his having been knighted by the Queen, parts were now few and far between. In short, he was broke.

For me, however, in those early days, he was still a well-known man and probably as close as I'd come to an English knight—even a penurious one. I tried his case, and we were successful. Over the years, since then, a number of clients, having lived through a trial with me and having obtained a good result, have given me a gift or a bonus over and above the fee. For example, when Jeffrey Katzenberg successfully sued Disney and had paid his significant legal fees, he handed me an extra check for one million dollars. But that was many years later.

Sir Cedric was pleased with the outcome of his case and wanted to do "something extra." But, of course, he could afford nothing of any material value. Indeed, I had excused his paying much of my fee. Given this dilemma, he took me aside and apologetically told me what I already knew. He was in no position to provide any kind of bonus. Except one thing. If I was interested he'd tell me his life's story—something he said he'd never done.

I was certainly interested. And so we went to lunch, had some wine and stayed all afternoon, while Sir Cedric gave me the only gift he could afford—the story of his life. It was well worth it, and, when he finally concluded his fascinating and moving story, I couldn't help thinking of "The Juggler of Our Lady."

12

The Tipping Point

Anne Bancroft, the brilliant actress, was a dear friend of Lydia's. When Anne married Mel Brooks, he became a friend as well. At the time, Mel was at the top of his career and Anne had won two Tony Awards for best stage actress, the first for *Two for the Seesaw*, the second for *The Miracle Worker*. There probably wasn't a more famous couple in America. We, on the other hand, were relatively unknown. Lydia was a successful fashion model, but I was a young lawyer, still in the early phases of my career.

We were in New York celebrating Lydia's birthday. Mel and Anne generously invited us to dine with them at Le Pavillon, then New York's most fabulous and expensive restaurant. Its chef was world renowned, and its patrons were pretty much limited to America's "A" list.

The four of us were shown to a table with a softly spoken, "Will this suffice, Monsieur Brooks?" "May I assist you, Miss Bancroft?" "And you, Madame?" And so we sat, surrounded by a troop of serious waiters, captains and a somewhat smarmy maitre d', who could have been played by Bela Lugosi.

After champagne, we ordered. And, for two hours, we dined magnificently, the staff hovering around, pouring wine, brushing crumbs from the table or bringing one splendid dish after another. My God, I thought, this must be costing Mel more than the budget of his latest film. For a moment, I considered offering to pay, but it would have been a silly gesture, and probably would have meant selling my car.

When the meal was over, the maitre d' presented the check to Mel in a silver box. Mel examined it and, taking out his pen, turned to the maitre d' who was standing directly beside Mel's chair rubbing his hands together, obviously waiting for a world-class tip.

Now Mel spoke to him in a serious tone. "Georges, I must congratulate you on a magnificent meal—more than that, a magnificent occasion. The meal, of course, was superb—perhaps the best of my life. But the service—the service surpassed anything I have ever experienced. And I know that this truly spectacular evening was due to your superb management of every detail."

The maitre d' was trying hard to suppress a triumphant grin. But Mel went on.

"My only regret, Georges, is that I have this firm policy against tipping."

The maitre d' turned white and, for a moment, I thought he would faint or cry. Instead, he gave the tightest, most stressed smile I have ever seen and muttered, "I understand Monsieur Brooks."

"No you don't," cried Mel, leaping from his chair and hugging the man. "I'm just kidding. Here, look." He held the signed check before the poor man's eyes, showing what must have been a tip exceeding my monthly earnings.

That was Mel, irrepressible and off the wall funny.

Although most people didn't realize it, Mel was also a serious filmmaker. It wasn't just *Blazing Saddles* and *Young Frankenstein*. Mel also produced serious dramatic films, but didn't put his name on them, because he didn't want the public to think they were comedies. One such film was *The Elephant Man*, the true story of a hideously deformed man, a one-time circus freak, those who were cruel to him and those who helped him find a decent place in life.

The problem was there was already a successful play running on Broadway about the same character; and it was also called *The Elephant Man*.

Not surprisingly, the producers of the play were enraged. They demanded that Mel "cease and desist" his production or, at the very least, change the name of his film. Mel refused; and that's where I came in.

The play producers filed a lawsuit seeking an injunction to stop release of Mel's film, which would have been a disaster, or, in the alternative, to prevent Mel's use of the name *The Elephant Man*. I represented Mel. The plaintiffs, of course, argued that Mel not only stole their story, but that he also stole their name and was passing off his film as being based on their successful Broadway play.

I argued that Mel's film was based on a book that was published many years ago and was in the public domain. Thus, they couldn't stop Mel from telling the story. I also argued that both the play and the film were about an actual, historical figure, and that even without the public domain book, the play producers couldn't monopolize his life's story any more than they could monopolize the life story of George Washington, Babe Ruth or Elizabeth Taylor.

But then came the more difficult part—the title. Plaintiffs argued that, even if Mel had the right to tell the story, he could have called his film many other things. He didn't need to use their title, which created public confusion and should be stopped.

I argued that, since the published book was in the public domain and was entitled *The Elephant Man*, the title also had to be considered in the public domain. Otherwise, if someone published a version of Tolstoy's *War And Peace*, they could stop anyone else from using that title. Would we have to call it *The Adventures of Pierre Bezukhov*? Would *Pride and Prejudice* have to be sold as *Darcy's Day Out* and *Hamlet* as *The Melancholy Dane*? Of course not, I argued. If a book is in the public domain, the public must be free to sell it under its original title.

The Judge took the case under submission, and issued his decision the following day. Since the book entitled *The Elephant Man* was in the public domain, he ruled Mel was entitled to release a film on its contents and to use the title of the public domain book as the title of his film.

"Injunction denied."

13

Judicial Dicta

Over the years, I've found that judges react badly to lawyers' maneuvers that, to use the British phrase, they consider "too cute by half."

In the early days of my practice, I represented a lovely middle-aged lady whose husband had filed for divorce. We had a hearing on temporary "alimony" (that was before we had to call it "spousal support"). We were quite successful. The Judge, a distinguished, greying man, simply didn't buy the husband's "poor boy" story. He awarded the wife an amount of alimony almost as large as what the husband claimed (I thought falsely) was his total income. He also awarded temporary attorney's fees in what, for those days, was a very substantial amount. Obviously, the Judge believed the husband was lying.

The next day, the husband tried a very cute maneuver. He dismissed his entire divorce case, which would ordinarily terminate the Judge's order on temporary alimony. Then, five minutes later, he filed a "new" action for divorce, which was automatically given a new and different case number by the court clerk. He then had me and my client served with the dismissal of his original divorce case and the "new" divorce case he'd just filed. It was a clever, but sleazy way of avoiding the court's order on temporary alimony while still suing for divorce.

To say I was enraged at this tactic would put it far too mildly. I gave notice of seeking what's called an ex parte order set for hearing the next day, asking the court to do something I'd never heard of before . . . to find that the husband's dismissal of his original case and immediate filing of a new case was a "sham" and to order that the new case be deemed simply an extension of the old case, with the temporary order for alimony and fees remaining binding, as if the original case has never been dismissed.

When we arrived at court for the new hearing, the Judge read the papers in chambers and then took the bench. The husband's lawyer screamed that there was no precedent whatsoever for such an absurd order, treating two different cases as one.

The Judge smiled. "It is unusual, counsel, but then so is your tactic of dismissing your original case to avoid my order—then filing a new case. I'm going to grant Mr. Fields' new order. Admittedly it's unique, but it's fair and right in these circumstances. Oh . . . and one other thing: I'm increasing the attorney's fee award."

With that, the Judge left the bench.

Bellowing that he was certainly going to appeal, my opponent angrily rushed from the courtroom.

While I was putting the papers in my briefcase, the Court Clerk said the Judge wanted to see me in chambers. I was surprised. I knew I shouldn't argue the case in the absence of my opponent. Still, I had to obey the Judge's direction.

As I entered the book-lined room, the Judge rose, smiling, still wearing his robe. I recall thinking how distinguished, how judicial, he looked. "You don't have to say a word Mr. Fields. Here's how I see it. That guy put his cock in the mashed potatoes. Let's see if he can get it out. That's it. You can go."

In any event, the husband didn't appeal. He got a new, competent lawyer, who advised him to pay the order and settle the case. That's what happened. The appeal would have been fun; but this was a far better result for my client.

I've heard and read many judicial opinions, some of which rank with the finest of prose writing. But even now, more than 50 years later, I still remember the surprising judicial dicta issued in that divorce case. And, when I do, I can't avoid picturing that arrogant husband doing just what that distinguished judge said . . . putting "his cock in the mashed potatoes."

The only other time a judge invited me into chambers without opposing counsel was in a proceeding to remove two sisters I represented as trustees of a trust established by their grandmother. The trust was to provide for the living expense of the girls' mother, who, after being divorced by their father, had become a 400-pound tyrant. For years, the mother had lived in a deluxe apartment house on what's called the "Wilshire Corridor," a stretch of Wilshire Boulevard in West LA that is occupied, on both sides of the boulevard, by deluxe apartment houses. The buildings are high-rises with ever higher rentals.

In any event, my clients' mother wanted to move to a newer, even more expensive building in the next block. She claimed that her daughters had unreasonably refused her request.

After establishing that what she wanted would have almost doubled her rent, the mother's cross-examination went like this:

"Q. Now you actually occupy two complete apartments in your present building—isn't that correct?

A. Yes, I need two apartments.

Q. And that's because you don't want your maid using the toilet in your apartment?

A. Of course I don't.

Q. And you're asking two apartments in the new building for the same reason?

A. Yes. Mr. Fields, you wouldn't let your dog live in my present apartment house. It's disgusting and cruel that my daughters make me live in that tenement."

After evidence, including pictures of the existing apartments were admitted in evidence, both sides rested; and the Judge, without hesitation announced his decision forcefully from the bench.

"Petition Denied."

We had won. The girls' mother and her attorney angrily left the courtroom. After thanking me, the girls also left.

As I finished packing up our documents and my briefcase, the clerk put down his phone and said the Judge wanted to see me in chambers. Surprised, I knocked and was told to enter. The Judge stood behind his desk smiling.

"I'll just take a second Mr. Fields. I wonder if you can guess which apartment house on the Wilshire Corridor my mother lives in."

"The one 'I wouldn't let my dog live in'?"

"That's the one. You're excused."

I'm sure we would have won the case anyway, but who could have predicted that?

14

SELLING A LAWSUIT

I WAS CONSULTED BY A POTATO FARMER who felt he'd been terribly wronged by a powerful financier. From the facts he told me, I agreed.

The problem was, the farmer couldn't afford the fee that would be required to try the case and handle a potential appeal. Compounding the problem, my partners were unwilling to take the case on a contingency.

I hit on the idea of "selling" a part of the potential recovery to third parties. At the time, I didn't know of anyone who had done that, but I didn't see why it should be unlawful or unethical. England had an ancient concept of "maintenance and champerty" that arguably was inconsistent with my thought, but I found no American case holding such a deal criminal or even improper.

So, after discussing the case, Jack Webb, the creator and star of the hugely successful TV series *Dragnet*, and Frank Rohner, then a key executive of CBS (and later my partner) each bought half of a one-third share of any recovery, in exchange for paying the fees and costs.

We filed the action. Jack and Frank paid some fairly minor costs and, after we overcame a motion to dismiss, the case settled on very favorable terms. Frank and Jack each got about ten times the costs they'd laid out, and the client, who got double their share, was thrilled.

Now, we see companies advertising on television, in newspapers, and elsewhere that they will finance your lawsuit on a contingent basis. So, evidently, we were violating neither law nor ethics. In any event, we did right by the client and certainly by Jack and Frank.

15

INVESTMENTS

WAYNE ROGERS, who, for years played Trapper John in the television version of *M*A*S*H* was a Princeton graduate and a careful and knowledgeable investor and investment advisor. He was also a friend and client.

But "careful" would be seriously understating Wayne's degree of caution in approaching any investment proposal. One weekend, Wayne and I and Frank Rohner, by then my partner, flew up north to Eureka, California to look at a vast tract of timberland that was for sale.

The land and timber were impressive, there were many, many acres, and the price per acre was low. Wayne was not ready to make a commitment. Instead, he intended to "pencil it out," i.e., to compute the cost, as well as the potential income and expenses, when we returned to LA.

After a lunch of crab cioppino and lots of wine, we headed for the airport. Driving through downtown Eureka, the real estate broker pointed out a four-story brick apartment building that he said was for sale. There was an excellent loan on the property, and, under California law, there was no personal liability on that loan. All that would be required to buy the building was making a down payment of $5,000.

It seemed like a "no brainer." Ever cautious, I immediately shouted, "I'm in." So did Frank. We turned to Wayne. "Three way split?"

Wayne looked at us with disgust. "You guys don't know the vacancy rate, the term of the leases, the annual expenses or the state of repair—much less the gross rental income. You can't just rush into buying a building like this."

"Come on Wayne," Frank said. "It's less than $2,000 each and we can be the proud owners of this handsome building."

Wayne frowned, "What the three of us could lose, Frank, is $5,000. Before I could recommend it, much less invest in it, I'd have to do my homework—know a helluva lot more."

The conversation went on until we arrived at the airport. Carelessly, Frank and I agreed to divide the $5,000 down payment and committed to buy the building despite Wayne's stern disapproval.

We stood to lose $2,500 each, but we laughed that we're now property owners in Eureka, California. In theory, Wayne was absolutely right. But sometimes luck trumps caution. A year later, Frank and I sold the building for a $40,000 profit. We never told Wayne. We didn't want to rub it in.

The one time I ever knew Wayne to plunge was about a year later. While on a trip to Texas, he'd encountered a bright and aggressive oil man whose name, not surprisingly, was "Tex." Tex told Wayne he'd come across what he thought was a likely area that could produce excellent results without a huge investment.

Wayne "penciled it out" and, if he, Peter Falk, Jimmy Caan and I each put up $30,000, we could swing it. That $120,000 would buy us two-thirds of the deal, with Tex owning the balance. It would also allow us to drill the first couple of wells. Again, I was ready; and so were Peter, Jimmy and, this time, even Wayne. After all, we'd heard of the millions that could be made in oil, so "Let's take a shot." Somehow, I scraped up $30,000, borrowing most of it from the bank; and we were in the oil game.

About five weeks later, we were all gathered around a loudspeaker phone to receive the report on our first two wells.

"Gentlemen," said Tex, "This isn't just a 'gusher.' This looks like we've hit what could be the largest single oil deposit in U.S. drilling history."

"My God," one of us said. "Tell us more."

"Well, I've already had a call from Standard Oil. They're offering $14 million for a quick purchase of the entire field."

"Fourteen million?" I croaked.

"Yes sir. You can accept it today. But, my advice would be to turn it down. $14 million is peanuts compared to what's in the ground here."

Wayne immediately said, "Guys, let's grab the $14 million. After the driller's third, we'd split more than $2 million each. For a $30,000 investment, that's not bad."

The rest of us immediately indicated that Wayne must be nuts.

"What? You heard Tex. Sell the largest oil discovery in U.S. history for only $14 million? That's insane!"

We deferred the issue to our Texas partner, "What do you think it's really worth?"

"Oh," he said, "you can never be precise about something like this. But this is one giant whale of a field. I'd say, if we drill a couple more successful wells, you're probably looking at 10 or 20 times what they offered—at least."

"Wow!" That decided the matter. We voted three to one to turn down the $14 million.

Hell, it was only going to cost us another $40,000 to drill the two added wells.

Delirious, we assured Tex, "You'll get the money right away."

We were rich! Yes! Really, really rich! It looked like about $50 million each, which, in those days, was huge!

So, somehow, I scraped up another $10,000, adding to my bank loan in the process.

Meanwhile, we had T-shirts printed for our wives with "Four Aces Oil Company" printed across the chest. And each couple thought long and hard about what they were going to do first with the money—a yacht? A private plane? A house in Malibu? Wayne, of course, was going to invest his share in a diversified portfolio of securities.

SUMMING UP: A PROFESSIONAL MEMOIR

Anyway, for the first few weeks, we got glowing reports. We continued in a state of euphoria. Then, over time, the reports slowed; and we were told that, maybe it made more sense to drill for natural gas, rather than oil. "What?" Tex assured us things were still very good. We'd just take a different approach. That "different approach" would, of course, require some costly new equipment; and thus an added investment from the "owners."

Now, I was getting suspicious, and so was Wayne. Without telling Tex, Wayne took a quick trip to visit our wells. You guessed it. There were no wells. There was no equipment, there weren't even any oil rights that we owned. We'd been taken.

I immediately suggested turning Tex over to the FBI. His fraud had been interstate and was, I pointed out, a form of theft and a serious federal crime. "Will that get us our money back?" my partners asked. Tough question. "Probably not," I said. "In fact, almost surely not. But you'll feel better knowing Tex got 20 years."

They asked why we couldn't just threaten him with jail if he didn't pay us back. I said that could be extortion, ending us in trouble with the FBI.

"Shit!" was the studied response from my partners. After a while they hit on the idea that a lawsuit accusing Tex of fraud would ruin him in his own state and might force him to pay us back. I was skeptical but agreed.

Without telling Tex of our plan, Wayne invited him to a meeting at the Beverly Wilshire Hotel, supposedly to give us a report and discuss the future.

He arrived with a blonde in the shortest miniskirt I'd ever seen and red cowboy boots. He introduced her as "Mama" and told "Mama" to watch TV in the bedroom, while "the boys" talked in the living room.

I told him immediately what we'd learned, and what we planned. I said we had to restrain Jimmy Caan, who wanted to throw him off the hotel balcony (we were on the 6th floor). But, I added that we were determined to get every cent of our money back. I said he'd be hit with a civil lawsuit for fraud in his own town. He'd be through, I said. And we'd at least take whatever assets we could find in Texas or elsewhere.

Tex continued to insist that he'd been honest with us, but that, even so, he didn't want "unhappy partners" and would be glad to "buy us out" by returning what we'd invested.

"When?" I asked.

"You gotta give me 60 days."

"We'll give you 30 days to raise the cash. Then, we're filing our lawsuit. Once we do, I don't think many Texans will be doing business with you . . . ever."

"Don't worry, you'll get the money," he said. You'll get it before then."

"Mama" was unhappy to leave the soap opera she was watching. But Tex insisted, collecting her from the bedroom and leaving.

We heard nothing from Tex during the next two weeks. Then Wayne discovered that his phone was disconnected and his home vacated.

"What?" Yes. A search by a local investigator reported that Tex had cleared out his bank accounts and had left for Argentina, taking with him "Mama" and what was left of our money.

I managed to pay the bank back and declared the loss on our income tax return. Sadly, I wasn't in the 100% bracket, so the net loss really hurt.

In a way, it was a sad experience. On the other hand, for Lydia and I just starting out in life, it was almost worth it to have believed—at least for a month or so—that we were among the rich—the <u>very, very</u> rich.

16

JONATHAN LIVINGSTON SEAGULL

YEARS AGO, the number one bestselling book for over a year was a unique story called *Jonathan Livingston Seagull* by Richard Bach. It was a simple tale of a seagull who shuns the flock, perfects his dive, evades a murderous hawk and flies on—bravely, but alone.

One day, I got a call from a lawyer I knew in a respected New York law firm. He was referring Richard Bach, who was in a desperate fight with Paramount over the film version of *Jonathan*.

A few days later, I met with Richard, who explained his problem. *Jonathan Livingston Seagull* represented his strongly held personal philosophy. Much like Ayn Rand, Richard believed that, if each person simply tried to perfect himself, society would be fine, and the world would be a better place. He deplored governmental attempts to create a better life for everyone.

And so, Jonathan Seagull tried to improve his dive, just to make it the best dive it could possibly be, while generally ignoring the collective rules, opinions and needs of the flock.

But Paramount had bought the film rights to the book and had changed everything for which Jonathan (and

Richard) stood. Paramount's version of the film, already shot and about to be released, had Jonathan diving, not to improve himself by becoming the best diver he could be, but to improve the diet of the flock—exactly the philosophy Richard deplored.

I read the contract and knew that it gave Richard the right to approve any material change in the story. But his approval was not to be unreasonably withheld.

I wrote Paramount, telling them they were violating Richard's rights. Essentially, they told me to go pound sand. Paramount then released its version of the picture in theatres all over the United States, as *Richard Bach's Jonathan Livingston Seagull*. I filed a lawsuit seeking a preliminary injunction against further showing of the film. I told Richard that, with the picture already in theatres, this was more than a longshot, but I'd try.

Everyone I talked to told me I was as crazy as my client. With the film already in theatres, Richard was simply too late, if he'd ever had a chance in the first place.

The Court set a hearing for 5:00 p.m., so that the Judge could consider it after his full day's schedule. That, in itself, was unusual; but this was no ordinary judge. His name was Campbell Lucas, and he was brilliant, hardworking and totally dedicated to dispensing justice.

At 5:00, I showed up for the hearing, along with Richard. The courtroom was packed with media, both print and television. Judge Lucas took the bench and announced that he had read the book, screened the film and had read the briefs and evidentiary declarations. Now, he was ready to hear arguments.

This, itself, concerned the Paramount lawyers, who had hoped the Judge would simply take the bench and announce, as everyone expected, "injunction denied."

So, we began. I argued that this was not just an author's unhappiness with some dialogue or the way a scene was played. This film took Bach's basic philosophy—the whole point and purpose of his writing the book—and completely reversed it, telling the public exactly the opposite of everything Richard Bach believed and wanted to say. The only reason he wrote the book was to express his views—and Paramount had completely reversed everything he stood for and wanted to express.

Paramount's lawyer, an experienced and skilled litigator, argued that tens of millions had been spent on the film, that Bach had been invited to screenings but failed ever to attend and that, with the picture already in release, it was too late for him to seek to punish Paramount's thousands of innocent shareholders by stopping further screenings, causing them a disastrous financial loss.

Besides, he argued, there was nothing insulting or degrading about Paramount's portrayal of Bach's book—Jonathan was portrayed as noble, even patriotic, thinking not of himself, but of the good of the flock. Bach should be proud of what this film said, instead of trying to muzzle it.

In reply, I argued, that was just the point. What the film said was the very antithesis of everything Richard Bach stood for. Its philosophy was hateful to him. Whether you agreed with him was not the point—he had the right to say what he wanted in his own book and not to have Paramount's version of his book say exactly the opposite.

By now it was 7:00 p.m. But Judge Lucas was ready to stay as long as it took to reach the right conclusion. He announced that he wanted to review the briefs and the evidence and would reconvene in about an hour.

We all filed out of the courtroom and scattered to restrooms and telephones. To keep Richard calm, I challenged him to a contest of lagging coins against the wall at the end of the corridor. The closest coin to the wall was the winner. And so, for the next hour, we lagged coin after coin. Richard beat me pretty regularly; and the contest took his mind off the critical decision we were awaiting.

At 8:00, we filed into the courtroom; and Judge Lucas took the bench. He glanced around the packed room and began. "This," he said, "is a difficult case, in that this film is already in release. But this is not some quibble about how a scene should be written or even a dispute about what ending is most effective. What's at stake here is a man's basic philosophy, the entire purpose of his writing his book, and whether he has to live with a film bearing his name that sends a message he despises to the public.

"So—I'm issuing the following order. Paramount will stop any and all exhibitions of the present film."

At those words, there was an audible gasp from the audience. Media representatives rushed for the phones. So did the Paramount executives who were present.

But Judge Lucas continued, "Unless"—he smiled, "unless, within 48 hours, the film is altered to conform to plaintiff's philosophy.

"I invite counsel to come into my chambers now to see if we can't agree on what those changes must be. We'll stay all night if that's what it takes."

"Wow," I thought. "How many judges would do that?"

"One more thing," Judge Lucas announced. "If the film continues to be shown in its present form during this 48 hour period, it must prominently state before the title 'This film is not Richard Bach's *Jonathan Livingston Seagull.*'"

Paramount's attorneys leapt at the opportunity to work out changes with the Court's supervision that could keep them from removing the film from the theatres or placing the humiliating announcement at its beginning.

For the next hour and a half, Paramount's lead lawyer and I sat in chambers with Judge Lucas reviewing those scenes that were offensive to Richard. Ultimately, we reached an agreement approved by both Richard and the studio, deleting or changing the offensive lines. It was almost 10:00 p.m. when we said good night and thanked Judge Lucas.

Paramount spent the rest of the night altering the soundtrack to conform to the newly agreed version.

Fortunately, this could be done, because the film had no human actors, only gulls and hawks, who were given human voices on the soundtrack.

Richard Bach's *Jonathan Livingston Seagull* was saved. Agree with Richard's philosophy or not, he was entitled to express it and ought not to have had a film of his book that expressed the opposite.

The next day, Richard wrote me, "Thanks for your flashing sword against the Palace Guard."

Sadly, Judge Lucas has died. He was one of the best.

17

Insider Information

SOME YEARS AGO, I was retained to represent the former president of Occidental Petroleum in his appeal from a decision by Judge Joe Wapner, later of television fame, in a case against Occidental that had been tried by another lawyer. I was convinced that Judge Wapner had committed numerous reversible errors in his conduct of that trial, and I wrote an appellate brief graphically setting out those errors.

The night before I was scheduled to argue the matter before the Court of Appeals, I received a call at home from lead counsel for Occidental. He offered my client a very generous settlement, far beyond what Occidental had previously been willing to pay. I phoned my client at home, and he happily accepted the last minute offer.

That was the end of the matter, except that, years later, I received information that probably explained Occidental's eleventh hour offer.

Based on the written briefs, appellate courts typically draft confidential and tentative opinions or at least memoranda of their likely rulings, even before oral argument. Sometimes, their tentative rulings are changed by the oral argument, but typically not.

I heard that, before the hearing in our case, Armand Hammer, then Occidental's Chief Executive Officer and major shareholder, had learned that the appellate court's tentative opinion was to reverse Judge Wapner's decision, and that this was what led to Occidental's generous offer the night before the hearing.

Was this true? Probably. Although if it was true, I was sure the "leak" to Dr. Hammer did not come from one of the appellate judges. I'm also sure that Occidental's excellent lawyers were not told why the company suddenly wanted to make their eleventh hour settlement offer. There were clerks and a number of other court employees who would have had access to the appellate court's tentative decision and could have directly or indirectly passed the result on to Dr. Hammer.

The matter had a happy ending, but I'll probably never know the whole truth.

18

My Worst Moment

By this time, I was beginning to gain something of a reputation for successful trials. Another New York firm referred a case involving David Merrick. David was probably the most famous and successful Broadway impresario since Ziegfeld. He typically had two or three shows running on Broadway at the same time, plus road companies performing Merrick shows all over the country.

David was also famous for his multiple divorces and his legendary temper, which could suddenly ignite into ferocity over almost anything.

I represented David in a contract dispute. I felt he had a much stronger position than our opponent; but this was an arbitration and, sometimes, the results could be hard to predict. On the other hand, the arbitrator was a retired judge, so I felt reasonably confident.

Our opponent put on his case first, and I was generally able to shred his witnesses on cross-examination. When their side rested, I was reasonably sure we were going to win. I called David as our first witness. I was reluctant to have him testify, because he was so uncontrollable. But I decided it was essential.

Surprisingly, his direct examination went well. He responded to the few questions we'd prepared with crisp, effective answers that we'd also prepared. When I turned from the lectern, saying, "Your witness," I felt even more confident that the case was won.

My opponent, a very nice, soft-spoken and competent lawyer, rose to cross-examine David. He began with a fairly routine question.

"What is your occupation Mr. Merrick?"

There was a long pause during which I saw David's face turn bright crimson.

Suddenly, he rose from his chair and bellowed, "I don't have to take this shit!" He then marched across the room and out the door. The rest of us simply gaped in amazed silence.

Finally I said, "Excuse me for a moment," and I left the room to look for my crazy client. Apparently, however, he'd already caught the elevator and was gone.

What could I do? My client had behaved outrageously. I was mortified. I returned to the hearing room, looking and feeling grave. I apologized to the arbitrator, telling him that Mr. Merrick felt so strongly about this matter that he just couldn't control his emotions. I pointed out that it was four o'clock anyway and suggested that we adjourn for the day, promising to bring my client back in the morning.

That night, I got a call at home from opposing counsel. "Bert, despite your client's bizarre conduct, I recognize we've got what clearly seems a losing case, and, unfortunately, we've got a solid arbitrator. Maybe I can still turn him around. But probably not. If you'll waive attorneys' fees and costs, we'll stipulate to judgment in Merrick's favor."

Thrilled, I quickly said I'd recommend that and would get back to him.

I immediately called David. "Great news, David. They just called. If you'll waive attorneys' fees and costs, they'll agree to judgment in your favor."

There was a long moment of silence, then, "See Bert, I know how to handle these Hollywood types. When I walked out, they knew they were beaten."

We accepted the settlement offer; but, to the day he died, David Merrick believed that, when he bellowed "I don't have to take this shit" and walked out of the arbitration, he'd won the case for us.

To him, his walking out was a personal triumph. To me, it was my worst moment in litigation.

David died years later. Before his death, he had a serious accident. He was hospitalized and in a wheelchair. Apparently, an orderly was taking him out for some air when, somehow, the wheelchair broke loose and David, still in the chair, plummeted down a steep hill, smashing into a lamp post. Naturally, given David's temper and proclivity to insult others, there was a rumor that he'd been pushed. Probably not. But who knows?

19

Treaty Obligations

ONE OF MY FAVORITE CLIENTS was Clement Hirsch, an ex-Marine and a pal of John Wayne. In his day, Clement owned the highly successful Kal Kan dog food company, as well as Stagg Foods, producer of the best canned chili then on the market, an outstanding stable of race horses, plus various other companies and assets. Many years ago, Clement was sued for divorce by his wife of several years, a strikingly beautiful woman named Claudia, but nicknamed "Coy."

I was still a young lawyer, and this was a _very_ big case. A breakfast was arranged at which Clement and I were to meet for the first time. Coffee was served and I took a big swallow. _My God!_ It was scalding! I spit the mouthful of coffee onto my plate. What a way to begin an introductory meeting! I said, "I'm sorry. That was absolutely boiling." Clement gave me a big grin. "You'd've been a goddamn fool to swallow it. I'll tell you that!" I knew from that point on that we'd get along fine.

The case was tried in Orange County, which meant the County Courthouse in Santa Ana. We retained Vernon Hunt, a local lawyer, as co-counsel. Coy was represented by two outstanding lawyers, David Harney, a nationally famous litigator, and Jack Trotter, a brilliant young Orange County attorney, who subsequently founded JAMS, the highly successful mediation and arbitration service.

The trial went on for months, during which I lived in a Newport Beach hotel, going home on weekends. There were many issues; but the principal point of contention was community property. Coy claimed that, even if Clement owned his companies before the marriage, all of his assets had been "transmuted" into community property, and that they were worth over $100 million, a huge sum in those pre-billionaire days. In terms of today's dollar, this probably would have been two or three billion dollars at stake.

One of the many disputed assets was Stagg Foods. Coy claimed she had even created the company trademark, a bow-legged cowboy figure. She described how she and Clement were sitting together in their bedroom on a rainy day and how, while doodling on a pad and thinking about "their" chili company, she invented and drew the well-known trademark figure. That testimony could have gone a long way in supporting her claim that the chili company had become community property.

On cross-examination, however, I handed her an official Department of Agriculture form depicting the same bow-legged cowboy trademark and showing that it had been registered by Clement two years before he'd even met Coy.

Many witnesses caught in a situation like that try to get out of the trap by frantically making up some phony explanation that just makes matters worse. Coy didn't. She did what I've subsequently advised clients to do if their testimony is completely impeached, as Coy's was. She just smiled beautifully and said, "Oh, I guess I was wrong."

Clement had a marvelous sense of humor and was irrepressible. He told me that, when they met, Coy had fudged her age, making her four years younger than she was, and that he had only learned the truth during the trial. While Coy was on the stand, being questioned by her attorney, she could see Clement, but the Judge's view of him was blocked by me and Vernon. This freed Clement to be the kid he was at heart. According to what Coy had told Clement, she was now 48. Suddenly, in the middle of testifying, she seemed to sputter. I looked back at Clement who was sitting behind me grinning and holding up a handmade sign that said, in big numbers, "52."

Later in the trial, Coy's lawyers called an "expert," a college professor of economics who testified to the value of one of Clement's newer companies that had been steadily losing money. The professor testified that the company was worth $10 million. His "value" was based on a chart showing that the company's losses had been less in the last two years than before and extrapolating the line of diminishing losses into the future so that, a few years from now, the company would show a sizeable profit, supporting the value to which he testified.

Clement whispered to me, a bit too loudly, "What bullshit!" The Judge frowned in our direction. When the direct examination ended, I whispered at length to Clement, and he nodded.

I rose to cross-examine, telling the professor I had only one basic question. I said my client had authorized me to offer to sell the company he'd said was worth $10 million to the professor for only $2 million. Did he accept that offer?

Coy's lawyers were both on their feet objecting that this wasn't a proper question and that the professor had no duty to buy anything. "Overruled," said the Judge, who evidently wanted to hear the answer.

The witness took a moment and then said that $2 million would be an exceptionally low price, but that he didn't have that kind of money. "After all, I'm just a college professor."

I said this was no problem, that Mr. Hirsch had authorized me to give the professor six months to pay. "Surely," I said, "since you testified under oath that the company's worth $10 million, you can raise the money to buy it for only $2 million." I repeated the key question—"On those generous terms, will you buy the company?"

Again, Coy's lawyers objected. Again the objection was overruled. The Judge was obviously not only interested, but amused.

The witness looked totally flustered. After a moment he said that he wasn't in the business of buying and selling assets, that he was an academic and stayed away from such things.

The Judge looked very skeptical, and I repeated the question—"So, you're saying that you won't pay two million for this company you testified was worth ten—is that right?"

"Yes."

"Your witness."

The Judge was smiling.

Toward the end of the trial, Harney and Trotter came up with their ace card, the 1848 Treaty of Guadalupe Hidalgo, which they claimed overrode California law, applied Mexican community property rules and made everything held by the Clement community property.

Ugh! It seemed a body blow. Could all of our work, all the cross-examinations, be down the drain because of a treaty made in 1848? A treaty made by the United States would take precedence over the laws of any state. They were right about that. Dave and Jack were smart, but the California courts had handled thousands of community property cases. How come no one had raised this before?

That night, I went to the Orange County Law Library, checked out the Treaty of Guadalupe Hidalgo and discovered why.

The next day in Court, the Judge asked if we had any response to their argument based on the treaty. I rose and told him that I had now read the actual treaty and had even brought a copy with me. I said the treaty did establish that Mexican community property rules applied in California and other territories. I paused there for effect. "But your honor," I said, "the treaty is absolutely clear that those rules only apply to residents of those territories in 1848 when the treaty was signed." I added that, "while there was some uncertainty as to Mrs. Hirsch's actual age, I'm sure she was not a resident of the treaty territories in 1848."

And that pretty much ended the case. The Court issued an order finding that all of Clement's companies and other assets (all $100 million) were Clement's separate property, except that Coy had a community property interest worth only $1 million, which was to be paid to her by Clement. On the other hand, Coy was required to pay her own attorneys' fees, which were $800,000.

It was a huge win for Clement, and it was the right result. Dave Harney graciously sent me a congratulatory note. Jack Trotter went on to the fame and fortune he deserved. They'd made a gutsy try with the Treaty of Guadalupe Hidalgo. It was a scary moment I won't forget.

20

"Just The Facts, Ma'am"

Jack Webb was a larger-than-life character, who created a television empire beginning with *Dragnet* and followed by others over the years. He personally brought the public six highly successful television series that ran for multiple seasons. Jack had been a client of David Tannenbaum and loyally stayed on for many years after David's death. I handled many legal problems for Jack, some with the network, some with his agency, some with his wives.

When I was still a young lawyer, Jack suggested that my son, who was then only three years old, might get a kick out of seeing his dad on television. Would I like to be in a *Dragnet*? Having been in school plays in high school and stage shows in college, I was a born ham. I leapt at the chance.

On the appointed day, having memorized my lines, I showed up at the sound stage where *Dragnet* was being filmed. It was 5:30 a.m. The early call was to allow time for makeup, wardrobe and rehearsals before the actual shoot. If you think actors don't work hard, you're wrong.

Jack directed other scenes from the program, in which I was to play an Assistant District Attorney prosecuting a fast-talking group of fraudsters. By the time my first scene was to be shot it was 11:30 a.m. and I was starting to get hungry.

In that first scene, I was to be at the counsel table during a trial. Sitting with me were Jack, as Sgt. Joe Friday, and his partner, played by Henry Morgan. Our table was surrounded by what seemed to be about 50 guys all doing different jobs—cameramen, light men, electricians, grips, teamsters, and others.

When Jack called "Action!" I started to speak the lines I had carefully memorized. Before I got out the first sentence, a huge guy holding a microphone on a long pole stepped forward. "Cut it Jack"—he bellowed, pointing at me. "His stomach growled! Can't use it."

It seemed like all 50 onlookers were laughing. I was not. I couldn't believe the guy's mike was that sensitive. But obviously Jack did, and time was money. So, without delay, he got everyone ready again, and, once again, shouted, "Action!"

Once again, I spoke my lines, or at least the first few words. But once again, the big guy with the mike shouted, "Cut it, Jack. His stomach growled again."

Now there was more laughter and finger pointing. But no one wanted delay. I wasn't laughing. I was embarrassed—fatally embarrassed. But Jack was unflappable. "Okay guys, we'll take ten." Then he turned to a craft service rep and said, "For God's sake, get Bertie Boy a sandwich! Otherwise we'll go broke trying to get the shot."

The sandwich came, and I wolfed it down. We resumed filming and my stomach cooperated.

If you look carefully at TV listings you'll see that my *Dragnet* segment is still playing every once in a while, decades after the embarrassing beginning of my television career.

• • • •

Later, Jack Webb was the head of Warner Bros. TV, a job he didn't like nearly as much as directing, producing and acting in television dramas. Jack didn't get on well with Jack Warner, the head of the studio, and Warner decided he wanted someone else in the job. The issue was that Jack Webb would have received a <u>very</u> substantial amount of salary over the three years he had left on his contract. And Warner Bros. didn't want to pay it. Still, Jack had done nothing wrong. They had no real grounds to terminate him.

First, they had the idea that, if Jack wanted to continue drawing his salary, he'd have to stay home and not compete with Warner Bros. They knew that Jack would never do that. He'd want to go back into the television production business, so he'd have to give up the Warner Bros. money.

I argued that to pay him to stay home and not compete would violate the antitrust laws. If he was actually working for Warners, I said, of course he couldn't compete. And if his contract called for a brief non-competition period at the end of its term, it might be enforceable. But Jack's contract had no such provision, and they couldn't legally pay him not to compete if he wasn't actually working for them.

Next, they said okay, Jack didn't have to stay home. He could work elsewhere, but he'd have to apply the money he made elsewhere to reduce what Warner Bros. owed him. That might sound reasonable, but I didn't agree. I argued that if they breached the contract by firing him they'd be right. If they did that, Jack would have the duty to "mitigate the damages," which would require him to apply what he earned elsewhere to reduce what Warner Bros. owed him.

But, I said, Warner Bros. denied that it was in breach of the contract, claiming to be exercising the "pay or play" clause of the contract. That clause allowed the studio to pay Jack, but not use his services. But, if that's what they were doing, they couldn't stop him from competing and they couldn't deduct what he earned elsewhere. I'd actually found case law supporting that position.

It seemed ironic that, by committing a breach of the contract, they'd get a credit for what Jack earned elsewhere in the three years left on his contract. But, if they didn't breach the contract and, instead, exercised their contract right simply not to use his services, they'd have to pay him, and they couldn't deduct his outside earnings.

Ultimately, the Warner lawyers came to the same somewhat ironic conclusion—in order to avoid having to pay Jack his full salary with no offset for what he earned elsewhere, they'd have to fire him in breach of Warner's contract, rather than exercising their contract right simply not to use his services.

Of course, I had warned Jack that this was what they were going to do in order to save all that money. But to Jack Warner, it wasn't so obvious. He was, of course, the powerful and undisputed head of Warner Bros.—in effect an absolute monarch. And, even though Warners would save all that money simply by saying that the studio was in breach of its contract with Jack, Mr. Warner announced that this would never happen. "Warner Bros.," he said, "does not breach its contracts." At his direction, the studio exercised its contract right to pay Jack, but not use his services. This allowed Jack to keep what he earned in his new job and also collect his full salary from Warner Bros.

I was amazed and, in a way, respectful. Jack Warner was one of the old Hollywood moguls, like Sam Goldwyn, L.B. Mayer and Harry Cohn. We tend to think of them as tough guys—certainly not guys ready to give money away. But here was Jack Warner refusing to follow his lawyers' advice to save millions by breaching the contract, because he insisted that "Warner Bros. does not breach its contracts."

You've got to admire that.

21

Green Underwear

Herb Yates was a tough, little guy. A former Boston newsboy and boxer, he was about 5'6", bald, bellicose and very rich. At 70, Yates was the owner and CEO of Republic Pictures; and he treated the Republic lot as his personal fiefdom. Yates was married to Vera Hruba Ralston, a tall blonde Czech, who'd been the Olympic ice skating champion four years before Sonja Henie.

After some 15 years of marriage, Yates believed (erroneously) that Vera had been unfaithful. Maybe, at first, Vera had been attracted by Yates' money and power. But, if so, she had come to love him; and she was deeply in love with him when he demanded a divorce.

She pleaded; but Yates was unmovable. He retained a major law firm and filed for divorce. Vera, in tears, became my client. Yes, she wanted to be protected; but, mostly, she wanted "Hoyb."

That was beyond my skill, so the case went on. The night before the trial, Lydia and I had dinner with Vera at the Bel Air Hotel, where she was staying. We tried to comfort her, but she was inconsolable.

Finally, Lydia hit on an idea. She announced that she knew what would bring Vera luck. It was green underwear.

"Green underwear?" I said, dismissively, and was swiftly kicked under the table.

"Green underwear never fails," said Lydia.

So, somehow, that night, we found a box of Rit and, borrowing a kettle from the hotel kitchen, we dyed our underwear green—all three of us.

The next morning, Vera and I, wearing our green underwear, were first to arrive in the courtroom. We were seated at the counsel table when Herb Yates entered, surrounded by a phalanx of high-powered lawyers carrying file boxes and even a film projector.

Yates looked across the courtroom at Vera. She looked back with tears in her eyes. Suddenly he rushed toward her, his arms outstretched.

"Vera! I can't live widdoutcha!"

Vera rose, knocking over her chair and threw herself into his arms.

"Hoyb," was all she said as he bent her over backwards for a long screen kiss.

I turned to Yates' lead counsel. "I guess this is a reconciliation."

"Sure looks like it."

Yates grinned, his arms still around his towering and beaming wife.

"You betcha."

So we knocked on the door to the Judge's chambers and told him the good news. Then, all of us assembled in his chambers. There weren't enough chairs, so Vera sat on her husband's lap.

"Well," his honor intoned. "Do you lovebirds intend a second honeymoon?"

Yates' lead counsel whispered to me, "Yeah, in Lourdes."

In any event, they ended up happily together for the rest of their lives.

And, for the rest of mine, I've worn green underwear. It didn't work with Lydia's cancer; but, if you were here and looked now, you'd see that's what I'm wearing.

22

A Near Miss

It was a very complicated case. There were plaintiffs, defendants, cross-complainants, cross-defendants and intervenors. At least six different claims and cross-claims were at issue. We represented only the plaintiffs.

After a closely fought trial, we stood awaiting the Court's announcement of its decision. The Judge adjusted his glasses, and, without even looking at the papers before him, announced, "Judgment for the cross-complainants."

We had lost! I was stunned and disappointed. I was sure my client felt even worse. Out of the corner of my eye, I saw my opponent grin and slap his client on the back. But, at that same moment, the court clerk jumped from his chair and raced up to the Judge, whispering excitedly. I had no idea what had occurred.

Finally, the Judge waved his clerk away and turned again to us. "Gentlemen," he said, "I must apologize. We had so many claims and cross-claims that I misspoke. Judgment is for the plaintiffs, not the cross-complainants."

Whew! We had won after all. My client looked relieved, but asked, "Shouldn't we find out if he's sure?"

"Absolutely not!" I said, packing my briefcase as quickly as I could. "Let's get out of here." And we did—to a nearby bar.

23

A Good Decision

Some years ago, Sid Sheinberg was the bright and effective head of Universal Studios. He and I were meeting in his office one afternoon to discuss a potential Universal film for a client.

Sid seemed distracted; and he took an incoming call during which he seemed to grow quite upset. When the call was over, Sid apologized and explained. "I've got this kid director back east somewhere, shooting on the water. He's got this mechanical shark that they can't get to work properly, and they're going way over budget. I've got to decide tonight whether to shut the picture down."

I didn't know it at the time, but Sid decided not to shut the picture down. It was a very good decision. The picture was *Jaws*, a massive hit for Universal that launched a great career.

The "kid director" was Steven Spielberg.

24

The Secret Case

Yes, a case can be "secret," even if filed in court. But only in extremely rare circumstances and, of course, only by order of the Court.

At the very inception of a very unusual case, I obtained an order signed by a courageous judge sealing the file and excluding onlookers from court proceedings. I still can't (and won't) disclose the identity of my client, except to say that he was famous, although perhaps not quite as famous as the man financing our opposition—Marlon Brando.

We had proceedings before various trial court judges, before the Court of Appeals and even before the Supreme Court of California—each time the courtroom was closed and the proceedings were sealed.

When our side won the first hearing, Marlon, whom I came to like, claimed that maybe we'd won the first round, but he was sure his side would ultimately win the case. I offered to bet him $100 on the ultimate outcome. He took the bet. But, much later, when the Supreme Court upheld the Court of Appeals' decision in our favor, which had upheld our win in the trial court, I asked Marlon to pay off. He responded with a friendly grin, "When we bet, I had my fingers crossed."

"You what?"

"I had my fingers crossed. You didn't say 'Crossies don't count.' So the bet doesn't count."

"Were we in kindergarten when we bet?"

"Doesn't matter. My fingers were crossed."

I saw Marlon from time to time after that; and he was always friendly. Certainly, he held no grudge over the outcome of our secret case.

Later, we became allies in suing the producer of *Superman* which was written by my client, Mario Puzo, and starred Marlon.

Just a few weeks before his death, Marlon called me. He was obviously out of breath and sounded weak.

"Bert," he whispered hoarsely, "I want to change my name."

"What?"

"Yes, I want to change my name, and I need your help."

Foolishly, unaware that this would be our last conversation, I didn't ask him what he wanted as his new name. I just said, "Okay Marlon, when you're ready, we'll get together and get the papers done."

That was it. Marlon died soon after that, and I never found out what new name he wanted.

Oddly, I miss him.

25

BEATLEMANIA

I WANTED TO SAY, "WOW, DO YOU MEAN IT?" But I didn't. I just said, "Of course." What the lawyer had asked was whether I'd be willing to represent The Beatles. Was I willing? They were the most famous musical group of all time, and I was a devoted fan. Of course I was willing.

The Beatles were in a fight against the producers of *Beatlemania*, a show the lawyer described as a rip-off of a Beatles concert performed by Beatles lookalikes and set against a background of 1960s history. The show, produced by a group of New Yorkers, had taken Broadway and then the world by storm, and The Beatles (or, as I learned, three of them) wanted it stopped.

That started one of the most exciting cases of my career—or anyone's. Not only was I a Beatles fan, like the entire world at the time, this was a fascinating, even groundbreaking case.

But first I had to fly to England to meet with Neil Aspinall, then CEO of The Beatles' management company, and George Harrison, who seemed to be the point man for the group in this situation. That started a friendship I treasured for years.

George and I met at Friar Park, George's estate in the English countryside. Between mad rides around the property in George's racing car, we discussed the case. I said we would base our argument on the "right of publicity," a badly named and, at the time, fairly new legal doctrine that allowed a celebrity to protect himself against the commercial use of his name, likeness or performance without his permission,

I explained that we would be sailing in uncharted legal waters and that our opponents were clearly relying on First Amendment protection by wrapping themselves in the cloak of history and biography. First they'd argue that *Beatlemania* showed, in each separate "act," The Beatles looking different in different stages of their careers, so that it was "biographical." And, second, they'd stress that each of their Beatles "concerts" was played in front of a "scrim," a kind of curtain on which they projected films showing the historic events of the '60s. Thus, the show was also historical.

They'd argue that this was both a history of an era and a biography of a famous group and, as such, it was clearly protected by the right of free speech under the First Amendment. We would argue that it was just a scheme to rip off a Beatles concert and a violation of their right of publicity.

George asked if our opponents could win. I said they could, that we had to recognize it; but that it would be my job to see that they didn't. George also warned me that, while John and Ringo, along with Neil Aspinall, were very much in favor of the lawsuit, Paul McCartney wasn't; and, in fact, Paul had told the press he thought *Beatlemania* was a very good show.

In any event, I returned to LA, read all the cases and articles on the right of publicity and filed our lawsuit in the state court in California. We plunged into a round of depositions and other discovery proceedings, during which John Lennon was tragically shot and killed in front of his home in the Dakota, a legendary New York City apartment house.

John's death was, of course, a tragedy for his wife, the other Beatles and Neil, and a source of worldwide mourning. It was also a serious blow to our case. First, John was to be one of our principal witnesses. Second, this gave the defense the argument that their show caused no real harm to The Beatles, because, without John, they could never play together again, so there was no lost revenue because of *Beatlemania*.

I tried to develop arguments to counter theirs and decided that our principal witness would be Neil Aspinall, who had been with the group from its inception, and an expert witness, the highly intelligent and articulate Jeff Berg, then chairman and CEO of ICM, a leading artists' agency.

Finally, the day of trial arrived. Our Judge was Paul Breckenridge, a fine man and a good judge. I'm sure he didn't remember it, and I didn't tell him, but I'd played two-man volleyball against him one afternoon at Stanford the summer I graduated from law school and was preparing to teach there.

Early in the trial, I called the main producer of *Beatlemania* as an adverse witness, which meant that I could treat him as if I were cross-examining him. He insisted that they were never looking for Beatle lookalikes, that they just wanted good musicians, and that it was just luck that the *Beatlemania* performers happened to resemble John, Paul, George and Ringo. The story didn't sound plausible, and I knew it wasn't true.

After he'd made his position very clear, I asked if his company hadn't posted flyers all over New York actively seeking Beatle lookalikes. He vehemently denied this, repeating that they were just looking for good musicians.

I then signaled my partner, Bob Marshall, who entered the courtroom accompanied by an associate. They were carrying an 8 by 10 foot blowup of a poster that said "Wanted Beatle Lookalikes" followed by the *Beatlemania* address and phone number.

"Sir, do you deny that this is the poster you put out all over New York City?"

At this point, there occurred one of those events in a trial that may have little to do with the merits of the case, but that, on a human level, has a significant impact on the judge or jury.

There was a moment of silence. The witness had been caught in what was obviously a lie. He seemed to be trying desperately to think of an explanation. Finally, he answered. "No, counselor. We did put out that poster. But we weren't really after 'Beatle lookalikes.' We just said that to keep out the black musicians."

There was a mass groan from the people in the courtroom, and Judge Breckenridge rapped for order.

"Any more questions, Mr. Fields?"

"No, Your Honor, that was enough."

But the case was far from won. The producers argued that there could be no harm to The Beatles because, John being dead, they couldn't perform again. I countered with the argument that the three survivors could license other Beatle lookalikes to perform as a group, just as the defendants did and that they were damaged by defendants' lessening the value of that right.

The defendants played film after film of The Beatles, as they changed from fresh-faced kids playing in a Hamburg club to what appeared to be jaded druggies sitting in someone's kitchen, playing sadly, with Yoko Ono sitting in front of them.

Clearly, the defendants were trying to create the feeling in the Judge's mind that he was dealing with a group of spoiled addicts who should hardly be allowed to destroy a gifted portrayal of an episode of modern history.

But, I felt it didn't work. When the group looked so tired and sad at the end, after having looked so fresh, young and vigorous in their early concerts, I thought I even saw some moisture in the Judge's eyes.

In any event, the trial went on and on, one witness after another. Finally, both sides rested, followed by lengthy arguments over the right of publicity and the First Amendment. When both sides were done, Judge Breckenridge announced that he would take the matter under submission.

A few days later, the Judge's decision arrived. It was a scholarly order, analyzing the factors that should be considered in weighing the right of publicity against the right of free speech under the First Amendment.

As to the decision itself, the Judge issued a permanent injunction stopping any further performance of *Beatlemania* and awarded The Beatles $12 million in damages, at the time a huge sum. Years have now passed, and a number of courts have faced the same type of issue. Yet, in my view, Judge Breckenridge's opinion remains the soundest analysis of all.

We were all very, very happy. I had gone through one of my most challenging cases and an experience I'll treasure my whole life. I last saw George one night when we sang together at a Karaoke party. He was a dear and highly talented man who died much too soon.

26

A Lack of Diversity

REMEMBER LEON SPINKS? If you're a boxing fan you do. He was one of the best, and, some years ago, he was a credible contender for the heavyweight title. But there were others. And, for the moment, the title was vacant.

I was retained by Jose Sulaiman, then President of the World Boxing Council (WBC). The WBC had sanctioned a heavyweight title bout between two outstanding contenders, Larry Holmes and Ken Norton. The public loved the idea of the bout, and it was about to take place in Las Vegas.

The problem was that, shortly before the Holmes/Norton fight, Leon Spinks filed a lawsuit against the WBC and others, seeking an injunction against the fight on the ground that Spinks should get the title bout against either Holmes or Norton, rather than their fighting each other.

I appeared to argue the WBC's case before Judge Roger Foley in federal court in Las Vegas. I was told that my opponent, representing Leon Spinks, was a celebrated civil rights attorney.

In the papers I filed, I argued that, while one might argue for Mr. Spinks' position, the WBC had the right to designate who should be the contenders for what was, after all, the "WBC Heavyweight Title." They had weighed all the relevant factors and come to a rational and reasonable conclusion. Although Mr. Spinks might disagree, it was their decision to make, not his. I cited cases supporting the WBC's position.

But Spinks' attorney had a very different view of the matter. In a lengthy and dramatic oral argument, he asserted that the WBC was a nest of racial discrimination, that Mr. Spinks, who came from a poor family in a ghetto environment, was being made an innocent victim of vile discrimination, right here and right now, and that the court should not stand for it.

After continuing what became a long and stirring attack on racial discrimination in all of its guises, Spinks' lawyer was finally interrupted by Judge Foley.

With a rather puzzled expression, the Judge said that, while he was certainly against racial discrimination, he was finding it very hard to follow counsel's argument. "I agree that Mr. Spinks is black," he said. "But Mr. Holmes is also black, and so is Mr. Norton. So, counsel, where's the racial discrimination?"

Spinks' lawyer never seemed to answer that question. He just went back to his argument against racism in general.

In my view at the time, he'd made no real case in support of the injunction Spinks was seeking. So, when Judge Foley turned to me for a response, I took a chance. I said, "I think we've covered it in our papers, Your Honor. Unless the Court has any questions, I'll leave it at that."

There was no question from the court. Almost before I sat down, Judge Foley announced, "Injunction denied."

27

"Tropicana Six"

SPINKS V. THE WBC was only one of the many legal problems that took me to Las Vegas. Years ago, the most elegant hotel in town was the Tropicana, and I was retained by the new owners to be general counsel to the hotel.

At least once a month I'd fly to Vegas to meet with the owner and his team. I'd walk through the casino in my midnight blue suit, imitating Humphrey Bogart in *Casablanca*. If I was wanted for a meeting or just to take a call, the hotel's loudspeaker would say "Tropicana Six,"—that was me—and I was to pick up the nearest house phone.

Over the years of representing the hotel, I learned a great deal about the gaming business, the methods of attracting "high rollers" and the intricacies of Vegas entertainment deals. It was enormous fun while it lasted. But it came to a sad end. The owner of the Tropicana was Deil Gustafson, known as "Gus." He also owned a bank, an insurance company and other businesses in Minnesota. Gus was totally honest, and, under his ownership, the Tropicana reported honestly and did not "skim," i.e., take unreported cash "off the top" when the night's "take" was counted.

The first problem was a guy who hung around the hotel with no job or authority. He was telling a Detroit branch of the Mafia that he was "working on Gus" and would convince him to "skim" and split the skimmed money with the mob.

It wasn't true; but he'd been telling them this for a while, and the mob was running out of patience. And these were guys you didn't want to make impatient. So, scared and desperate, this sleazebag told them Gus had finally agreed. This was completely false. Gus had flatly turned down any skimming and any relationship with the mob.

But the second problem was that the sleazebag didn't want to risk a hotel operator or anyone else at the Tropicana overhearing his conversations with the mob. So, to avoid making these calls from the hotel, he made them from a pay phone on the Vegas Strip. Why was this a problem? Because the FBI had tapped every public phone booth on the Strip!

That's where the third problem came into play. When the Tropicana ran short of cash, which could happen from time to time, Gus would transfer money temporarily from the Minnesota bank he owned. He'd temporarily use it to fund the hotel he also owned. "My bank, my hotel. What's the problem?" I guess that was Gus' attitude. But there was a problem. What Gus did violated federal law. It may have been a victimless crime; but, nevertheless, it was a crime. And the local U.S. Attorney was pursuing the case.

Ordinarily, this would have led to a plea deal, a significant fine and a suspended sentence. But the FBI and the U.S. Attorney had the recording of the sleazebag's phone call falsely telling the Detroit mob that Gus had agreed to skim and split with them. Armed with the recording of that call, plus a clear violation of the banking laws, the U.S. Attorney went after Gus with a vengeance.

Gus hired a well-known criminal lawyer, but he had plainly violated the federal banking laws; and, because of that horrible, lying phone call, the U.S. Attorney and the federal court believed him to be in bed with the Mafia.

Suspended sentence? Hell no! The U.S. Attorney pushed for twelve years. The Judge, thinking he was dealing with a mob associate, gave Gus eight. His lawyer's appeal went nowhere, and Gus went on to serve his time. It ruined his life. The hotel was sold, and my time as "Tropicana Six" was over. The memories are bittersweet.

28

The Missing Film

Elaine May is a brilliant woman and a favorite friend. She first became famous when teamed with Mike Nichols as the extraordinary comedy team "Nichols and May." Get one of their recordings if you can. They're marvelous.

Later, Elaine became a successful screenwriter and director—indeed one of the few directors that was given the coveted right of "final cut," the right, usually retained by the studio or a powerful producer, to determine what would be the final version of a film released to the public.

That was the problem. Elaine had written and directed a film called *Mikey and Nicky*, starring Peter Falk and John Cassavetes. Her contract with Paramount gave her the right of final cut, on condition she delivered the film by December 31st of that year. She had, however, obtained the studio's oral consent to extend that delivery date to February 28th of the following year.

But the studio grew unhappy with what they'd seen of Elaine's cut, and Elaine was unwilling to make the changes they wanted, believing those changes would seriously weaken her film.

Unfortunately, someone at the studio made a dishonest and unforgivable decision. With no warning to

Elaine, the studio's lawyers had gone into court in New York during January and obtained a court order to take the film, and final cut, away from Elaine, on the ground that she had failed to comply with her contractual duty to deliver the film by December 31st.

You'll say, "What about their agreement to extend the delivery date to February 28th?" Sure, but the studio filed papers that only showed the Judge the original written contract with the December 31st delivery date. They didn't disclose their oral agreement to extend the date to February 28th.

Elaine's New York lawyer tried unsuccessfully to get the Judge to change his ruling, and Paramount was going to pick up the film at Elaine's offices late that afternoon.

That's when Peter Falk and Elaine got me into the case. When I heard what the studio had done, I was outraged. I'm not going to talk about what, if anything, I did. I'll just tell you what happened.

At the end of the day, when the Paramount lawyers arrived with the sheriff to pick up the film, Elaine wasn't there. More importantly, neither was the film. In those days, a film was thousands of feet of celluloid rolled up in numerous metal cans. How could it be gone? And where was Elaine? They were told she'd been out of the office all day, visiting a friend in Connecticut.

Where was the film? No one knew.

The studio and its lawyers were crazed. "That's millions of dollars worth of film. Where the hell is it?" Elaine didn't know. She'd been in Connecticut. Apparently, no one knew.

Finally, Peter Falk spoke out. Peter was a brilliant actor, a co-star of the film and a dear friend of Elaine. As he later testified in a deposition, he knew that Elaine wasn't really late in delivering the film and that the studio wasn't really entitled to seize it. He was worried that enraged friends of Elaine might take the film and unintentionally damage it. He knew there'd be a vigorous court battle over it. So, to keep the film safe pending the outcome, he rented a pickup and drove the film to the home of an old friend, the mayor of a small New Jersey town whom Peter described as "the soul of integrity." There, Peter said, the film would be completely safe until the court decided the case.

Hearing Peter's story, the studio lawyers breathed a sigh of relief and rushed out to New Jersey to collect the film from the small town mayor. The problem was, by the time they arrived, the film wasn't there. Neither was the mayor. He was on a trip to the West Coast. The mayor's wife was there; and she tried to be helpful.

Yes, she told them, Peter Falk had indeed brought the film to her husband, and they'd stored it safely in their garage. But, after her husband left on his trip, a very nice man came from Paramount. He said the Court ruled that the studio was entitled to the film, and he'd come to pick it up. So, she helped him load it all in the trunk and the seats and floor of his car; and he left, telling her the studio was very grateful for her assistance.

"Did you get the license plate?"

The mayor's wife shrugged. "No, the guy was from the studio. I didn't see any need."

"That person was <u>not</u> from the studio!" shouted the lawyer.

"Oh? He certainly said he was. Anyway, the car was a black limo. Does that help?"

"Hardly. There are probably 2000 black limos in New York."

It was a dead end. The lead lawyer for the studio was boiling with anger and hurling threats, but it didn't help. He took the depositions of everyone involved. They all testified that they had no idea where the film was. It was just gone.

At about this time, I called the head of the studio, who was not only a friend, but a very decent, very smart guy who was also a friend of Elaine. I was sure the studio's deceptive tactics had not been his idea. I'm still sure of it.

I told him my hunch was that partisans of Elaine had the film, that they probably intended only to protect Elaine's right to final cut and that, if the studio released a story in the trade papers that it had agreed to Elaine's right of final cut and to extend her delivery date to March 31st, I felt certain the film would be promptly returned.

My friend said, "Are you sure of that?"

"I can virtually guarantee it."

"You've got a deal."

"Hey," I said, "it's not my deal. It's just my belief."

"Sure," he said, sarcastically.

The next day, both *The Hollywood Reporter* and *Daily Variety* had a story released by the studio, just as I had described it to my friend. And, as if by magic, the film was returned to Paramount in pristine condition. It had been a scary time, but with a happy ending.

Meanwhile, the angry Paramount lawyer had filed papers seeking to hold Elaine, Peter Falk and me in contempt of the Court's order. Our friend, the studio head, ordered their lawyers to dismiss that claim; but the Judge refused. This was decades ago. Peter's dead; but Elaine and I may still be "wanted" according to some long-forgotten New York file.

Elaine and I have remained good friends over the years. She lives in New York and, for a time, was with the hugely talented director, Stanley Donen (*Singin' In The Rain*, *Charade*, etc.). Elaine knew that I loved to sing and so did Stanley. So Elaine hired a pianist and scheduled a "sing off" in her apartment of songs by George and Ira Gershwin, Jerome Kern and Cole Porter. Without warning, I showed up in white tie and tails. Having no top hat, I borrowed one from my friend Ira Reiner, whose father had been a vaudeville magician. Formerly, he'd pulled a rabbit from my new hat.

Anyway, when Stanley answered the door and saw my attire, he raced down the hallway of their apartment, appearing 15 minutes later in a splendid tuxedo.

Then, suitably attired and, ultimately, a bit drunk, we sang the night away.

Stanley died in early 2019; but Elaine goes on and on, winning a Tony Award later that year for *The Waverly Gallery*.

29

CONSUMER LITIGATION

Did I ever sue a food manufacturer for a consumer? Yes, at least once that I can recall. That time involved our Corsican housekeeper, Julie Reichle. It occurred many years ago.

How Julie came to America is a story in itself. During the Second World War, she fought in the French underground and lived in a small French village. When the Americans arrived she fell in love with an American soldier and they were married in the village church—very romantic.

The problem arose when it was time for Julie's soldier husband to return to America. As he boarded the train, he told her that there was something she should know—he was already married to someone else in America.

So, Julie went to work to accumulate enough money to travel to America. When she had enough, she boarded a ship carrying in her suitcase the small axe she had used to kill German soldiers during the occupation. She had only one goal: to find her "husband" and kill him.

Somehow, she traced the guy to a town in upstate New York. But when she arrived (the axe still in her bag) he had gone. From what she was told, he was in Minnesota. It took her six months to earn enough to pay for her fare to Minnesota. But, in that time, she'd lost her determination to split his skull. So she was in America with her reason for being there gone.

She worked a few months more and made her way to Los Angeles, where she got a job working for Jack Webb and his then wife. When the Webbs split up, Julie came to us. She worked for us for years, ultimately becoming a U.S. citizen. She still had the axe, but it lay peacefully in our hardware drawer.

Of course, we always wondered what Julie put on her naturalization form when it asked "Reason for coming to the United States." We liked to think she wouldn't have lied on such an important form. But, the truthful answer, "to kill my 'husband,'" would probably not have gone over big with the Immigration and Naturalization Service.

Anyway, some years later, we went on vacation, leaving Julie in charge of the house. When we returned, we found her in tears. She explained that, while we were gone, she'd seen an ad on television saying you could lose weight by eating Profile Bread. So, Julie, who stood five foot four and weighed about 180 pounds, had been eating at least a loaf every day—and, instead of what they promised on TV, she'd <u>gained</u> weight. What a surprise!

I watched the Profile Bread commercials, and they didn't really say so; but you might get the same idea Julie got—if, like her, your English wasn't that good. Moreover, one of their commercials even said there were less calories in a slice of Profile Bread than any other bread on the market. Asking around, I found that this was true, not because Profile Bread had less calories, but only because it was sliced thinner!

So, we sued the makers of Profile, and, ultimately, we settled, getting Julie what to her was a cash bonanza. She bid us a sad goodbye and retired to an apartment in Hollywood, where she spent all day watching movies and eating candy bars, which she liked much better than Profile Bread.

30

Post-Production

My longtime client and friend, Dustin Hoffman, was engaged in a bitter dispute with First Artists Corporation and its Chairman, Phil Feldman. They were making a picture together, and Feldman had taken very tough positions concerning Dustin's creative rights, which Dustin felt would ruin the film. Not being shy, Dustin confronted Feldman with a metaphor. "I know you," he said, "you're the bully in the first grade who pushed my head into the fountain when I was trying to drink."

And that was on a good day. Anyway, when shooting and even most of the editing had been completed, Dustin had an appointment to dub a few lines of dialogue in time for a screening of the rough-cut of the film that night for First Artists' executives and investors.

"Dubbing," for those of you who might not know, is a marvelous process by which an actor can totally change a scene or the plot of the entire film by changing the lines he says while the camera is focused on someone else, so the actor's lips can't be seen. He simply records the new lines over the old ones on the soundtrack, and the new lines become part of the film.

"I adore you" can be converted to "I hate you" just by dubbing. The actor watches the film and, at the right moment, simply says the new lines, which then become part of the soundtrack of the film.

On this day, Dustin was to be in the dubbing room by 2:30 in the afternoon. We were having lunch that day and, it being a Friday, we both had some wine with our food. When we were ready to leave the restaurant, Dustin asked if I'd like to come with him to the dubbing session. I said "sure," and we headed for the studio.

In the dubbing room, I noticed that the two of us were alone. Dustin had been given the script with the new lines he was to say; and, as an old pro, he knew just what to do. As he was about to pick up the intercom to tell the technician to run the scene to be dubbed, I asked Dustin if we shouldn't send a special greeting to Phil Feldman, rather than just dubbing the new lines.

Dustin loved the idea; and he improved on it. "How about a filthy song?" "Great idea." Together, we quickly composed new dirty words for an old tune and Dustin sang them as his dub of the prior lines.

That night, the film was played for the investors. At the moment of Dustin's key scene, instead of dramatic lines, he appeared to be singing an old, filthy song about Columbus. The words, however, were new. "Phil Feldman runs a sinking ship where talent is no factor. He filled his ass with broken glass and circumcised an actor."

You can imagine Feldman's rage when, instead of reciting the expected lines, his star appeared to be singing this crude song about him in a screening for the people he wanted most to impress.

Was it irresponsible? Yes. Juvenile? Of course. It was probably my most irresponsible act in years. But was it fun? You bet.

• • • •

Later, I represented Dustin in negotiating his contract to play Willy Loman in a Broadway revival of Arthur Miller's classic play *Death Of A Salesman*. Toward the end of the run, we filmed the play with an eye to a possible showing on television.

Over the succeeding months, Dustin and I received numerous requests from teachers all over America. Could they have a video of the film to show their class? The rights were owned jointly by Dustin and Arthur Miller. Each time Dustin replied "Of course." Each time, Arthur, who'd grown up in the Great Depression of the 1930s, said, "Only if they pay." Finally, I got sore and told Arthur that, if he wouldn't agree, I'd begin telling the teachers that Dustin wanted to give them the video free, but Arthur Miller refused and insisted on payment. It didn't take Arthur a minute. "Go ahead," he bellowed, "Fuck the little bastards!"

Arthur was unquestionably a great writer. But his explanation of his own plays was sometimes puzzling. He once told me, for example, that, in *Death Of A Salesman*, he was really portraying "the inside of the human brain."

And he wasn't kidding.

31

AN EXTRAORDINARY OPPONENT

REMEMBER *THE ELEPHANT MAN* CASE for Mel Brooks? I had a similar case much later—similar in that it also involved the concept of what was in the public domain and thus usable by anyone, as opposed to what was protected by copyright or other laws.

A woman named Barbara Chase-Riboud had written a book about an uprising of captive Africans who took over a slave ship called The Amistad, killing the captain and crew. Later, Steven Spielberg produced and directed a film called *Amistad* based on that same historical incident.

Pierce O'Donnell, a brilliant, world-class lawyer (now a member of my firm), brought a lawsuit against Spielberg for copyright infringement, seeking an injunction against the showing of Steven's film.

I was asked to represent Spielberg. The pressure was enormous, because the injunction hearing was the morning of the night on which Steven's film was to be premiered at the Kennedy Center in D.C., with the President and most of Congress in attendance. If the Court were to issue an injunction against showing the film, the embarrassment for Steven (and for me) would be unimaginable.

Pierce argued brilliantly that his client had written an original view of what occurred on that historic slave

SUMMING UP: A PROFESSIONAL MEMOIR

ship and that Spielberg had simply stolen her work. I argued that the Amistad mutiny was an important part of American history, that no one could monopolize history and that there was no way to tell the actual story other than the way Steven had skillfully told it, which was significantly different from the scenes created by Ms. Chase-Riboud.

When we finished, the Judge announced that she would render her decision from the bench in a few minutes. She retired to her chamber, and I was worried. Did this mean she was framing the terms of an injunction and wanted it to be issued before the premiere that night? Fifteen minutes later, she retook the bench. I held my breath. The Judge first explained that historical events, like the Amistad mutiny, were in the public domain and announced her ruling that Spielberg was entitled to make and exhibit his film. Injunction denied.

When Pierce and I left the Court, we were met with what looked like 50 microphones and 200 reporters. I spoke first, telling the media how pleased we were at the Court's ruling that completely cleared Steven Spielberg and allowed that night's Presidential premiere to go forward.

Then Pierce, always ingenious in dealing with the press, stepped up to the microphones. I thought to myself, "The guy lost. What can he say?" But that didn't stop Pierce. "What you should remember," he said, "is that the Judge said that this was a very close call. Obviously then, Ms. Chase-Riboud's claim had considerable merit."

That afternoon and evening, while most of the media reported that Spielberg had won, Pierce had successfully misdirected some, who reported, "Spielberg barely gets by" or words to that effect.

Pierce's client gave him a handsome present, which he richly deserved and still treasures.

32

Recruiting

MARVIN DAVIS was a 450-pound Denver oilman who moved with his family to Beverly Hills and bought 20th Century Fox. Yes, Marvin bought the entire studio. The "D" page of the studio's telephone book included a listing for "Marvin Davis . . . Owner."

After Marvin took over, I represented Fox in a number of matters, something I enjoyed very much. A film studio is an exciting place; and it's a heady experience to be one of the "insiders" charged with making it function properly.

One day, Marvin was complaining about some of his key executives and how he should replace one or more of them. Suddenly, he asked me who was the best and brightest motion picture executive in town.

I thought a moment, mentally running through a few names. It took me only seconds. "Barry Diller," I said. "No question. But he's at Paramount."

"Can you get him to come over here?"

"I don't know what Barry's contractual situation is; but, he's a friend, and I can try."

That led to months of my trying to persuade Barry to leave Paramount and come over to Fox to become its Chief

Executive. I met him at his home, at restaurants, wherever and whenever I could. I painted a glowing picture of what it would be like at Fox and of the advantages he would enjoy there as CEO. Finally, Barry agreed, and his contract with Fox was negotiated and signed.

I was right. Barry was terrific. Where the executive hallways had been dark every day by 4:30, the lights now burned past midnight. The entire culture was changed. Fox was alive and well again.

The only problem was that Barry and Marvin didn't get along, and that's putting it mildly. Each of them had an ugly name for the other that I won't repeat. Fortunately, at just the right time, Marvin sold the studio to Rupert Murdoch, who recognized Barry's genius and kept him in place.

When Barry came to Fox, there were only three television networks, CBS, NBC and ABC. Even ABC, the third network, had experienced a very difficult time establishing an audience to catch up with its older, established rivals. It seemed impossible that anyone could successfully establish a <u>fourth</u> network. But Barry did it. Rupert financed it and justifiably gets credit for what the Fox Network became. But, to a great extent, it was Barry's genius and hard work that created it.

When Barry announced that he was leaving Fox, I attended a small dinner for him at Giorgio's in Santa Monica Canyon. I asked him what he planned to do. He said he was going to study computers. "What?" I said in a tone of disbelief. "You're giving up being the head of a major studio to study computers?"

"Yes," he said. He added that computers were the future of most industries and particularly entertainment and the media. With my usual foresight, I thought to myself, "Poor Barry. He's nuts."

And, of course, Barry took his new-found knowledge of computers and built one successful media company after another, achieving an enormous and well deserved success. I like to think I played a small part in Barry's meteoric rise. After all, what if he'd never left Paramount? Who knows? I suspect he'd have accomplished great things anyway.

33

I Screw Up

Rita Hayworth was, for many years, one of my favorite actresses. When I was asked to represent a studio in handling a problem she was creating, I was reluctant. But, when I heard about her behavior, I agreed.

The studio reported that Ms. Hayworth was starring in a film, but was showing up each day late and apparently under the influence of what seemed to be drink, drugs or both. She didn't know her lines and would become angry if reproached about it. Her conduct seemed grossly unprofessional, and the production was falling seriously behind schedule. This was costing money, and the studio was becoming impatient. I understood their feelings.

On behalf of the studio, I took a very tough position. Ms. Hayworth would have to shape up or be replaced. I even threatened to sue her for the added expense caused by her "deplorable conduct." Before any suit was filed, however, her daughter, Yasmin Khan, became involved, and Ms. Hayworth voluntarily withdrew from the project. Nothing further was said.

Years later, I learned that I had been terribly wrong about the entire situation. Rita Hayworth's conduct was not caused by drugs, drink or negligence. It was the onset of Alzheimer's disease, which apparently was the cause of her subsequent death. In those days, we didn't know about Alzheimer's, and we made (I made) a terrible mistake that caused her and her daughter extreme anguish and embarrassment.

There's nothing I can do about it now, except to apologize to her daughter and to make it as clear as I can that Rita Hayworth was a splendid actress who was always totally professional, even trying her best to perform when it was simply impossible for her.

I'm sorry—really sorry—that I played a part in making her life even more difficult.

34

Saying the Unmentionable

THE PEPSI COLA COMPANY had its headquarters in an attractive building in a rural area of Purchase, New York. I was there at a table with a dozen Pepsi executives trying to make a multi-million dollar advertising deal.

When the principal parts of the deal had been worked out, an attractive woman asked each of us if we'd like "refreshments." Without thinking I said "a Diet Coke please." Suddenly, a dramatic hush fell over the room. Each of the Pepsi representatives seemed to be staring at me with a mixture of amazement and horror.

I got it quickly. There in the heart of Pepsi-land, I'd expressed a preference for something I should never have even mentioned, much less requested—the product of their bitter rival. It was as if I'd cried "Hurray for Hitler" in a synagogue.

I tried to make it better by saying that I use "Diet Coke" generically to mean any cola product. But that only made it worse, implying that, whenever I think of a cola drink, what comes to mind is not a Pepsi, but the despised product of their competitor.

Despite my gaff, we closed the deal. But the atmosphere remained frosty. I should have learned long before this to think before I speak—even about something as seemingly unimportant as my choice of beverage. Obviously, I hadn't.

35

A Dramatic Life

David Begelman was a delightful man, well spoken with a keen sense of humor. He had been a powerful agent, then an enormously successful head of Columbia Pictures, then a convicted felon, then the head of MGM, then an independent producer and then . . . well, you'll see.

When David had his criminal problem—forging endorsements on checks—his lawyer was Frank Rothman, the gracious young man who'd been chief prosecutor in the City Attorney's Office at the time of my first civilian trial. Frank had become one of the country's leading lawyers; and his brilliant work had kept David out of jail.

Later, Frank's long-time client Kirk Kerkorian made Frank the CEO of MGM, a studio Kerkorian then owned. Frank hired David Begelman as head of production. David made some good pictures and some that were not so good. It was by no means a terrible record. But it wasn't a great one either. In any event, Frank and Kerkorian made the decision to replace David. Surprisingly and without warning, they notified him that he was fired "for cause," which meant he could get no further compensation of any kind. Not only that, the studio had David's Rolls-Royce (which the studio owned) towed away, creating an embarrassing situation for David.

Why did Frank do these things? I'll never know. It wasn't like him. Maybe Kerkorian insisted. Maybe Frank was embarrassed that he'd suggested David to run the studio. In any event, when David came to me, I could see nothing he'd done that could possibly constitute "cause" for his discharge.

There was an arbitration clause in David's contract, so we had to arbitrate his claim against MGM, rather than try it in court. The arbitrator was a distinguished retired judge. Both Frank and I had appeared before him in the past.

David testified and successfully weathered cross-examination. There seemed no real "cause" for his termination. Then it was MGM's turn. Their key witness was Frank Rothman, himself, the head of the studio. Their problem was that, having been a hugely successful trial lawyer, Frank evidently felt no need to prepare for his testimony. It was a critical mistake.

Frank testified that David had driven MGM into bankruptcy, putting the studio in a position in which it couldn't even meet its payroll. Not only that, Frank testified that David had allowed a drunken director to ruin an MGM film. And he swore that, in France, during the making of an MGM film directed by Blake Edwards, Edwards had complained to him that Begelman was not only ineffective, but that his negligence and interference were preventing Blake's doing his job and would cause the ultimate film to be a huge loser.

When Frank finished testifying, David turned to me stunned. He insisted that nothing Frank said was true—nothing! Fortunately, this was a Friday, and there was a weekend before I had to cross-examine Frank.

I was immediately faced with a problem. I needed desperately to talk to Blake Edwards. But I had previously represented Dustin Hoffman in a bitter dispute with Blake and, although the matter had ultimately been settled, my impression was that Blake wasn't speaking to me.

Well, I had no choice. I called Blake that evening. Surprisingly, he took the call, probably intending to give me a vehement scolding. I just said that I needed to speak to him urgently on a critical matter. Could I come to his house in the morning. Surprisingly, he agreed. Probably his curiosity got the better of him.

The next morning I drove out to Blake's home on the bluffs overlooking the sea in Malibu. We spoke for almost an hour, after which, to his credit, Blake agreed to testify on Monday.

Sue Mengers was an extraordinary agent and a friend whom I had represented in the past. I knew that Sue's French husband, Jean-Claude Tramont, also had key information that could rebut some of Rothman's claims. I had confirmed this with him, and he had also agreed to be at the arbitration Monday morning.

Sunday night, as I was preparing for my cross-examination of Frank Rothman, I got a call from Sue. She told me that her "darling Jean-Claude" couldn't be a witness the next day. She was very sorry, but he couldn't testify against the studio. It would be devastating to his career. I tried to persuade her, but it was no use. He just wasn't going to do it—or she just wasn't going to let him do it. It didn't matter. I'd have to do without Jean-Claude.

On Monday morning, I began the cross-examination of Frank Rothman. My career has included hundreds of cross-examinations, but this one was extraordinary. I asked Frank when it was that, as he'd testified, David Begelman had put MGM "in bankruptcy" so it couldn't even "meet its payroll."

He said it was in February of that year.

I then handed him MGM's quarterly report to the SEC for the period January, February and March. I asked if he saw where the report stated that the quarter had been "highly successful" for MGM and that the future of the company looked "rosy."

"Do you see that?"

"Yes."

"Do you see who signed the report—that it's signed by you?"

"Yes."

"That's exactly the time when you testified that MGM was bankrupt and couldn't meet its payroll. Was your report to the federal government false?"

"No, of course not."

There was nothing else Frank could say. Obviously, his testimony about Begelman driving the company into bankruptcy and rendering it unable to meet its payroll was, to put it charitably, totally wrong.

I pointed out some other things that were "wrong" in his testimony and I had him repeat what he'd said about his conversation with Blake Edwards. Then I asked if he was "sure" about that conversation—wasn't it possible that he wasn't remembering it correctly?

No he testified. He recalled it clearly.

Finally, I turned to what he said about David allowing a drunken director to ruin an MGM film. I asked for the specifics of this episode. Frank replied that it was all set out in a lengthy written report on Begelman. He motioned to his lawyers who handed him a very thick loose-leaf binder.

I asked Frank to point out the part of his "report" that showed a drunken director ruining an MGM picture. We all sat there in silence while Frank leafed through page after page of the lengthy report. After about five minutes, he finally said, "Here it is!"

I asked to see what he was pointing at. Then I read it aloud. "This says that, at 5:00 o'clock, after shooting was concluded, Mr. Toback (the director, James Toback) was seen with a glass of champagne in his hand."

"That's it?" I asked. "That's your evidence of the 'drunken director' ruining a picture?"

Again, Frank had to say it was. But he said it quietly.

And that's where I ended the cross-examination.

There was no redirect, and MGM rested its case.

I didn't have Jean-Claude; but, after Rothman's disastrous testimony on cross-examination, I didn't think I needed him. Moreover, I had Blake Edwards. In our rebuttal case, I called Blake to the stand. He flatly denied saying any of the things to Frank that Frank had claimed or saying anything even close to what Frank had testified. On the contrary, Blake said David Begelman was enormously helpful and effective in the organization and making of Blake's film.

In closing argument, I presented a chart with a very rude title itemizing Frank's provable misstatements. But it wasn't necessary. There was no question now as to the outcome—a complete win for David.

About a year later, I ran into the retired judge who'd been the arbitrator. We reminisced about the case, and he said, "Frank Rothman was as good a trial lawyer as I ever saw, but he was certainly the worst witness."

Frank's dead now. He was a superb trial lawyer and I liked him. I still don't know why he tried to fire David "for cause." I'd like to think it was Kerkorian's order. As to Frank's testimony, I think he was busy running the studio and, overly confident from his many years as a litigator, he simply took no time to prepare. I'm a little sorry I made that chart with an ugly title itemizing Frank's misstatements. It was piling on—unnecessary roughness. The Judge "got it" without the chart.

Anyway, to Frank's credit, he didn't hold a grudge. All of our interactions after the Begelman arbitration remained cordial.

Blake Edwards, with whom I was hardly speaking before the arbitration, became a client and remained one for years.

David Begelman founded an independent production company, which had some success, but, in the long run, encountered considerable difficulty. I was aware that David was under severe financial pressure. But I didn't realize the toll it was taking on him.

One morning, I arrived at my office to find a sealed envelope that had been delivered to my desk. Curious, I opened it to find a handwritten note from David Begelman saying thanks and goodbye.

A few minutes later I learned that, the night before, David had checked into the Century Plaza Hotel and blown his brains out.

36

How Times Change

Now, famous men are accused almost daily of multiple instances of sexual harassment, as in the case of Harvey Weinstein, or illicit sex, as in the case of Bill Clinton. In earlier years, most such matters were kept secret, except from insiders, as in the case of Franklin Roosevelt with Missy LeHand or Dwight Eisenhower with Kay Summersby.

One rising politician was an exception—and a sad one for the United States. That was Gary Hart. Gary, who became a friend, was the handsome, articulate and highly intelligent Senator from Colorado. He seemed a sure thing to win the Democratic nomination for President and very likely to win the election itself.

Only two things destroyed that chance—a girl and a yacht. Gary, a married man, was photographed with an attractive young woman sitting in his lap about to board a yacht named "Monkey Business" for a weekend of what appeared to be just such "business." The unfortunate name of the yacht appeared boldly behind Gary in the photo of the girl sitting on his lap.

Immediately, that deadly photo was published in virtually every American newspaper, as well as others throughout the world. These were different times. Gary's future as a presidential candidate appeared to be over.

At this point, Gary's friend, Warren Beatty, asked me to see if I could prepare Gary for his participation in a prime time network interview, with the hope that something he could say would resurrect what appeared to be a dead political career or at least one on life support.

I spent hours with Gary, trying to prepare him for the interview, trying to find a way to explain the seemingly unexplainable. The best way appeared to be the truth: Gary was sitting in the chair about to be photographed, when, without warning, the girl simply jumped into his lap. Gary knew he was being photographed and had only two choices. He could shove her off his lap onto the pavement, which would have been not only ungentlemanly but a disastrous photo, or he could let her sit there. He'd elected to let her remain.

Okay, I thought, maybe the audience would buy that explanation. But he still had a serious problem. He and the girl were about to board the yacht "Monkey Business" for a weekend cruise. Yes, he could point out that others would be aboard, that this was to be a weekend of political strategy and that he had a separate stateroom and planned to sleep alone.

But, we realized going in that no one was likely to believe our claim, that, given the girl's appearance, no one would buy she was on the trip to provide political advice. And they didn't buy it. Gary was literally laughed out of any possible run for the presidency. If only the yacht had a different name—but "Monkey Business"—come on!

Gary became a successful businessman and author. But, in my view, it was the nation's loss that he never became president.

How things change.

37

Local Counsel

I HAVE ALWAYS BELIEVED THAT, when trying a case in another city, it makes sense to associate with local counsel who's familiar with the judge and with local practices, procedures and prejudices. And there have been many situations in which I've relied totally on lawyers in other states. One instance was a land dispute in a rural Arizona town. This was no place for some hotshot "Hollywood" lawyer. Not even a lawyer from Phoenix. The local lawyer I used was a huge, aging fellow, famous in the area for his dramatic trial wins. When I heard from our mutual client that he'd won a terrific jury verdict, I called to congratulate the lawyer.

"Hell, Bert," he said, "it wasn't no damn surprise. My cousin and my dentist was on the jury!"

• • • •

Once in a San Francisco case many years ago, I hired Jake Ehrlich, then a famous criminal lawyer, to be co-counsel. I was surprised to see that Ehrlich's office had an old-fashioned front door, with a glass transom at the top. When I asked about it, Jake explained that, when he was a younger man, he, like many criminal lawyers, had trouble collecting fees from his clients. That's where the transom came in. Even with the door closed, you could carry on a conversation through the open transom, and Jake said he always kept the front door locked, but the transom open. When a potential client knocked, Jake would ask about the case. Then, he'd state the fee he was asking. If the fee was agreeable, Jake would shout, "Throw the money over the transom!" If the money didn't fly over the transom and into the room, Jake didn't unlock the door.

• • • •

I represented Madonna in a case brought in the Delaware Chancery Court by Warner Music. I filed a motion to dismiss the case on the ground that the proper venue was not Delaware, but California. I retained excellent local counsel, but traveled to Wilmington to argue the motion before a very distinguished Vice Chancellor, as Delaware calls its judges.

Before the case was called, my local counsel said he was planning to introduce me to the court, as is customary with out of state lawyers anywhere. I said "fine." But he added that he was going to mention the books I had written on Richard III and Shakespeare. Concerned, I said that the Vice Chancellor might resent that as irrelevant and an attempt to curry favor. "Wait," he said, "you'll see."

Our local counsel did introduce me just as he said he would, giving a few items of legal background and then mentioning some of the books I'd written. I remained concerned that this could backfire.

When I rose to argue our motion, the Vice Chancellor spoke even before I did. "What's your opinion Mr. Fields, did Richard the Third really kill his nephews in the Tower of London?" After I replied, the Vice Chancellor asked one or two other questions about my books. Obviously, he was fascinated by history.

Finally, he asked that I turn to our motion, which, after extensive argument from both sides, he granted.

Was he more inclined to grant the motion because I wrote books on English history? I'm absolutely sure he was not. He impressed me as a very bright judge who lived to apply the law correctly. I had no doubt that he ruled for my client because he thought my position was legally correct. Did it hurt that the local counsel mentioned my books knowing the Vice Chancellor would be interested? Not a bit. He knew his judge.

• • • •

To handle a federal criminal case in Texas against the daughter of a longtime client, I retained Percy Foreman, a legendary Texas criminal lawyer. It was said that Percy had successfully tried 100 murder cases. Maybe he did. In any event, when I arrived at his office, I found that it was actually a bank—except that the bank was no longer operating. There was a receptionist sitting near the door. But, although the building was huge, there was no one else in sight. When I introduced myself and asked for Mr. Foreman, the receptionist pointed to the rear of the bank.

I walked in that direction, passing numerous empty tellers' cages and loan officers' unoccupied desks. It was spooky.

Finally, I came to an office marked "President." I knocked, and a stentorian voice boomed, "Come on in." I did and there was the famous Percy Foreman. Strangely, he was in his shorts, darning a hole in his trousers.

We discussed the case and later had lunch at his club. During our talk, the headwaiter approached and whispered something in Percy's ear. Percy rose and announced, "Gotta take a call from 'the Big Man.'" He left and returned a few moments later with a huge smile.

I assumed that the "Big Man" was Lyndon Johnson, a fellow Texan and then President of the United States. I never found out. I returned to LA; and, a few days later, I got wonderful news from Percy. All the charges against my client's daughter had been dropped. I hoped that the U.S. Attorney for that district had concluded that the girl was innocent or at least that the government's case was too weak to go to trial.

Of course, the U.S. Attorney's respect for Percy's skill may have played a part. Who knew? In the back of my mind though, I've always wondered if there'd been some friendly intercession by the "Big Man" as a favor to his old Texas buddy. I'll never know. I never asked; and Percy, God bless him, has gone to the big courtroom in the sky.

38

"Calling The Kettle Black"

Peter Morton founded the Hard Rock Cafes, then a novel concept combining contemporary music, sporty food and fun. The cafes were a huge success, and the chain spread throughout the U.S. and England.

Some years later, after ownership of the Hard Rock chain in America was split between East and West, Peter hit on the brilliant idea of a Hard Rock Hotel and Casino in Las Vegas. The primary owners in the East were "Shocked, shocked! . . . gambling connected with the sacred Hard Rock name? Appalling!" They filed suit to enjoin Peter's Vegas project.

It was a close case, with the Eastern owners testifying to how gambling and the evils that follow it would ruin the valuable Hard Rock name. Then, on cross-examination, I asked the key executive of the Eastern Hard Rock chain what their principal business was.

My opponent leaped to his feet.

"Objection, your honor, irrelevant and immaterial. What could our clients' other business have to do with whether the valuable Hard Rock name is besmirched by gambling?"

I asked the Judge for some leeway, promising that the relevance would quickly be established.

The Judge paused—thinking—and then overruled the objection.

And it did quickly become obvious why the question was not only relevant but critical.

Reluctantly, the witness conceded that their principal business was "gaming."

"Gaming?" I asked, "doesn't that mean gambling?"

"Yes."

"So you operate the Hard Rock Cafes in the East, even though it's known that your principal business is gambling all over the world?"

"Yes."

"But you want to stop Mr. Morton from conducting a perfectly legal gambling business in just one city, Las Vegas, on the theory that an association with gambling will harm the Hard Rock name?"

"Yes, that's our contention."

"No more questions."

The request for an injunction was denied. The Hard Rock Hotel and Casino opened. It was, and still is, an enormous success. And whenever I see Peter Morton, he still says, "Thanks."

39

FOREIGN ADVENTURES

MOST OF MY CASES have been in the United States, including, of course, California, but also Hawaii, Nevada, Arizona, New York, D.C., Massachusetts, Ohio, Illinois, Delaware, Colorado, Florida, New Mexico, Texas, Pennsylvania and New Jersey.

In addition, there have been some very interesting matters overseas. Quite a number of the cases have been in England, where I worked through English Barristers and Solicitors. Two were in France, two in Germany and one in Mexico. But in each of those cases I also worked through local attorneys.

I did try a case against a Yugoslavian bank; but it was in federal court in Los Angeles. Much of the testimony was in Serbo-Croatian. This frequently resulted in dueling translations between two interpreters, each with a different version of what the witnesses had said. In the end, the case turned out fine; but I suspect I may never be welcome in the area that was formerly Yugoslavia.

I've had a number of cases for Japanese clients, some of which took me to Tokyo. One, however, took me to Nicaragua. I was retained by a Japanese bank to represent them in their claim that they were being cheated by a rich and powerful Nicaraguan owner of vast cotton farms with whom the bank had invested.

I was to travel to Nicaragua to investigate and, if possible, to find a Nicaraguan lawyer willing to sue the powerful farm owner on behalf of the Japanese bank. The problem was that the farm owner was rumored to be very close to Somoza, then the ruthless and murderous Nicaraguan dictator. Indeed, there was some thought that Somoza had a substantial interest in the farming operation I was about to investigate.

My partners (and my wife) were worried about my safety. But, I had a good friend and client in the oil business in Nicaragua. He spread the rumor, not only in Managua, but in the countryside as well, that I was Mafia and that, if any harm should come to me in Nicaragua, not only the men considered responsible, but every member of their families, down to the smallest child, would be hunted down and killed. I may have needed that.

I traveled to Nicaragua three times on the case, going far out into the countryside to the area of the farms in question, which was fairly near the area where the Sandinista revolution began. I was finally able to examine "the books" of the farming operation and, although I'm sure there were *two* sets of books, even the records I saw were enough to convince me that my Japanese client was not getting an honest count. I tried to see the records of the farm owner's bank account, which I felt would support what seemed the truth. Naturally, the Nicaraguan bank stonewalled me. I'd need a court order, they said.

My problem was finding a Nicaraguan lawyer who'd take the case. The man reported to be the best lawyer in Managua gave me words of encouragement, but to go into court suggesting that this farming operation, and possibly Somoza himself, was cheating? "No señor, not with the present administration." I could see his point. If Somoza was involved in the operation or even wanted to protect the owner, then taking the case could lead to the lawyer's "disappearing."

I tried the local newspapers. At this time, there seemed to be no opposition press. Still, I thought, this could be a big story. I asked if a scandal that potentially involved "El Supremo" would be a matter of interest? No dice. I was shown the door.

I reported the situation back to my clients in Tokyo. They thanked me for confirming the likelihood that they'd been cheated and said I should await further instructions.

The bank concluded that "self-help" was their best course. A month later, a freighter carrying an enormous quantity of cotton under the Panamanian flag docked in Hong Kong Harbor. The bank had learned that the ship and the cotton were owned by the Nicaraguan farm operator in question. The bank's Hong Kong lawyers seized both the ship and the cotton. They sold both, got the money that was due the bank and perhaps even more.

It was a fascinating adventure that had a happy ending. Was I in real peril? Given the rumor my friend spread, I didn't think so—except one time. That was in a torrential rainstorm having lunch in a shack that served Chinese food far out in the wilds of the Nicaraguan countryside. The place had no walls, but we were sheltered from the deluge by the palm frond "roof." The food was surprisingly good—chicken sautéed with garlic and hot red chiles. But, as a gringo, I noticed that there didn't seem any place to wash the dishes, much less the chopsticks. Perhaps rainwater, I thought; but I didn't want to ask. I didn't want to know. As it turned out, I was fine.

• • • •

Another time, I received a phone call from a major Japanese company asking if I could come quickly to Tokyo to help them negotiate a contract with a sophisticated American who they felt was trying to take advantage of them.

It sounded interesting, and I took a flight to Tokyo the next day. I arrived on a Sunday morning to find a message waiting at the hotel advising me that there would be a meeting at my client's headquarters that afternoon. A company car would pick me up.

At the meeting, I found not only the four or five key executives of my client but also the entire Board of Directors. They were all in dark suits and ties. A translator began to discuss the problem I was there to solve. He kept referring to "the unfortunate terms of the contract." I interrupted him to point out that I had come to negotiate the contract. What "contract" was he referring to?

Everyone looked embarrassed. At this point, the company's President addressed me in English. "Fields

San," he said, "we are embarrassed to tell you we have already committed to the contract."

"In writing?"

"No, but we agreed on all points and said we had a 'deal.' The shorthand reporter took it down."

I realized what had happened. In those days, educated Japanese, being extremely sensitive and polite, did not like to give anyone bad news. And the fact that they had already agreed to the contract I had come to Tokyo to "negotiate" would have been bad news indeed.

The fact was that, after reaching agreement, they had realized that the contract was extremely unfair, and they wanted me to find a way out. That's why I was there. They handed me a translation of their notes on the contract. I took them to my hotel to study.

Later that afternoon, I phoned my client's President and asked him to set up a meeting with the American who'd signed the contract and his lawyer. I said to make sure the meeting would be transcribed. I thought I might have a way out, but it was a longshot.

The next day we met. Again the room was filled, except that now our American "partner" was there with his lawyer, as was a shorthand reporter. I had given instructions on how my clients were to act.

After the necessary exchange of pleasantries, I told the American and his lawyer that I considered the contract ambiguous in one critical respect—that it didn't specify whether or not my client could exercise a particular right. I knew the exercise of that right would be extremely disadvantageous to the American. I said, "The contract needs to be clarified to make clear that my client can exercise this essential right. It's critical to them," I said. "Without that clarification they could never agree."

Here the American got angry and, being angry, made the mistake I was hoping for. His lawyer tried to speak to him, but he wouldn't listen. In an angry, impatient tone, he said, "Listen, Mr. Fields, if your clients insist on what you're asking for, we have no deal—just forget about it."

I believe the man was convinced that the Japanese really wanted the deal and that I was just trying to improve on what they had negotiated. I'm sure he didn't realize that what we wanted was to be out of the deal entirely.

"Well," I said, "I agree with you. Without that critical provision, we have no deal."

He stood up and made the situation even better. He held up his notes on the contract and said, "As far as I'm concerned, we can just tear this up!"

As I had instructed, my client's executives and Board members bowed politely and quickly left the room. I shook hands with the American and his attorney and also left the room, before the lawyer could enlighten his client. As I left, I turned to the shorthand reporter, "Did you get all that?"

"Yes sir, I did."

That night, I confirmed in writing to the American's lawyer that, regretfully, no contract between our clients had been concluded.

Also that night, the top executives of the company took me and my wife to a late dinner. There was a bottle of excellent scotch and a glass full of ice in front of each place, and the Kobe beef was superb. It was a happy group. Toast after toast was made. As the night wore on, I started to glance nervously at my watch, because we were to board a late JAL flight to Los Angeles. I had been told by a Vice President that the flight was at juuichi ji-han or eleven thirty. It was by now after ten and the airport was a long drive from our restaurant. Suddenly, another Vice President jumped up, ran to the President and whispered in his ear. The President turned to me in embarrassment. "It seems Fields San that your plane is at jugi-han, ten thirty, not juuichi ji-han as you were told."

I said, "Well, there's no way to get there in ten minutes, so I guess we're out of luck." This was a serious problem, because, as the Japanese knew, I was to start a trial the morning after I arrived back in LA.

The President rose and barked an order in Japanese. Quickly a phone was rushed to his side. He dialed a number he seemed to know by heart and launched into a rapid fire speech. I saw him smile and say something that sounded very nice. He hung up and turned to me. "You have no problem; but you need to leave right now. That was the President of the airline on the phone. The plane will be held for your arrival."

Wow! I doubt that the President of the U.S. could have an American airline hold a plane for someone arriving very, very late, because he'd been drinking and dining. But, at least in those days, the governing class in Japan was a far more closely knit group than in the States. I found out later that the President of our client and the President of the airline had known each other since childhood and played tennis together every weekend.

In any event, we said our goodbyes quickly and were rushed to the airport. It was almost eleven-thirty before we finally boarded the plane, to be greeted by angry muttering and enraged looks from our fellow passengers, who'd been kept waiting in their seats for over an hour.

The story had a pleasant sequel. The next time the President of my client was in California, he invited us to an intimate dinner at which, with considerable ceremony, he presented my wife with a large emerald from the company's mines. He added that, while grateful for what I had accomplished for the company, he was sure the quiet support of Mrs. Fields was to a great extent responsible. Okay, it was a bit sexist; but she loved the gift.

40

A Royal Tragedy

It was August 1997 and I had just started representing Mohamed Al-Fayed, the Egyptian-born former owner of Harrods, the giant London department store, and the legendary Hôtel Ritz in Paris. Barbara and I were vacationing at our mill in the French countryside. But we awoke early. We were to catch a helicopter at a nearby landing strip for a trip across the Channel to an airfield near London. From there, a car was to take us to a meeting with Mohamed. The principal subject of discussion was to be the media's treatment of Dodi Fayed, Mohamed's son, who was then the constant companion of Princess Diana in a widely publicized romance.

Just as we were leaving our home, the phone rang. There would be no meeting. Dodi and Princess Diana had been killed a few hours earlier in a terrible automobile accident in a Paris tunnel. Their French driver had also been killed.

Later, when I spoke with Mohamed, he insisted this was no accident. There were certainly many questions. Was their driver drunk? Who had been in the other cars that seemed to be pursuing the couple? Were they paparazzi or were they assassins? From a paint sample and the few witnesses who could be found, the French police determined the make and year of the car that had apparently caused the accident, by forcing Dodi and Diana's car into the tunnel wall. Yet, despite a nationwide search, the car was never found. How could that be?

There was a widespread rumor that the English royal family had arranged for the killing through MI5, in order to prevent Diana's marrying Dodi, who was dark complected and of Egyptian origin. Things were quite different then, and Diana was the mother of a future King of England. Would they allow her to marry such a man?

I thought the rumor was almost certainly untrue. But Mohamed didn't share my view. He was certain Dodi and Diana planned to be married, and that someone had tried to prevent their marriage by killing them. And who, he thought, but the English royals were motivated to do this? I felt there was no way the Queen would ever have authorized such a thing and that the idea of MI5 "going rogue" and arranging the murder of Diana on its own seemed absurd.

In any event, Mohamed was determined to pursue the matter; and we parted ways over his refusal to pay a detective who was unable to prove the conspiracy Mohamed was sure existed. Still, I liked Mohamed and felt sorry for his loss. I hope he's finally been able to put aside his anger and suspicion and get on with his life. But I doubt it.

I've tried to put myself in his place. If my son had been killed under those circumstances, I'd probably never let the matter rest. I doubt that Mohamed ever will.

41

Negotiation

I'VE PROBABLY NEGOTIATED a thousand contracts involving deals of every sort—motion picture agreements for actors, directors, producers, distributors and others, cotton farming agreements, corporate acquisitions, collective bargaining agreements, commercial leases, financing agreements for a regional shopping center and just about every other kind of agreement you can think of.

I teach negotiation to my students at Stanford Law School, and I've lectured on the subject at Harvard. But most of my negotiating tactics have been learned over the years from others.

Eli Broad taught me the value of asking, "Is that your best and final offer?" Usually, it's not. But if they say it's not, it shows there's a better deal to be made. Yet, most people are afraid to say "yes that's it" for fear you'll just leave.

Lester Roth, a superb lawyer and later an appellate judge, taught me to preface a question with, "Are you trying to create the impression that . . ." The best answer would be, "I'm not trying to create any 'impression.' I'm just telling you what it'll take to make a deal." But most people can't come up with that answer on the spur of the moment. Rarely will they say "yes," which makes their position seem a pose. But "no" suggests you haven't reached their bottom line.

But it was two people who taught me the use of anger—or at least feigned anger—in negotiations. One was Lew Wasserman, in the early days of my practice. The other was Peter Falk—much later.

Many years ago, I was representing Jack Webb in a dispute with MCA, then Jack's agent, over the sale of rights to the original *Dragnet* series. We were threatening a major lawsuit; but Jack really wanted a settlement, and I arranged a meeting with Wasserman, then CEO of the agency, in the hope of concluding a deal.

In those days, being a young lawyer, I called him "Mr. Wasserman." It was years before calling him "Lew" felt comfortable. In any event, I was ushered into Wasserman's office in MCA's handsome Beverly Hills building, situated on its own square opposite the Post Office. Like most offices in the building, Wasserman's was furnished with English antiques and splendid paintings.

He rose and greeted me cordially. I opened my briefcase, removed a lengthy memorandum covering the points of a potential settlement. As I went through points numbers one through eight, I got generally positive responses, a few clarifying questions, but no resistance. We were making real progress.

Then, I raised point number nine, expecting a similar response. Suddenly, Wasserman jumped to his feet and seemed to turn red. He pointed his finger at me and shouted:

"Get the hell out of here . . . right now! How dare you? We're through here. Take your settlement and shove it. We'll see you in court!"

I was stunned. I quickly packed my briefcase hoping he couldn't see my hands shaking. I stood up not knowing what to say.

But Wasserman wasn't through.

"You heard me," he bellowed. "Get out of here; we've got nothing more to say."

So I left.

Twenty minutes later, I called Jack.

"Well Bertie Boy, did you guys settle?"

"Not exactly."

I explained what happened, and Jack took it well. It looked like there was no choice but to litigate.

That night I got a call at home from Al Dorskind, one of Wasserman's top lieutenants. "Listen Bert. Whatever you said really infuriated Lew. He just wants to go to court. But most of us still see the sense in a reasonable settlement." Then, after a pause, he added, "If I can get Lew to sit down with you again, would you be ready to be somewhat more flexible?" I replied that I didn't think I'd been inflexible, but I'd be ready to sit down and try again.

Another meeting was arranged just a few days later. Wasserman was polite, but cold. We went over all my points, but when I got to point nine, I presented something I thought he would be more inclined to accept.

We ultimately reached a settlement that I thought was a good one for Jack. But, to this day, I still don't know if Wasserman's rage over "point number nine" was real or just a clever negotiating ploy.

• • • •

Years later, I saw an even more devastating use of rage in a negotiation. Peter Falk was a good friend as well as a client. He was the star of the immensely successful television series *Columbo*, produced by Universal and broadcast on NBC.

The current season of *Columbo* had just ended. Universal had Peter under contract for the coming season. But I had the theory that Universal had committed a material breach of the contract. If so, Peter had the right to cancel the contract and not perform in the series during the next season.

But, that situation had a more practical effect. It allowed me to demand a significant pay raise for Peter as the price of his waiving his right to terminate the contract and agreeing to continue performing in the series. Universal and NBC were, of course, desperate not to lose *Columbo*, a huge hit. They realized that, without Peter, there'd be no series.

After weeks of unsuccessful negotiations with Universal's business affairs executives, there was to be a final attempt to reach a settlement. Sid Sheinberg, Universal's President, and Herb Schlosser, then CEO of NBC, were to meet face to face with Peter and me at my office. We were quite far apart on the new terms; but Sid and Herb felt that, if they could speak directly to Peter, they could convince him to reduce the huge raise we were demanding.

The meeting began cordially. Although it was only eleven in the morning, Herb announced that he'd arranged for a special lunch to be delivered. We all nodded approval. Then, Sid turned to Peter and said, in a very polite tone, that what Peter was asking would create a large potential loss for the shareholders of Universal and NBC, and, since we all wanted this highly successful series to go forward, surely there was a way to compromise.

Suddenly, Peter jumped to his feet, his face bright red. "Compromise?" he shouted, waving his arms. "Compromise my career . . . compromise my life? Compromise? Fuck you!"

With that, he rushed from the room, slamming the door behind him.

Sid and Herb both started after him, but, in his haste, Sid knocked over a small bookcase and books came tumbling to the floor. I started to say something, but, instead, opened the door and went after Peter, only to be told by my receptionist that Mr. Falk had rushed out of the reception area.

I ran to the elevators, but it was too late. Peter was gone.

I returned to my office and apologized to a still shocked Herb and Sid. "He's gone?" "Yes. I'm afraid he's gone." Sid just stood there, shaking his head. Finally, he said "Bert, have you got an office where Herb and I could talk in private for a few moments?"

"Sure," I said and led them into the vacant office of my partner, Frank Rohner, who was out of town.

Ten minutes later, Sid and Herb knocked on my door and filed in. Standing in front of my desk, Sid spoke quietly. "We've decided that the best thing is to give Peter what he's asking. I assume this will get him to come back for next season." This last was said more as a question than a statement. I told them I thought they were being very wise, that I'd do what I could to make it work. But, I said, you heard Peter. I can't promise anything.

When they'd left, I called Peter's home. He'd arrived only minutes before. I told him of the conversation after he left and asked if he was okay, adding that I was really worried about his emotional state.

His response was ambiguous. "You don't need to worry. Don't forget, I'm an actor." He certainly was. If he was playing rage that day, he certainly fooled me. Anyway, we closed the deal on Peter's terms, and the series continued.

• • • •

I came to represent Ray Stark after he and I had some ferocious battles. The battle that I particularly remember was when I represented Jimmy Caan, then a huge star, in negotiating a deal for Jimmy to star in a film Ray was to produce.

The negotiations were more difficult than usual, and there was one major point on which Ray's then lawyer and I were unable to reach agreement. Meanwhile, Jimmy had participated in rehearsals and shooting was ready to begin the next day. I hand delivered a letter to Ray's lawyer, saying that, while Jimmy would be glad to shoot the first week without a contract, he wouldn't go beyond that unless and until we reached agreement.

Ray's lawyer wrote back that we'd reached agreement on virtually everything, and Jimmy was bound. I said that's nonsense. With our disagreement on a very significant point, there can't be a binding contract. Jimmy's completely free not to do the picture unless you agree to what he's been asking.

It must have been a bitter pill to swallow; but Ray's lawyer knew I was right; and, much as Ray hated it, they had to give in. They did; and Jimmy did the film, which was a commercial and artistic success.

After shooting "wrapped," Ray sent Jimmy a small but very expensive piece of bronze sculpture. The card read, "Please tell Mr. Fields to shove this up his ass."

• • • •

Every year, the leading players in many, if not most, successful television series ask for raises. Some openly say that they ought to get more money, since the series is doing so well. Others will come up with phony claims of an illness that quickly is cured if they're paid more money. Still others will claim the production company committed some kind of breach, allowing them to terminate their contracts if they're not paid more money.

My client, Aaron Spelling, always followed the policy of granting generous raises when the series was successful (and Aaron's always were), even when the actor raised some phony claim of illness or breach.

I advised Aaron that, when the series was over, he could sue to get the money back from any actor who made a phony claim to coerce Aaron into paying him more. But Aaron never agreed. "Nope," he'd say, "the series is a big success, and I agreed to pay more. Yes, the guy tried to force me to pay it, but so what? I'm making enough."

That was Aaron; and that's why more people loved him than loved me.

There was at least one instance in which I was able to push a TV production company into holding firm against a coercive demand. This was the case of James Gandolfini, the star of *The Sopranos*. In one of the last years of the series, Gandolfini's attorney said that, unless his agreed pay was enormously increased, he wouldn't be back for the next season of *The Sopranos* because of California's unusual "seven year rule," which provided that an employee couldn't be held to an employment contract beyond seven years.

This time my clients were tougher than Aaron Spelling had been. I wrote back that the "seven year rule" was strictly a matter of California law, that Gandolfini was a resident of New Jersey, the series was shot in New Jersey by a New York production company, the contract had been made in New York and the only "contact" with California was the office of Mr. Gandolfini's lawyer; which would hardly make California's "seven year rule" applicable.

Gandolfini abandoned his argument and showed up for the balance of the series.

• • • •

Was what I did in Jimmy Caan's case or what Peter Falk did in the *Columbo* negotiation any different from what I criticized in the actors' tactics with Aaron Spelling or Gandolfini's ploy regarding *The Sopranos*? I say there was a big difference. In the Caan matter, it was demonstrable that no contract had ever been reached and that Jimmy remained free to perform or not. In the *Columbo* case, there were solid legal arguments that the studio was in breach and that Peter Falk had the right to refuse to render any future services in the series unless he got a significant raise. By contrast, there was no breach of contract by my producer client in the Gandolfini situation or by Aaron Spelling in the regular end of season claims against his company.

I like to think that I've never just "held up" any employer, using an unjustified refusal to perform to extort greater payment. Am I fooling myself? I don't think so. But I'm sure there are networks and studios that wouldn't agree.

42

The "Ad"

Tom Cruise, a longtime client and dear friend, is a Scientologist. The world knows that. Tom believes that Scientology has been an enormous force for good in his life.

Some years ago, the government of a German state went on a kind of crusade against Scientology. They passed laws excluding Scientologists from government jobs and even their children from public schools.

I was enraged. Whatever your views of Scientology might be, they didn't deserve this kind of harsh governmental discrimination. I called studio heads, key agents and some principal actors. I said that what the Germans were doing to Tom's religion was despicable, that it was like the early days of the Nazi regime, when they were cruelly discriminating against Jews—before they started killing them.

I said I was going to take a full-page ad in the *International Herald Tribune* calling out the Germans and pointing out that, today, it was Tom's religion, tomorrow, it might be theirs. I asked to use their names in the ad. To a person they agreed. I bought the ad and it ran in the *Herald Tribune*, creating a furor in Germany.

Some Germans angrily responded that I was falsely accusing them of building concentration camps and murdering innocents, as the Nazis had. I tried to point out that the ad said no such thing, but only compared their anti-Scientology campaign to the early days of Nazi rule, when Jews were cruelly discriminated against, but not yet imprisoned or murdered.

In any event, I think the ad had the desired effect. It captured the attention of most Germans to a deplorable policy and, I believe, helped to at least mitigate the policy.

A copy of the controversial ad is included in the illustrations (page x).

You can draw your own conclusions.

43

Remembering A Code Section

Judge Jerry Pacht was a lovely man and a fine judge.

I was in his courtroom one morning, waiting for my case to be called. Judge Pacht was hearing argument on another case about which I knew nothing.

As I looked up, I noticed that the plaintiff's attorney seemed frustrated at his inability to convince the Judge of the merit of his argument. "But," he told the Judge, "what possible response could there be to Civil Code Section 2611.21?"

Judge Pacht looked at the lawyer with a smile. "Counselor," he said, "my mind has only limited capacity; and I've noticed, over the years, that, when I remember the number of a code section, I forget a line of poetry."

44

The Least Happy Fella

ONE AFTERNOON, I got a call from Gore Vidal in Italy. Gore was furious. The studio had submitted the proposed writing credits for a picture called *The Sicilian*. Gore had written one draft of the screenplay, a draft he considered the best of several. According to the studio, Gore was to receive co-screenplay credit on screen and in paid advertising. This meant significant added money for Gore. However, at the request of another writer who had submitted another draft of the screenplay, the Writers Guild (WGA) had conducted an "arbitration" to determine the screen credits, and the arbitration panel had ruled that Gore wasn't entitled to any credit at all. The other writer was to receive sole screen credit as writer of the screenplay. The added money to Gore, conditional on screen credit, was out the window.

"You've got to get that changed, Bert. It's not just the money. It's the idea. This ruling is crazy! My name must be on that picture. I wrote it—or at least co-wrote it."

I told Gore I'd do what I could. But that didn't seem like much. The arbitration panel had ruled, and its ruling would be difficult to overturn.

Then I remembered that, under the WGA rules that governed such arbitrations, the identity of the arbitrators was kept a secret. I recalled an earlier case in which Universal had argued that this was an unfair and improper procedure. I remembered that because I'd been on the other side, representing Mario Puzo in a WGA arbitration, and I had successfully argued for Mario that the WGA procedure was perfectly proper—indeed, was essential.

Now, I realized I had to get around the very precedent I had established and argue instead that the WGA procedure was unconstitutional, because it deprived Gore of his writing credit (and the money that went with it) without due process of law.

So I filed an action in state court to declare the arbitration invalid as a violation of Gore's rights under the due process clause of the U.S. Constitution. I argued that the WGA procedure deprived Gore of basic fairness, because it refused to disclose the names of the arbitrators. For example, it could turn out that one of the arbitrators was his opponent's brother-in-law. He'd never know. I argued that couldn't be due process.

The WGA was outraged. Their attorney argued that this procedure had successfully existed for years, that my own Puzo case against Universal squarely upheld that procedure and that, in the Puzo case, I had argued the exact opposite of what I was arguing now.

I said "not so." The WGA arbitrators were always other writers. To a great extent, they were dependent upon studios to get jobs. The Puzo case involved a dispute between a writer and <u>a studio</u>. In those cases, I argued, there was a strong policy reason to protect the writer-arbitrators against the studio's latent threat to harm their careers if they ruled against the studio. That policy reason applied in disputes between the writer and <u>the studio</u>, as in the Puzo case. In those cases the identity of the writer-arbitrators had to be kept secret, so that they could feel free of studio pressure.

But, in Gore Vidal's case, I argued, the dispute was between <u>two writers</u>, with no studio involved. Thus, I said, my argument in the Puzo case didn't apply, the arbitrators had no fear of studio retaliation, and the ordinary requirements of due process had to be followed. That is, Gore had to know who his judges were.

After lengthy and heated argument, a courageous judge, Dzintra Janavs, ruled for Gore, holding that the WGA arbitration procedure was a violation of Gore's constitutional right to due process and, therefore, invalid.

The Writers Guild and its lawyers were crazed. The entire WGA arbitration structure that had decided thousands of cases over many years was out the window.

Of course, the WGA appealed. I argued the case before the Appellate Court, making essentially the same argument I had made as in the trial court. Again, the Guild's lawyer pointed out what he called my "flip flop" in arguing the opposite of what I had argued in the Puzo case. About a month later, the Court of Appeals issued its opinion affirming Judge Janavs' decision and holding that the WGA arbitration procedure was an invalid denial of due process. This meant that the credits originally proposed by the studio would stand, including a writing credit for Gore. We had won—wow! The entire Guild procedure, one that had been accepted and used for years, was out!

I was thrilled. My due process theory had been a long shot; but, thanks to a courageous trial judge and a thoughtful appellate panel, it had paid off. As soon as I read the appellate opinion, I called Gore at his home in Italy.

"Great news, Gore," I said. The Court of Appeals upheld Judge Janavs' decision. You won a knockout victory. The WGA procedure that was followed for years has been held illegal. Your name will be on every print of the picture and in every ad."

Instead of the expression of joy and praise I anticipated, there was a long, surprising silence. Finally, Gore responded. "I saw the picture last night, Bert. Keep my name off that piece of shit!"

45

Foreign Affairs

Once at a dinner, someone asked if, with the exception of The Beatles, my clients were mostly American. I responded that with the exception of Japanese, English and Canadian clients, that was essentially true.

Barbara didn't want to contradict me publicly, but, on the way home, she pointed out that I was goofy. "How about Bertolucci?" she said. "You had a long case for him. And how about Zeffirelli? Claude Lelouch? Isabelle Adjani? And have you forgotten Gerard Depardieu?" Yes, I had completely forgotten.

One morning, I received a frantic call from the agent for Depardieu, the marvelous French actor. American newspapers were carrying a story claiming that Gerard had participated in raping a girl in the South of France. "It never happened," the agent cried, "Gerard swears it."

I got the papers and saw that it had become a hot story. One thing was strange; most of the stories said Gerard had "assisted" in the rape, and some said he'd "helped" rape the girl. What was particularly bad was that they all quoted Depardieu seemingly admitting this. How do you "assist" a rape?

I read Depardieu's quote to my wife, who's fluent in French. She quickly told me that Gerard had used the verb "assister," which sounds like it would mean "to assist." In fact, it means "to witness." What Gerard had related to the media was a story about seeing a girl raped in Marseille when he was young. Apparently a crowd had watched. Gerard had not said he'd participated in the rape or helped the rapists. He had simply watched. Not great, but certainly better than what the media was reporting.

I quickly got out letters to all the wire services and newspaper syndicates pointing out the correct translation of "assister" and demanding a correction. The correction appeared widely and the storm that threatened Depardieu's career blew over.

He's a great actor, and I was pleased to help. Last time I heard of Gerard, he had moved to Moscow to avoid French taxes. Okay, maybe that's not admirable; but it beats assisting in a rape.

• • • •

Isabelle Adjani's case led to an actual trial. The French film star was—and still is—an extraordinarily beautiful woman. She asked me to help her with a claim against Time Inc. and Young & Rubicam (Y&R). Time Inc. was, among other things, the publisher of *Time*, then a hugely popular and immensely powerful news magazine. Y&R was the nation's biggest ad agency and they were the agency for *Time* magazine.

A few months earlier, *Time* had published a picture of Isabelle as part of a news story. No problem. Now, however, *Time*, working with Y&R, had published an advertisement for *Time* magazine featuring the same photo of Isabelle and captioned "She's bright, she's vital, she reads *Time*."

This didn't seem right to Isabelle, and it didn't seem right to me. We filed a lawsuit in federal court alleging a violation of Isabelle's right of publicity. The defendants were represented by Tony Leibig, a classmate of mine at Harvard Law School and a skilled trial lawyer. Tony argued that a publication could properly take a photo it had previously published as part of a news story and feature that photo in an ad for the magazine, in effect using the photo as a sample of its work. A case involving Bette Midler had held just that. It allowed an earlier news photo of Ms. Midler to be used in an ad for the magazine.

I argued that our case was different, that *Time*'s ad featuring Isabelle didn't just use her photo as a sample of its work, as in the Midler case. It falsely represented her as a <u>reader</u> of *Time* magazine and thus as someone who, at least impliedly, <u>endorsed</u> the magazine. That, I argued, was what the words "She's bright, she's vital, she reads *Time*" clearly meant.

Tony argued that "She" in the sentence referred to the general *Time* reader, not Isabelle personally, so it wasn't an endorsement by her—that it was just like the Midler case.

I called a professor of linguistics as an expert. He testified that the words of the ad just below the photo of

Isabelle plainly told the reader that "She" in the sentence referred directly to Isabelle and meant to ordinary readers that Isabelle Adjani read and endorsed *Time* magazine. Tony slightingly referred to the professor as "the Guru," but was unable to shake him on cross-examination.

I also called a longtime agent in the business of licensing star's endorsements for use in advertising. He testified that *Time*'s wording at the bottom of the ad was a typical form of endorsement, for which the actress pictured would ordinarily receive hundreds of thousands of dollars.

In any event, the Judge decided the case for Isabelle, finding that *Time* and Young & Rubicam had used her name, likeness and endorsement without her permission and in violation of her right of publicity. He awarded her very sizeable damages. A very pleased Isabelle went back to France, just as beautiful, but considerably richer.

• • • •

So, next time someone asks, I'll try to remember that The Beatles were not my only foreign clients.

46

A Hollywood Meeting

OVER THE YEARS, I've been a part of countless meetings—some cordial and productive, others rude and antagonistic. Sometimes I'm asked my most memorable meeting. It's hard to pick one from a few contenders. But the meeting I call "Chinatown" comes readily to mind.

Chinatown was (and is) a great movie. It starred a superb actor, Jack Nicholson, as private eye Jake Gittes, and it was written by Bob Towne, possibly the all-time greatest screenwriter.

Following the enormous success of *Chinatown*, Paramount hit on the idea of a sequel. Why not? Towne was still around, and so was Nicholson. So Towne went to work on a sequel screenplay. It was to be called *The Two Jakes*; and Towne was to write and also direct it. One "Jake" was the same detective, Jake Gittes. Of course, he was to be played again by Nicholson. The other "Jake" was a new character written by Towne. And that's what caused the problem.

Bob Evans, a very nice man, started in his family dress business, became a successful film producer and, for a time, had even been a successful head of Paramount

Pictures. More than anything, however, Evans wanted to be an actor. Unfortunately, he had tried acting in films; and, putting it mildly, he'd had limited success. Indeed, in the view of most people who'd seen him act, he couldn't.

But Evans was a good friend of both Nicholson and Towne, and he was desperate to play the other Jake in Towne's new film. Since Towne was a client and a friend, we discussed this. Towne was sure he could make Evans a good actor. I disagreed. "Have you seen his work, Bob? *The Fiend Who Walked the West*, *The Sun Also Rises* and *The Best of Everything*. Bob, get real. I like Bob Evans—very much. He's a good guy and a fine producer; but he can't act. And you can't change that."

"Bert," he said, "you're wrong. The talent is there. It's latent; and I can bring it out."

Well, we just couldn't agree; and, after all, he was the writer-director, not I. I was just the lawyer. So, Towne held a couple of rehearsals with Evans playing the second Jake. Pretty soon, I got an early morning call. "Okay, okay, you were right. I can't make Bobby an actor. I've tried, and it's hopeless. He can't be the second Jake. It'll break his heart, but I just can't do it. I've got to tell Paramount and, worse, I've got to tell Evans."

Well, that part wasn't as easy as Towne thought. Evans put up a huge fight for the role, and Paramount didn't know which way to turn. So an "all hands meeting" was called at Evans' home to hear both sides and reach a decision.

The meeting was held in the very large room behind Evans' swimming pool. As I walked toward the meeting room, I passed at least three gorgeous young girls in bikinis lounging by the pool. "Okay," I thought, "even if he doesn't get the part, Evans' life isn't so bad."

The meeting was extraordinary. Frank Mancuso, then head of Paramount, was there, flanked with a covey of Paramount executives and lawyers. And, of course, so was Jack Nicholson. Representatives of every major agency were present, as were the top entertainment lawyers. It seemed everyone had a stake in this game.

As I entered the room, I saw Bob Evans. Remarkably, he was wearing an orange terrycloth bathrobe and a brown fedora hat—strange attire from this guy who was something of a fashion plate.

I walked up to him, saying, "Hi Bob." Looking at the floor, he mumbled, "Hello Bert," extending a rather limp handshake. This was not the Bob Evans I was used to, whose grip was firm and whose response was always filled with vigor.

In any event, Mancuso called the meeting to order and indicated that Bob Towne would speak first. Bob did, and he was eloquent and effective. He said he had a duty to the studio and its shareholders to cast the film in a way that gave it the best chance of success, that he had thought his friend, Bobby Evans, being a brilliant filmmaker, would be a brilliant actor as the second Jake. But, he said, he'd been very wrong and that he would be acting irresponsibly and betraying his obligation to the studio and its shareholders if he allowed Evans to play that key part.

"It was an extremely hard thing for me to do," he said. "But I had to tell Bobby 'no.' And, without a doubt 'no' was and is the only responsible answer—both artistically and commercially."

I could see the heads nodding all around the room. Seemingly, Towne had pulled it off. There was no overcoming the points he'd made. Evans had to be out.

At that point, Jack Nicholson raised his hand, and was recognized by Mancuso. "Jack, do you have something to add?" He did indeed. Nicholson rose, looked slowly around the room and began. "I'll be brief. Commerce is important," he said. "And, of course, so is art." So far everyone was in agreement. "But," he said, his voice rising, "friendship is more important than either art or commerce. And, if my friend, Bobby Evans, isn't in this picture, then I'm not in it either!"

The room exploded. Nicholson *was* Jake Gittes. Without Nicholson, there was no picture, and everyone there knew it. They broke up into separate groups. I happened to be drawn into the Paramount group, whose thoughts can be summarized as, "What the hell do we do now?"

The separate discussions went on well into the night with no resolution. I left, disappointed in Nicholson, a very smart guy, who surely realized that Evans would wreck the film and yet called himself a close and loyal friend of Bob Towne.

The next morning I got a call from Towne. I angrily blasted away at Nicholson, who I said had flat out betrayed him. "You should never speak to the son of a bitch again!" Towne interrupted me. "You don't understand," he said. "Jack's here now. I'll put him on. He'll explain."

"Listen," said Nicholson, "We've got to do this. We can't just reject Bobby. We've got to let him down slowly. Towne'll shoot a few scenes with him in the part and then, after viewing those scenes, Towne can reluctantly let him go."

Now I understood. The problem was Paramount didn't. They didn't know what Nicholson had in mind, and they'd lost confidence in the entire project. The next thing I read, *The Two Jakes* was indefinitely postponed. Towne and Nicholson went on to other things.

A long time later, the project was revived with Nicholson acting and directing. Evans was <u>not</u> the second Jake, and Towne was not involved.

Like so many others, the picture failed. The entire situation recalled the great, but ambiguous last line from the original picture . . . "It's Chinatown."

47

My Friend, Mario

MARIO PUZO, who wrote *The Godfather*, was a dear friend as well as a client.

We first met when Mario gambled at the Tropicana, then the premier hotel in Las Vegas. I represented the hotel at the time and had to travel there from time to time on hotel business. I say "had to"; but the fact is it was always exciting, with never ending, unusual problems to solve. Strolling through the casino in my dark suit and silver tie, I felt like I was a character in a film.

Anyway, Mario had written a film called *Earthquake* and a Writers Guild arbitration had held that he was not entitled to screenplay credit, which meant that Universal could pay him much less money. Mario was at the Tropicana when he got the bad news. He was hurt and angry. The hotel management suggested he talk to their lawyer, and he did. That's how we met.

The Writers Guild had an appellate process, and I filed an immediate appeal. Fortunately, we were able to get the decision reversed, and a new arbitration panel held Mario entitled to screenplay credit—and much more money.

We became good friends. I handled other cases and contracts for Mario and attended fantastic afternoon celebrations at his Bay Shore, Long Island home, playing bocce ball and stuffing myself with lasagna and other delicious Italian dishes brought by Mario's relatives and neighbors.

Of course, we talked a lot about *The Godfather*. Mario was fierce in telling me I must have nothing to do with the Mafia. "Let me tell you what'll happen," he said. "One day your dog will die. The next day, there'll be a knock at your door—it'll be a young guy in a dark suit with a puppy in his arms. He'll say 'Don Carmine heard about your loss and wanted you to have this little fella.' 'Wow,' you'll think, 'what a nice thing to do.'

"Then, five years later, you'll be about to start trying a case and you'll get a call. 'Mr. Fields, Don Carmine wants you to lose this case.'

"You'll say, 'Are you crazy? I'm going to win—big time!' Then, in an ominous tone, he'll say, 'Mr. Fields, remember the puppy? Remember how you took Don Carmine's gracious gift in your time of grief? Don Carmine would be seriously offended if you refused to respond to his generosity.'

"Anyway, you'll get the implied threat, and they'll feel justified in making that threat, because 'you took the money.' Only, in this case, you took the puppy.

"So," Mario said, "Don't take the puppy! And don't hang out with them. They may seem fascinating—even fun. But they can be deadly—especially when they feel you 'owe them' and don't pay your debt."

All of this was surprising from the guy who wrote *The Godfather*.

• • • •

Some years later, Mario wrote a screenplay for Warner Bros.' film *Superman*. The film was to be produced by Alexander Salkind, a somewhat mysterious European, brilliant and charming, but something of a rogue.

The picture was an enormous success and made a huge amount of money. Mario had a percentage of the distributor's gross receipts, and it appeared he'd make a bundle. But time passed, and Mario got no payment.

Mario's contract was with Salkind's UK company. When I complained, I was told that Salkind's argument was, first, that Mario's screenplay was so bad it constituted a material breach of his contract, and, second, that, even though I might think Warner Bros. was the "distributor" of the picture in whose gross revenue Mario was to share, the real 'distributor' was, in fact, Salkind's Costa Rican company. So, even if he won, Mario would get a share of the Costa Rican company's gross revenue, not the gross revenue of Warner Bros. "Unfortunately," they said, "the Costa Rican company didn't make a dime from *Superman*."

"Absolute bullshit!" I replied, with some heat—and we sued. Others, including Marlon Brando, had not been paid either; and they also sued. The litigation turned into an amusing, and quite wonderful adventure.

We served notice of taking Salkind's deposition in Los Angeles, i.e., his sworn testimony recorded by a court reporter. On the day of his deposition, Salkind failed to show. I filed a motion asking the Court to compel his testimony at my office in LA on a new date. I also asked for monetary sanctions for his failure to show.

By coincidence, the judge was Campbell Lucas, who'd been the judge in the *Jonathan Livingston Seagull* case. Salkind's lawyers begged Judge Lucas to be lenient. Salkind, they said, could not fly. He was terrified of flying and never, ever flew. He was in Mexico—in Acapulco—and he would be glad to have his deposition taken there.

Judge Lucas was understanding—more understanding than I'd hoped. "If the man can't fly, okay, I'll order his deposition in Acapulco. But Mr. Salkind will have to pay Mr. Fields' flight there and for his meals and lodging there and also for the court reporter."

Gratefully, Salkind's lawyers arranged for a new date in Acapulco and had no problem with the order to pay all of my expenses.

Two weeks later, I had a lovely dinner with my wife in Acapulco. When I arose the next morning ready to take Salkind's deposition, there was a knock at the door of my hotel bungalow. It was one of Salkind's lawyers. He looked embarrassed—actually, he looked mortified. He told me there could be no deposition that day. "Why not?" I asked. "Because," he said, "Alex isn't here."

"Isn't here?" I said. "Where is he?"

There was a long silence. The lawyer looked at his shoes. "Actually, he's in Europe."

"He's in <u>Europe</u>?"

"Yes."

"How'd he get there?"

There was an even longer pause.

"He flew."

"He <u>what</u>!"

"He flew."

Well, back we went before Judge Lucas. His questions were the same as mine. "He flew? You told the Court he couldn't fly. Obviously he can. Where is he?"

"In San Remo, Italy."

I demanded that Salkind be ordered to return to Los Angeles within a week to be deposed. My opponents pleaded. Finally, Judge Lucas asked if I would be willing to go on a European trip at Mr. Salkind's expense. I said, "If I could be sure to get his deposition, I would."

So, the Judge ordered that Salkind's deposition be taken in San Remo on a specified date and that Salkind must pay my first-class round trip fare, hotel and expenses to take his deposition there, as well as the expenses of the court reporter.

With Lydia, I arrived in San Remo at a stately 19th Century hotel overlooking the Mediterranean. Salkind and his lawyers also arrived, and we arranged for his deposition to be taken at a large table on the hotel's vast lawn overlooking the sea. Our table was separated by a tall hedge from the other hotel guests relaxing in lounge chairs.

Meanwhile, I had made a secret plan with Mario that was to play a dramatic role in the litigation. He was to fly secretly to San Remo and then, at the designated time, wait behind the tall hedge until I gave a signal.

I had heard that Salkind could be a tough guy when talking to his lawyers. But, when his adversary was present, Salkind's desperate need to be liked would make him relent and try to win the other guy's approval. That was the basis of our plan.

We began the deposition and covered a number of subjects. Soon though, I got to Salkind's claim that Mario had never done what the contract required because, supposedly, his screenplay was so terribly bad.

At that point, I gave the pre-arranged signal, and Mario stepped out from behind the tall hedge, shambling like a big bear and carrying his usual unlighted cigar. As he came to the table, Salkind jumped to his feet, and hugged him. "Mario, my dear friend. What a wonderful surprise!"

Mario grunted and sat down. The deposition resumed.

I immediately asked Salkind—under oath—if there was anything Mr. Puzo was to do under the contract that he didn't do.

Salkind's lawyers got it at once. They jumped up demanding a recess. I said, "I'm proceeding," but they just grabbed Salkind and dragged him far across the lawn "to talk." They stayed there for five minutes. I could see the lawyers gesticulating broadly and Salkind shaking his head over and over again.

Finally, the lawyers returned, looking disgusted. Salkind took his seat, the reporter reminded him that he was under oath and then read him back my question. Salkind looked over at Mario and smiled. Mario smiled back. "My friend Mario," he said "not only did everything required of him by the contract, he did it brilliantly."

That was the end of defense number one. I had an expert, a distinguished producer and writer ready to testify that Mario's screenplay for *Superman* was one of the best he'd read in a long career. But now I didn't need him. I had Salkind's critical admission.

I asked Salkind some more questions. I knew that he'd recently been arrested by Interpol in Germany, but had flashed a Costa Rican diplomatic passport, so they had to let him go. I asked if he had the passport with him. He did. It really was a Costa Rican diplomatic passport, and it contained a photo of a much younger Salkind.

"When were you last in Costa Rico, Mr. Salkind?"

"1942."

"And you are still a Costa Rican diplomat?"

"Absolutely."

After an afternoon of questioning on the lawn in San Remo, Salkind's lawyers said he had an urgent need to be in Venice. The deposition of another witness was scheduled to be taken there, and, since I had more ground to cover, we could complete Salkind's deposition while there. They offered, of course, to pay all our expenses. I agreed. Why not? I love Venice.

The problem was that, when I got to Venice and checked into the Gritti Palace, ready to resume Salkind's deposition, he wasn't there. What a surprise! Where was he? Sheepishly, his lawyers said, "He's in Marbella," a resort town on the coast of Spain, just across from North Africa. What the hell, I thought. I even agreed to go to Marbella at their expense; but I warned them that I intended to tell the Court that Salkind was abusing the system and abusing me.

And so the entourage went to Marbella, where we continued Salkind's deposition on the patio of my villa. I completed my questioning and turned him over to the lawyers for the other plaintiffs. Because it was extremely hot, I was wearing a Speedo; and when I wasn't examining the witness, I stretched out on a recliner to listen.

We had many adventures in Marbella. I won't relate them all. One of the attorneys, whom I knew to be a gracious, Southern gentleman, calmly poured a full pitcher of ice water onto the lap of the court reporter while we were dining in a restaurant. Why? He felt that, basically, she wasn't a nice person.

Then when we were at the small Marbella airport, ready to board a flight to Rome, John Schulman, then Warner Bros.' chief counsel, was late. There was no air traffic problem. Ours was the only plane on the field. Still, the pilot said he wouldn't wait for John.

Lydia, who was fond of John, and had something of a temper, simply sat down in front of the plane's single forward wheel. Her arms were folded, her expression determined. While she sat there, the plane couldn't move.

"Senora, you must move."

"You'll have to move me."

Well, he wasn't going to try that. I didn't blame him. I wouldn't have tried it either.

When the police were about to be called, John finally showed up. All was forgiven. We boarded the plane, headed for Rome and then, by Alitalia, to LA.

Back in LA, I went to court to seek further sanctions against Salkind for "abusive conduct," never keeping his word and making me traipse all over Europe. Salkind's lawyers brought in a blown up picture of me in a Speedo spread out on a recliner in Marbella.

"Here's Mr. Fields being abused," they said.

Judge Lucas just smiled. He didn't award further sanctions.

We finally settled the case in a way that got Mario all the money he was due. I had become friends with Alex Salkind's lawyers and with his key aide, Pierre Spengler. I even became friendly with Alex. I'd see him collecting his mail at the Hotel Raphael in Paris, where I've stayed for many years. Occasionally we'd laugh about the good old days, about San Remo, Venice and Marbella.

There were those who angrily called Alex a scoundrel. But, if so, he was a charming scoundrel. And that's the best kind.

Bert Fields in Malibu
Photo courtesy Jim McHugh

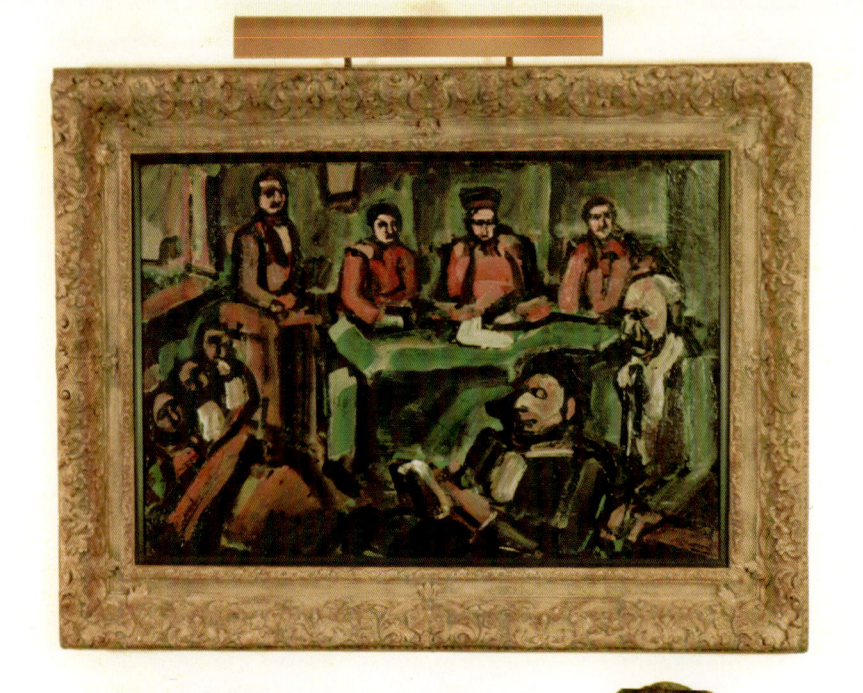

Edward G. Robinson with his paintings
Photo: Moviepix/Getty Images

Wayne Rogers and Sherry Lansing (circa 1970s) in Catalina
Bert Fields Personal Collection

Snapshots (1968) of Lydia, Mel Brooks & Anne Bancroft
Bert Fields Personal Collection

IV

Lydia
Bert Fields Personal Collection

MARIO PUZO

The Godfather

For Bert Fields

Who snatched victory from the jaws of defeat And who could be the greatest Consigliere of them all

with admiration
Mario Puzo

Dedication from Mario Puzo
Bert Fields Personal Collection

With Mario Puzo
Bert Fields Personal Collection

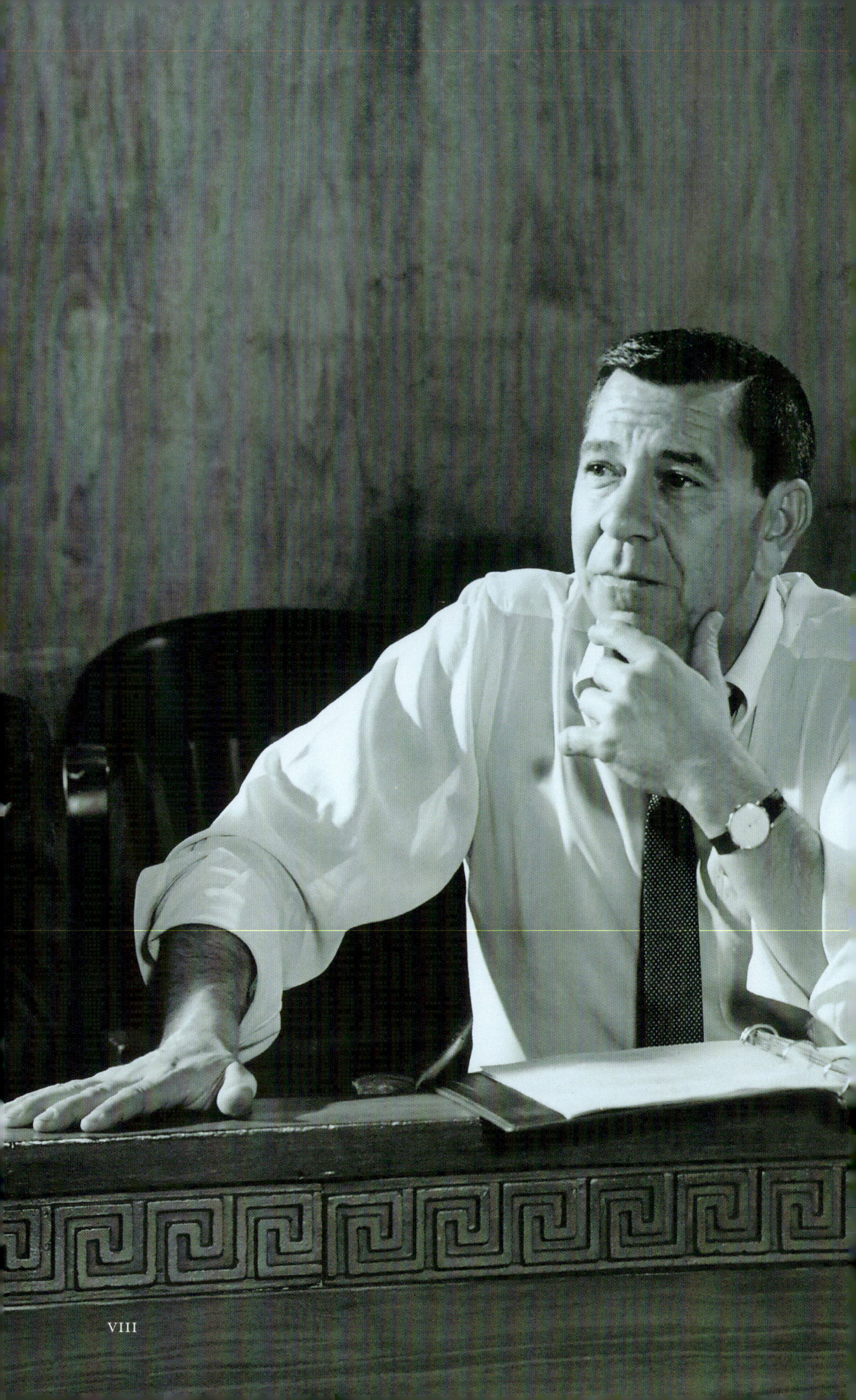

Appearing with Jack Webb on *Dragnet*
Bert Fields Personal Collection

AN OPEN LETTER TO HELMUT KOHL
Chancellor of the German Federal Republic

Dear Chancellor Kohl: December 1996

We have signed this letter to indicate our deep concern at the invidious discrimination against Scientologists practiced in your country and by your own party. We are not Scientologists, but we cannot just look the other way while this appalling situation continues and grows.

In the Germany of the 1930s, Hitler made religious intolerance official government policy. Jews were at first marginalized, then excluded from many activities, then vilified and ultimately subjected to unspeakable horrors.

The world stood by in silence. Perhaps if people had spoken up, taken a stronger stand, history would tell a different story. We cannot change history, but we can try not to re-live it.

In the 1930s, it was the Jews. Today it is the Scientologists. The issue is not whether one approves or disapproves of the teachings of Scientology. Organized governmental discrimination against any group on the basis of its beliefs is abhorrent even where the majority disagree with those beliefs.

And, when individuals hold personal beliefs that they consider their religion, it is not the place of a democratic government to proclaim by fiat that they are not a religion in order to evade laws against religious discrimination. Besides, the German courts have held more than once that Scientology *is*, in fact, a religion.

Individuals guilty of no crime but believing in Scientology are banned from German political parties, including your own. Scientologists cannot obtain employment by your government or contracts with that government. Children have been excluded from schools because their parents are Scientologists. Your Minister of Labor proposed the adoption of a ban on Scientologists from all positions of public service. And – like the book burning of the 1930s – your party has organized boycotts and seeks to ban performances of Tom Cruise, John Travolta, Chick Corea and any other artist who believes in Scientology.

These acts are intolerable in any country that conceives of itself as a modern democracy. This organized oppression is beginning to sound familiar ... like the Germany of 1936 rather than 1996. It should be stopped — now, before it spreads and increases in virulence as it did before.

You may feel that, as non-Germans, this is not our business. But today's World is a smaller, different place. We are far more dependent upon one another. When a modern nation demonstrates its unwillingness to protect the basic rights of a group of its citizens, and, indeed, exhibits a willingness to condone and participate in their persecution, right thinking people in other countries must speak out. Extremists of your party should not be permitted to believe that the rest of the World will look the other way. Not this time.

Those who seek to gain political power or to indulge personal hatreds by repeating the deplorable tactics of the 1930s cannot be permitted that luxury. This time voices will be raised.

We implore you to bring an end to this shameful pattern of organized persecution. It is a disgrace to the German nation.

Robert Bookman	Dustin Hoffman	Michael Marcus	Casey Silver
John Calley	Alan Horn	Doug Morris	Tina Sinatra
Sanford R. Climan	Kevin Huvane	Rick Nicita	Aaron Spelling
Constantin Costa-Gavras	Larry King	Morris Ostin	Sheldon Sroloff
Bertram Fields	Lawrence M. Kopeikin	Mario Puzo	Oliver Stone
Andrew M. Fogelson	Arnold Kopelson	Jack Rapke	Robert Towne
Larry Gordon	Raymond Kurtzman	Terry Semel	Gore Vidal
Goldie Hawn	Sherry Lansing	Sid Sheinberg	Paula Wagner
Barry Hirsch			Fred Westheimer

An Open Letter To Helmut Kohl
Full page ad in the *International Herald Tribune*, January 9, 1997

LAW OFFICES OF
GREENBERG GLUSKER FIELDS CLAMAN & MACHTINGER LLP

BERTRAM FIELDS

1900 AVENUE OF THE STARS
21st FLOOR
LOS ANGELES, CALIFORNIA 90067-4590
TELEPHONE: (310) 553-3610

October 25, 1996

14290-000.09
85365-000.02

VIA FEDERAL EXPRESS

PERSONAL AND CONFIDENTIAL

Donald Trump
The Trump Organization
725 Fifth Avenue
New York, New York 10022

Dear Donald:

We have now established just what occurred and when. In summary, I assured my friend ▮▮▮▮▮ you wouldn't mislead him, and you did.

Ordinarily, there would be nothing wrong with your bidding and getting Miss Universe. That's business. In this instance, however, when you had breakfast at ▮▮▮▮'s, you concealed the fact that you had already submitted a bid to buy the property at $10 million, that your lawyers had even worked out the written sales agreement and were pressing the sellers to close. What you said, among other things, was that you had only a casual interest in the property, that there was nothing imminent on your part, that you were sure the sellers would never get the $10 million they wanted and that you'd find out who the bidders were and what they'd bid and would phone ▮▮▮▮ with that information.

None of that was true. It was said to prevent ▮▮▮▮'s making a bid that would jeopardize your secret $10 million deal.

Okay, that's your style. Mine is I don't represent people who do that to my friends. I'm withdrawing from the LAUSD case as of today. I will, of course, cooperate with whatever substitute counsel you may select.

Please have Barbara Res call me to arrange the transition.

Very truly yours,

[signature]

BERTRAM FIELDS

BF:rjd

Letter to Donald Trump
Dated October 25, 1996

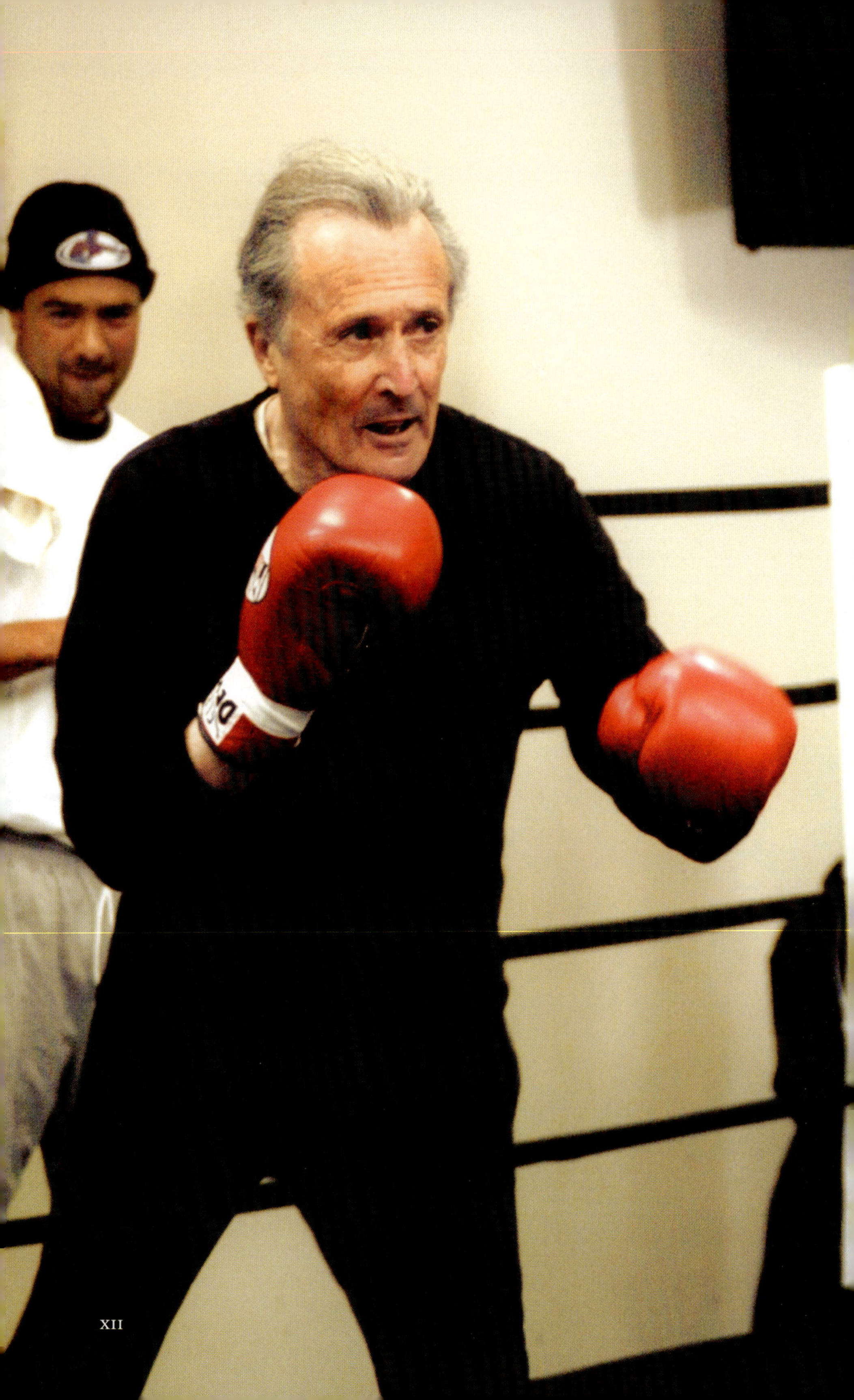

Going three rounds with Oscar De La Hoya
Bert Fields Personal Collection

Peter Falk & Elaine May
Photo: The LIFE Picture Collection/Getty Images

Polaroid of Dustin, Warren and me hanging in Dustin's office

52   NEW YORK POST · SUNDAY, JULY 11, 1999

CHAMIQUE INC. Page 54

Sunday Business

CYBERINK Page 54

HE'S A STAR WARRIOR

The Hollywood superlawyer who nailed Disney's Eisner

MICHAEL Eisner has crossed paths with Hollywood superlawyer Bert Fields before.

And the result was the same — the powerful chairman of Walt Disney was forced to back down.

Fields — who's never lost a case — beat Eisner last week to help Jeffrey Katzenberg settle and collect his disputed $250 million bonus from Walt Disney.

Dustin Hoffman said of his lawyer and friend, "He works for the studios, but he can't be bought. That's what makes him so feared."

But the 70-year-old attorney did more than win a case — he settled an old score with the chief Mouseketeer.

Eisner issued an impulsive, industry-wide blackball against Fields in the late 1980s — an unthinkable act even then.

"I was barred from the lot," Fields explained to The Post. "Michael didn't want to do business with anyone who did business with me. I was *blackballed* by Disney. I can't even remember exactly what caused it, we just had a lot of tough times with Eisner — it was always difficult negotiating with them."

The blackballing lasted only a few days, Fields said. No one in Hollywood wanted it to go any further. "It was resolved quickly," he noted.

No doubt, Fields' impressive client list made Eisner's decree impossible to carry out. The roster ranges from Michael Jackson to Warren Beatty. Fields, a Harvard law graduate, has represented every studio but Disney — and also sued all of them at one time or another.

Joni Evans, the literary agent who's also a friend and client, said, "He's everyone's secret weapon."

David Geffen, a DreamWorks SKG partner who helped broker last week's settlement, said he hired Fields as his lawyer several years ago after being on the losing side against Fields in a case.

"After that," Geffen said, "I realized I was being represented by the wrong lawyer."

Fields also said the blackball never would have stuck. "The people who are the heads of studios, the key agents and a few others, all tend to be friends with each other — and many of those people are my friends, and even though we fight from time to time, we remain friendly. I even have friends at Disney."

But Eisner? "He's probably the only one in Hollywood I don't speak with."

Fields, an actor, boxer and football player at UCLA, compares the law to a "highly complex chess game" and sees each courtroom performance as "being an actor, director and writer all at the same time."

He proved his theories at the Eisner trial. When Fields put an already ner-

Profile
BERT FIELDS
By Paul Tharp

vous Eisner on the stand, Fields got him to admit his infamous midget slur against Katzenberg ("I hate the little midget.")

"I'm sure Michael is very, very angry at me," Fields said. Fields also checked the Disney legal team into a corner on his legal chess board — by getting them in the awkward position of lowballing their profits so they could pay out a smaller profit-sharing to Katzenberg. Their lowballing strategy backfired among Wall Street investors who had always believed profits were much rosier.

It was enough to force Disney to settle, and guard their corporate secrets from further cross-examination damage.

"I'm in favor of settling most cases, and if you don't have insane clients, you should be able resolve just about any case," Fields said. The three-year trial almost broke the record as his longest case, and was one of his shining moments. He got congratulatory calls from all over the entertainment industry and beyond.

Fields, a man of 70 who looks 20 years younger, and his wife, art consultant Barbara Guggenheim (not *that* Guggenheim) religiously avoid the gossip columns, but they're at the center of Hollywood's most glamorous and powerful circle.

In the month of August, they're taking their annual one-month holiday to their sprawling compound at a mill house south of Paris, where they'll joined by close friends including Warren Beatty and Annette Bening, Dustin and Lisa Hoffman and Neil and Diane Simon. Fields' newlywed son, James, who's a lawyer and investment banker at Donaldson Lufkin & Jenrette in Manhattan, also will be there.

Of all the Hollywood couples, it's an invite to the Fields' brainy weekends or summers in France that signals you're arrived at the epicenter of Hollywood's inner circle.

Unlike many of Hollywood's rich and powerful, Fields is something of a scholar, preferring to spend time on his oil paintings (portraits and a Modigliani copy he painted hang in their Hollywood Hills and Malibu homes) or delving into research on his newest Shakespeare book.

Fields already published a scholarly work on "Richard III," and his latest book project is to prove the real identity of Shakespeare. He compares it to litigating the centuries-old mystery.

"It's going to be a great deal of fun to analyze each of those arguments to see which are strong and which are weak," Fields said.

After his first wife of 26 years, Lydia, died of cancer in 1986, Fields buried himself in work and spent all of his free hours writing and painting. He wrote three detective novels under the nom de plume D. Kincaid, with the main character, Harry Cain, as his, alter ego. Among women he dated was Andy Warhol groupie/actress Viva, who did a painting of Fields without hands and feet. "She's still got it," he said.

When his friend, superagent Mike Ovitz, introduced the urbane widower to art expert Barbara Guggenheim, Fields helped her fight off a lawsuit by Sylvester Stallone over a painting she sold to him. It was love at first sight, and they soon married.

Fields, the son of a Los Angeles surgeon, said he was going to be a doctor, too, but switched to pre-law at UCLA after an aptitude test said, "I would probably kill half of my patients if I became a doctor."

One of his first cases was helping Edward G. Robinson through a messy divorce. Fields' most harrowing experience came when he was representing producer Mike Todd, who invited Fields to join him on a private plane one stormy night. Fields couldn't make it. The plane crashed and killed all aboard.

Acting has been a passion for Fields since his days in school plays. In the 1960s, client Jack Webb cast Fields as a prosecutor in his series, "Dragnet." "You still see the episode occasionally in reruns," Fields said.

In his chauffeured black Bentley, Fields rides home from his Century City office each day and cooks gourmet lunches for the couple. After putting in

CHECKMATE: Attorney Bert Fields approaches each trial as if it were a chess match. *Ismael Roldan*

a 12-hour day, he cooks again at night.

Each Sunday morning, he and Barbara walk miles across downtown Los Angeles to the beach. "We never see any other walkers — no one else is crazy enough to walk across the city."

But when they stay in their Central Park South apartment —about four months of the year — they fit right in. "New York loves to walk," Fields said.

Of all the decisions Fields says he's pondered, the one he returns to frequently is turning down offers twice to run major studios. "I think about it, and then I realize how much I really love what I'm doing."

Personal profile
Name: Bertram Harris Fields
Age: 70
Career: Lawyer
Family: Married, one son
Lives: Malibu, New York, France
Education: B.A., UCLA; J.D., Harvard
Clients: Dustin Hoffman, Warren Beatty, Neil Simon, David Geffen

---

Article in the *New York Post*, July, 1999
© New York Post

XVI

¡Hola Falso!
Courtesy The Woods Family Archive

XVII

BLAKES
LONDON

With Tom Cruise and Dustin Hoffman in London
Bert Fields Personal Colletion

Barbara in Mailbu
Photo courtesy of Jody Cobb

xx

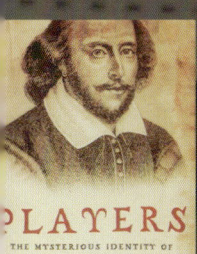

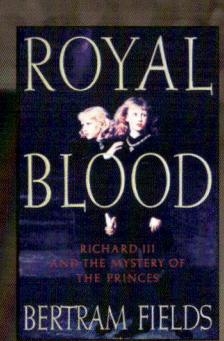

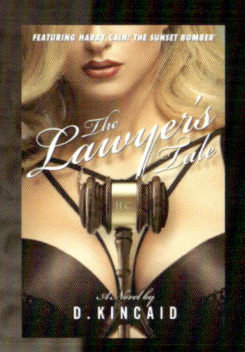

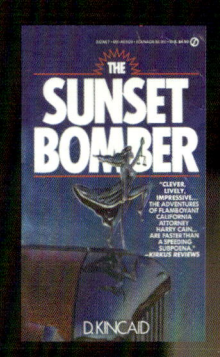

A reading and books by Bertram Fields
Photo: Kelly Balch

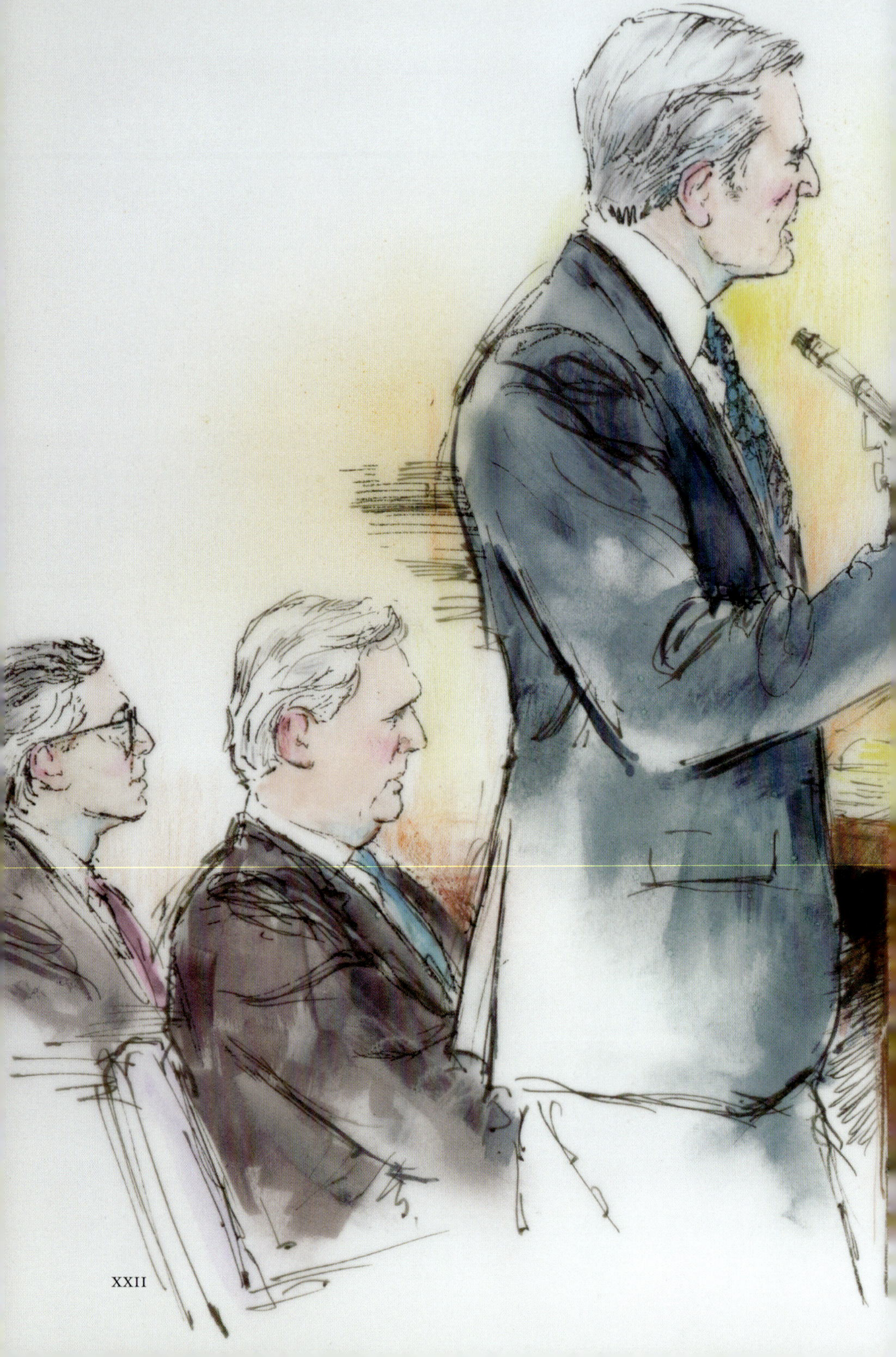

Courtroom sketch of the Sterling Trial
Bert Fields Personal Collection

In Japan 2019
Photo by Barbara

SUMMING UP: A PROFESSIONAL MEMOIR

48

GOOD PEOPLE AT A BAD TIME

INTERVIEWERS OFTEN ASK ME if my famous clients are selfish, egocentric individuals. I always reply "not mine" or "That hasn't been my experience." And, in fact, it hasn't been. Quite the contrary.

Warren Beatty, for example, is a remarkably good man. When my late wife, Lydia, was diagnosed with lung cancer, Warren, an amateur doctor, advised me to have her checked for a brain tumor, saying the two often go together. What I needed, Warren said, was a brain scan.

I asked Lydia's oncologist if that was necessary. He asked who suggested that, implying that it wasn't. I was embarrassed to answer "a movie star," so I just mumbled that I was curious. While the doctor was rather vague, I gathered that he didn't think a brain scan was necessary. He certainly didn't order one.

Later that month, I was on business in New York, and Lydia was with me. Given her condition, we tried to stay together as much as possible. I got a call from the hotel's front desk. "Mr. Beatty wants to speak with you." "Put him on."

"Hi Warren, what's up?"

"I'm downstairs in the lobby. Get down here with Lydia right away. I've got a car waiting to take us to a radiologist.

She's going to have a brain scan in half an hour. It's all arranged."

She did have the brain scan Warren had arranged, and it showed that she had a dangerous brain tumor. Thanks to Warren, we found it in time. It was removed surgically, and her life was prolonged for over a year. Sadly, in the long run, it wasn't enough. But Warren had flown across the country, insisted that the radiologist see Lydia at once and accompanied us to the scan.

That was just one instance of Warren's goodness. There are many. For example, when Hal Ashby, the talented director, was fatally ill, Warren and Dustin Hoffman chartered a private plane to take him to a specialist in New York. And, I've heard of Warren doing other such things for other friends—although you'd never know it, because he never talks about it.

As Lydia's illness progressed, Warren and Dustin took it on themselves to keep her spirits up and to ensure that she got the right care. When she was hospitalized, they vied with each other to see who could bring her the funnier or more luxurious presents. And, for critical procedures, one or both were always on hand.

Sherry Lansing, then a successful executive and assistant to the head of the American Cancer Society, bullied and threatened hospitals and medical schools all over the country to admit Lydia to their experimental studies or to speed a potential cure on which they were working. When Lydia was first diagnosed, Sherry was single and going with Wayne Rogers. Although they broke up during her illness, they continued, in visit after visit, to her various hospital rooms, to pretend they were still together, because they feared Lydia would be upset at their separation.

At one point in Lydia's illness, the lab at UCLA Hospital was to report on the results of a medical test that we believed would likely determine whether she would live or die. It was Friday afternoon and, although that critical test had been done on Thursday, the lab still hadn't issued the test results.

At about 4:30 on Friday afternoon, I went down to the lab and asked when the test results on Lydia Fields would be available. A young man in a lab coat said they were just closing for the weekend, that we'd get the results Monday.

I was ready to punch someone. But I tried to calm down enough to say, "You can't make this lady wait over the weekend to see if she's going to live or die."

It did no good. The guy apologized, but said that their policy was to close somewhat early on Fridays and that, with the key lab people already gone, there was no way to get the test done and results analyzed. He continued storing equipment and closing closets and drawers.

I've always avoided using influence to gain advantage or asking favors of clients or anyone else. But I was angry, upset and desperate. I recalled that Mike Ovitz, then head of CAA, was on the Board of UCLA Medical School. I phoned Mike, who left a meeting to take the call. I told him the situation. His reply was brief and to the point.

"Pal," he said, "within fifteen minutes, the Dean of UCLA Medical School will be in that lab doing Lydia's test."

I told Mike I didn't need the Dean, just a lab technician doing the test would be swell.

"Never mind," he said, "just wait at the lab."

I did and, in about 15 minutes, I heard the click, click of heels coming down the hallway. It really was the Dean of the Medical School.

"Are you Mr. Fields?"

"Yes."

"Come on in."

He ushered me into the lab, asked around and then, personally, completed and analyzed the test. He promptly handed me the results, which, at least for the moment, were hopeful.

When Lydia finally died, Warren and Dustin turned their attention to nurturing me. When they were working together with Elaine May on *Ishtar*, they kept me with them in the editing room and pretended to solicit my opinion on every issue.

Then, when I finally saw the picture in a theatre, I was stunned to see, on the screen in big letters, "This Film Is Dedicated to the Memory of Lydia Fields."

I tried hugging all three of them at the same time; and, to this day, 30 years later, I remember what marvelous friends they were at a time when I desperately needed them. So when people ask if my entertainment clients have been selfish and self-centered, I'm pretty vehement in saying "No."

49

AN ENCOUNTER WITH GENIUS

A FEW WEEKS AFTER LYDIA DIED, I had to attend meetings in London and Paris. I was a wreck, particularly in Paris, where Lydia and I had spent so much time together.

On the day after my meeting, I simply roamed the streets of Paris in a miserable emotional state. At noon, I stopped at a sidewalk cafe and sat there watching the passersby and drinking vodka on the rocks—two or three of them—hoping to diminish the pain.

Finally, I started walking in the direction of my hotel. As I entered the Place de la Concorde, I heard loud shouting from the direction of the American Embassy. I looked down the small street on which the embassy was located, where I saw a huge mob gesturing and screaming at the embassy gate. It seemed as though they might break through at any moment.

I thought, "My God, they're storming our embassy." I was just drunk enough and sad enough to take action. "I'm not going to let these bastards storm our embassy. I'll stand with our Marines! I don't care what happens." I really didn't.

I started sprinting down the street toward the embassy—ready to fight! When I got closer, I stopped. I realized the entire mob was screaming, "Michael! Michael! Michael!" What? I discovered that Michael Jackson was in the embassy, and the crowd just wanted to see the young man who, at that time, was probably the world's biggest star.

Feeling foolish, I headed up the Champs-Élysées toward my hotel.

• • • •

Some years later, I got a call from my longtime client, David Geffen. Would I like to represent Michael Jackson? You bet I would. And that started a remarkable period in my law practice. I liked Michael, as soon as I met him. And I quickly became involved in his numerous business and legal matters.

It was an extraordinary experience. When I negotiated Michael's record contract, my friend, Jon Dolgen, then an executive of the record company said, "Listen, you can get whatever you want. Just please don't embarrass me."

Then, there were the multiple transactions involved in Michael's world tour. We had discussions at Neverland, the fantastic home, theatre and theme park Michael had created in Santa Barbara County. There were giraffes, apes, zebras, Ferris wheels, bumper cars and a theatre with all the candy a kid could eat. Michael regularly brought busloads of poor kids up from the city to enjoy these delights.

I attended recording sessions with Michael, as well as screenings of his videos. I became his fan as well as his lawyer. I had remarried by this time; and Barbara and I traveled with Michael on his tour to the Netherlands, Russia and Romania. There were numerous problems to deal with; but Michael was brilliant, and just watching him perform night after night was an amazing delight.

One problem was that Michael wanted more than anything to star in a film—particularly something serious, something dramatic. Unfortunately, that was not an easy goal to achieve. To say the least, Michael was not easy to cast in a serious drama. His speaking voice was extremely soft, and his appearance, so wildly famous throughout the world, would make it difficult for the public to think of him in character. His agents at CAA tried. They tried very hard. But without success.

One evening, Mike Ovitz and Ron Meyer, then the principal officers of CAA, and I had dinner at Michael's home, while a young CAA agent reviewed for Michael a long list of film possibilities.

As a delicious tomato soup was served, the young agent did his thing. "Well, in this one, you play a tough sergeant of a battalion trapped in the jungle."

No response from Michael.

"And here's one where you're the aging manager of a major league ball club."

This went on for about fifteen minutes, with the young agent describing one seemingly impossible role after another.

Soon I heard a sound like a sob. Ron Meyer, who was sitting opposite me, nodded his head toward Michael, who was sitting on my right. I tried to look over at Michael without being obvious. I saw that he was actually looking down and sobbing, presumably at hearing all these monumentally unsuitable roles.

None of us knew what to do. And, while we sat there shrugging at each other as Michael quietly sobbed, the young man kept dutifully reciting potential parts. "Here's one where you're a Greek warrior defending Athens against the Persians."

I heard stranger sounding sobs and looked to my right. Michael's face was now in his soup. Yes, literally, in his soup. I thought, "My God, he's going to drown himself in tomato soup." But, that's when it ended. Suddenly, Michael jumped up and rushed from the room.

I followed him into the library and tried to comfort him. It was no go. He was inconsolable. Finally, I returned to the dining room and told Mike, Ronnie and their associate that we might as well just leave. And that was the end of Michael's career in feature films.

But it was not the end of his troubles. Next came the episode of "the boy." Michael had never had a real childhood—not as the rest of us would understand a childhood. His dominating father had him on the stage at five; and he transitioned not into an ordinary teenager, but into a young megastar and the prime source of family income.

He had no childhood friendships, as most of us do; and he sought such friendships in later life. He delighted in having kids around—lots of them, busloads of them. And he'd form friendships with some of them—sometimes even had "sleepovers" as most of us did with our close friends when we were kids.

But Michael was an adult having sleepovers with kids. Of course, rumors started. I was convinced that the sleepovers were harmless, that Michael loved having kids around and that his relationships with them, while certainly unusual, even bizarre for an adult, were an innocent catching up on what he'd missed as a child.

Then came "the boy," the claim and, ultimately, the lawsuit. Michael and the young son of a dentist were buddies. With the father's knowledge and, I believe, encouragement, they had sleepovers. After a time, however, the father claimed that Michael had sexually abused his son. He filed a lawsuit and wanted a huge sum to settle.

The case never went to trial. I won't go into all the facts that convinced me Michael was innocent. But I believed that at the time, and I still do. For example, when we had a settlement conference, Michael and I were seated when the father of the boy entered the room. Michael politely stood up. The father said, "Michael!", quickly crossed the room and gave Michael a big hug. Was that the conduct of a father toward a man who's sexually abused his son? I don't think so.

In any event, there were split views in the Jackson camp. By then, Michael was taking much of his advice from his close friend, Elizabeth Taylor, who, I'm convinced, told him to pay whatever it took to get rid of the case. I could imagine her saying, "You've got all the money in the world, Michael. Just pay this man off and get on with your life."

I felt strongly that this was a serious mistake, but no one seemed to agree. So, at about this time, I wrote Michael resigning as his lawyer. He had good criminal lawyers, but he seemed to be relying on Elizabeth Taylor's advice. He was about to settle and pay a huge amount of money, which I thought could be disastrous for his career. Perhaps, I was foolish; but I didn't want to be a part of it.

Shortly after that, the settlement was concluded. You could certainly argue that, given the circumstances, Elizabeth Taylor's advice was sound. Michael could well afford the payment, and it would avoid the public circus of a civil trial and, of course, possible conviction and imprisonment. But I don't agree. I was convinced of Michael's innocence; and I thought the massive payoff was a serious mistake. Paying a huge sum that soon became widely known (as most such payments do) created the impression in the minds of the public that Michael "must have been" guilty of sexually abusing a young boy. ("Otherwise, why'd he pay that kind of money?") I still believe that the public perception of this huge payment was severely damaging to Michael's career.

Years later, another boy made similar claims against Michael. This time, Michael fought the claims in court, as I believe he should have done the first time. After a hard-fought trial, Michael was found not guilty, as I'm convinced would have been the result the time before.

Of course, I could be wrong. But I don't think so; and I feel very sad about Michael, a uniquely talented and, in his last years, a very unhappy man. Still, I'm thankful to have been a part of his life in a much happier time.

50

What's a "Sequel"?

Generally, a sequel to a film is a second film with at least one of the principal characters from the original film in a new story.

Easy to say. Not so easy to apply.

I represented James Clavell, the author of *King Rat*, *Shogun*, *Tai Pan* and *Noble House*, fascinating novels that were enormous best sellers. There were profit participants in the film version of *Tai Pan* that would also participate in profits from any "sequel" to that picture. That's where the problem arose.

Tai Pan, set in the 19th Century, was the story of a bold English merchant-adventurer who, facing dangers and obstacles of all kinds, established a vast international trading company based in Hong Kong. He was called the "Tai Pan" which meant "Chief" or "Main Guy." A film version of the novel was very successful.

Noble House took place in 20th-Century Hong Kong. The principal characters were the descendants of the Tai Pan and other characters from the earlier book. Naturally, the great Tai Pan, having been dead for a century, played no active role in *Noble House*.

The problem was that the film version of *Noble House* had a scene in the 20th-Century boardroom of the vast trading company established by the Tai Pan in the 19th Century. And what was hanging on the wall? That's right—a splendid portrait of the Tai Pan.

And what did the profit participants in "the original" *Tai Pan* film claim? Of course. They claimed that this portrait was an "appearance" in the film version of *Noble House* of a character who appeared—indeed starred—in the film version of *Tai Pan*. Accordingly, they argued *Noble House* was a sequel to *Tai Pan*, so that they should share in its profits.

I argued "no," that to make the second film a "sequel," the character from the first film had to participate in the plot of the second film, not just be someone seen in a photograph or oil painting.

This caused a number of problems, however. I realized that the classic definition of a sequel required an actual character from the original work to appear in the second work. But couldn't it be argued that a second work based on the children or grandchildren of the central character in the first work should be considered a "sequel"? And, even if an actual "appearance" in the second film was required, what if the character in the first film was described in the second film as having been murdered; and we only saw him lying dead on the floor? Was that an "appearance"? Was that a sequel?

And what if a character in the second film played a copy of the original film including action by a character in the original film?

SUMMING UP: A PROFESSIONAL MEMOIR

No one can be sure of the answers to such questions.

Fortunately, the various claims of the *Tai Pan* participants were settled with no payment being made for their "sequel" theory. But this issue continues to create problems.

Years later, Bob Weinstein, a longtime client, released a film called *Piranha* about the tiny but deadly fish that devour the flesh of animals (or humans), leaving nothing but their skeletons. *Piranha* was successful, so Bob wanted to make *Piranha II*. Virtually as soon as this was reported, the claim was made on behalf of a profit participant in the original *Piranha* that *Piranha II* was a sequel, because the razortooth fish were the principal "characters," and they appeared in both films.

Not so, I argued. The humans in the two films were different, and, even though the fish are of the same species, they're not the same fish. In fact, the fish in *Piranha II* were in a totally different part of the world than the fish in the original film. I said that calling *Piranha II* a sequel would be like saying that, if there were humans in the first film and humans in the second, the second film would be a "sequel," which would be nuts.

I was concerned they'd argue that the piranhas in both films would appear to the audience to be the same fish even if they were in a different place. Fortunately, they didn't press the issue, and I never had to deal with it.

But the problem of defining a "sequel" is still out there; and, believe me, it will rise again.

51

A Major Threat

Did I ever defend an entire industry? Not really—not all of an industry and not alone. But there was the time all the major motion picture studios were sued in a widely publicized class action brought by Jim Garrison, the former New Orleans District Attorney who had become famous for his views on the Kennedy assassination.

Garrison had a participation in the "net profits" of a film, but "surprise!"—there were no "net profits," as carefully defined in his contract. But Garrison was not a guy to be pushed around. He quickly filed a very public class action on behalf of everyone who ever got a "net profits" deal. Every major studio was a defendant. Garrison made two basic claims: first, that all of the studios violated the antitrust laws by "combining" to define net profits in a way that prevented anyone from ever getting such profits; and, second, that the definition of net profits used by all the major motion picture companies was "unconscionable," and thus void. In addition to a declaration by the court on these two points, Garrison sought massive damages from every studio payable to everyone whose contracts had ever called for a share of net profits. Obviously, billions of dollars were at stake.

It was a scary time. I represented Paramount in the case. Frank Rothman represented Fox and Lou Meisinger represented Columbia. We were aware that the financial viability of the major studios could well depend on our efforts.

As the required first step, Garrison moved to have the class certified. We all worked on the brief opposing certification. At the hearing, Frank argued the antitrust issues, I argued the unconscionability claim and Lou batted "clean up," dealing with any other questions the court might have.

After Garrison's lawyer presented his opening arguments, Frank skillfully summarized the way the definition of net profits had gradually come about, that it certainly did not result from any clandestine meeting of the major studio heads and explained why Garrison's antitrust allegations were not only unavailing, but not appropriate for class determination.

I argued that unconscionability had two essential parts, "substantive unconscionability" (was the deal fundamentally unfair?) and "procedural unconscionability" (was it made in an unfair way?). I said that we could argue for days over whether the definition of net profits was substantively unconscionable, but there was no way that "<u>procedural</u> unconscionability" could ever be determined on a class-wide basis, since it required extreme and consistent unfairness in the way hundreds of thousands of individual contracts were made. This was not a situation in which all members of the class were uniform in their abilities, as, for example, if 50 women who couldn't speak English were sold defective vacuum cleaners. Here, we were talking about a massive and diverse class of potential plaintiffs of widely varying degrees of education and experience, many of whom were represented by highly skilled attorneys and agents, others by attorneys and agents with differing levels of experience and skill, some with agents, but no attorneys, others with attorneys but no agents, and others with neither, but, even then, with every imaginable amount of education and experience, so that, in summary, there was no possible way to decide the issue of whether there was procedural unconscionability on a class-wide basis.

I couldn't read the Judge's reaction to what either Frank or I had argued, and he asked no questions. After Lou summarized the positions of the two sides showing why ours was the correct position, Garrison's lawyer argued in rebuttal that our various arguments were simply wrong.

When he was done, the matter was "submitted" for decision. We anxiously—<u>very anxiously</u>—awaited the court's remarks, which we expected would be an announcement that he was taking the matter under submission and would send us his written decision in a few days. But he didn't do that. He surprised us by ruling from the bench that class certification was denied and that he'd be issuing a written order to that effect.

We breathed a huge and collective sign of relief. So did every major studio. In a very real sense, their economic future could have depended on that decision. Garrison was now on his own. Faced with the sizeable cost of pursuing his individual lawsuit against a single major studio, he settled. Is the issue still out there—awaiting another Jim Garrison?

No comment.

52

The Liar In Chief

I ONCE REPRESENTED DONALD TRUMP or, more accurately, his company. Yes, <u>that</u> Donald Trump. It was about some real estate litigation. I fired him. Yes, I fired the guy who became President of the United States.

After I had represented Donald's company for a time, an opportunity to acquire the Miss Universe pageant became available. There was to be an auction of the rights; and Donald and a longtime client of mine separately expressed their interest in acquiring the Miss Universe rights.

Rather than see the two bidding against each other, I suggested that they join together in acquiring the rights. Both seemed to like the idea, and we scheduled a breakfast meeting at my client's Park Avenue apartment.

During the first part of the meeting, we spoke of the two acquiring the rights together. Later, however, Donald began to say he might decide not to be involved with the pageant, but that he was sure the rights would never go for as much as $10 million and he would keep my client informed as to what he thought would be a winning bid.

Some time after that, my client got a call from Donald telling him that he had definitely decided not to participate in the bidding for the pageant. Naturally, my other client bid the amount Donald said would do the job. Sadly, he was informed that his was only the second highest bid. Someone had bid $10 million. Who was the successful bidder? Donald Trump! Not only that, his lawyers had apparently prepared the documents for Donald to buy the rights even before our breakfast meeting. Donald had simply lied from the beginning in order to keep my client from making a competitive bid.

I immediately wrote Donald a letter telling him that, in light of his deceitful behavior I would no longer represent him, or his company. This letter appears in the illustrations (page xi).

Donald's partners in the real estate litigation and Donald's key associate urged me to relent—to continue with the case. I refused, saying that under no circumstances would I ever represent Donald Trump or his company again.

Fortunately, I had put my firing of Donald in writing, because, two years later, he wrote a book in which, among other lies, he said, "Bert Fields...I fired him...he's highly overrated."

I wrote the publisher telling them this was simply another lie, and a defamatory lie at that. At first they said Donald stood by the quote. But when I sent the publisher my letter firing Donald, they quickly said that his statement about me would be deleted in all future printings of the book.

For a day or two I contemplated suing Donald for libel. But I decided that the less interaction I had with him, the better I'd feel.

53

Making Movies

I'VE PARTICIPATED IN THE DEVELOPMENT of a regional shopping center, the launch of a communications satellite and, as you've read, the operation of a Vegas hotel and casino. But, to my mind, nothing beats the creation and making of a movie. I've been fortunate enough to be involved in quite a number. My favorite? There are just too many, and it's too difficult to choose. But one I've been reminded of recently, due to the success of the Broadway musical version, is *Tootsie*.

It wasn't called that at its inception. It wasn't even about a difficult actor who couldn't get work as a male. Dustin Hoffman and Murray Schisgal originally thought they'd tell the story of an unsuccessful tennis pro who, unable to beat his male opponents, decides to pose as a female in order to become a champion. Ugh! That was my reaction and, finally, that of Murray and Dustin.

Then Dustin hit on the winning concept—why not use his own domain, to some extent even his own background, as an actor, so bound by principle that he can't play a tomato that moves from stage left to center stage as the play requires, because "a tomato can't move."

The character's professional rigidity prevents his success (or even being cast) as a male. So what does he do?

He reinvents himself as a female—and becomes a sensation as "Tootsie," only to fall in love with his female co-star.

I loved the idea! So did Dustin's wife, Lisa, and Mike Ovitz, his agent.

Columbia Pictures was somewhat unsure about it, but Dustin was then as big a movie star as you could find, and he wanted to do it. So we didn't have to work very hard to get them to move ahead.

We made a deal for the project's "development," i.e., creating a screenplay. Dustin and Murray had worked on an outline and Murray did a draft. Then Larry Gelbart went to work on it.

Meanwhile, we made a deal for Sydney Pollack to direct —and Sydney went to work on the screenplay with Larry, consulting along the way with Dustin, who continued to consult with Murray and, from time to time, when he wasn't otherwise occupied, would even listen to me.

It worked—and how! Teri Garr was cast as Dustin's comic girlfriend, Jessica Lange was the co-star with whom he falls in love and Bill Murray was his sardonic roommate. Finally the picture was "greenlit." That meant that Frank Price, then head of the studio, committed to its actually being filmed, an expensive decision, particularly given the magnitude of Dustin's "deal," as well as Sydney's, Larry's, and Bill's.

But the screenplay remained a work in process, and some issues began to arise between Sydney and Dustin, who was not only a hugely talented actor, but an able and experienced director as well. That was nothing particularly unusual—such issues are often a part of filmmaking.

Given Dustin's makeup and female attire, Sydney felt strongly that he had to be limited to interior scenes only, that on the street, he would immediately be perceived as a man "in drag." Dustin strongly disagreed, feeling Sydney's view would seriously limit the film and confident that he could make it work, even outside the studio.

What did Dustin do to resolve the issue? In a typically Dustinian move, he went to lunch at the Russian Tea Room in New York—in his costume and makeup as a female.

The popular restaurant was crowded as Dustin and Sydney passed through the waiting diners to be shown to their booth. No one—not one person in the crowded restaurant—recognized Dustin. Sydney introduced him as "Dustin's aunt."

It was complete vindication for Dustin, whose reaction was interesting. After years of being immediately recognized as a movie star anywhere he went, he was surprised to see that everyone's eyes "just slid off me," quickly seeing that this unattractive lady was no one they knew—or even wanted to know.

This scene was recreated for the film.

As filming progressed, we could see from the "dailies" that something extraordinary was being created. Still, issues arose, as they often do. I had meetings with Dustin and Sydney, some in New York, some in LA. Some in the afternoon, some at night, all to resolve problems that arose as the shoot continued.

Finally, it was "a wrap," i.e., filming was over and the process of editing and scoring began.

When I finally saw a print, it seemed that everyone in the cast was marvelous—even Sydney, who, while directing, also played Dustin's agent. Previews indicated that we had something remarkable. And, they were not wrong. When the film was released, it proved a massive hit. Columbia, Dustin, Sydney and others did very well.

I hoped for a Best Picture Academy Award and Best Actor for Dustin. We got close, but *Gandhi* won Best Picture, and Ben Kingsley won for Best Actor in the title role. Jessica Lange did win for Best Supporting Actress, but that was it.

Dustin, of course, made many splendid and incredibly successful films, finally winning Best Actor for *Rain Man*, which also won the Academy Award for Best Picture (and two others besides).

Somehow, though, my memory of the *Tootsie* experience seems more vivid. Maybe there were more problems to solve, and maybe there was more satisfaction in solving them. Or maybe it all came back when I saw the excellent Broadway version.

54

WERE YOU WRONG THEN OR ARE YOU WRONG NOW?

I'VE BEEN ASKED A NUMBER OF TIMES if I've ever had to argue the opposite of something I'd previously argued. The answer is "yes—you bet I have." Three times—three potentially embarrassing times—I've had to argue for a position directly opposite to a position I took very publicly in an earlier case.

There was, of course, Gore Vidal's case involving *The Sicilian* in which I seemed to reverse the position I'd taken earlier in Puzo v. Universal—that it was perfectly proper for the Writer's Guild to keep the names of its arbitrators secret. In Vidal, I argued that this violated the Due Process Clause of the Constitution. But there was a distinction. The Puzo case involved a writer vs. a studio, where the need for confidentiality to protect the writer-arbitrators from studio pressure or retribution outweighed the need to know the names of the arbitrators. The parties to the Vidal case didn't include a studio, but only writer vs. writer, where there was no need for such confidentiality. Accordingly, Gore was entitled to know who was deciding his case. It was not really an inconsistent position; and the courts agreed with me both times.

But there were other "reversals of position" that could be considered more embarrassing. I represented Warren Beatty in many situations; but the most fiercely contested was Warren's dispute with Paramount and ABC over the final cut of Warren's brilliant film *Reds*, for which he won an Academy Award as Best Director. Warren's contract as director gave him final cut of the film; and he'd spent a year cutting it.

After the film became a great success in its theatrical run, Paramount naturally wanted to sell it for television exhibition. ABC was a more than willing buyer, offering Paramount many millions of dollars in which Warren would have shared. The problem was that *Reds* was a bit too long for the network's schedule. ABC would have had to eliminate the 11:00 p.m. news or significantly delay it, something the network was not prepared to do. But there was an easy solution. All Warren had to do was cut 2½ minutes from the film in order to play it on television.

Despite the huge amount of money at stake in which he would share, Warren refused to cut another minute from the film. He said that, in the year he spent cutting the film, he'd taken every second out of it he could and that trying to take out another 2½ minutes would necessarily damage its quality.

Since neither side would relent, the case went to arbitration. Paramount and ABC argued that this was a film almost three hours long, so that, obviously, a mere two and a half minutes could be cut without harming the story.

SUMMING UP: A PROFESSIONAL MEMOIR

I argued that the right of final cut means just that, "<u>final</u> cut," the absolute right to determine what the film will be—with no exceptions. ABC, of course, disagreed, even suggesting a scene to be cut in order to meet the network's needs. John Reed, played by Warren, leaves his wife, Louise Bryant, for a long stay in Moscow. At that point, Warren inserted a montage of brief cuts showing Louise growing more and more lonely and depressed—walking alone on the beach, sitting alone on a park bench, getting into bed alone—becoming more and more lonely and upset with each shot. Finally, after this sad montage, Eugene O'Neill, played by Jack Nicholson, comes up the front walk and soon seduces the lonely, miserable Louise. Now ABC suggested eliminating the montage.

That sequence had worked beautifully in the film as Warren cut it. When you'd experienced the montage, you believed what happened and even had sympathy for Louise. But, I argued, if you did what Paramount and ABC suggested and eliminated the montage, Louise said goodbye to her husband and immediately jumped into bed with Eugene O'Neill. Her character was totally changed—and we lost all sympathy for her, which ruined the film. That's why Warren included the montage, I argued; and it's why final cut is sacrosanct.

I contended that even ten seconds can change a creative work. I cited Beethoven's 5th Symphony—da da da DAH! We all know those four notes. But shave even a second off and it's "da da da" with no "DAH!," which completely spoils it—and that's only <u>one</u> second. Paramount's talking about cutting out 150 seconds—an eternity in filmmaking.

In the end, the arbitrator ruled for Warren and issued an injunction against Paramount or ABC cutting anything from the film.

Now, fast forward several years to *The Sicilian*, the same picture that led to overturning the Writers Guild arbitration procedure—until Gore Vidal changed his mind. The battle over the writer's credit was only part of the war. The director, Michael Cimino, had a contract that gave him final cut. But the contract also provided that his cut could not exceed two hours and eight minutes. Anything materially longer would cost the theatre owners an entire "play" of the film each night, which meant the loss of significant revenue.

Cimino had been cutting *The Sicilian* for about six months, and, when he turned in his final cut, it was <u>two hours and forty minutes</u>, much longer than his contract permitted. Fox, the studio that financed the film and was to distribute it, refused to accept the film at that length.

Cimino, whose temper sometimes affected his judgment, went into the editing room for just one night and cut every action scene out of the film. In the morning, he told Fox, "Here's my final cut. You wanted short, I've given you short."

When they viewed what Cimino had done, both Fox and the producers rejected this new, truncated version. Another arbitration was the result. And what an arbitration it was. Cimino's attorney naturally pointed out to the arbitrator that the rule been firmly established "by

Mr. Fields himself" in the *Reds* case that the right of final cut was sacrosanct and unlimited. Now, he argued, Mr. Fields wanted to switch positions entirely, violating the director's right of final cut that he previously established was "sacrosanct."

I responded that final cut was indeed sacrosanct, so long as it stayed within the broad outlines of the basic story being told, as was the situation in *Reds*. But when it departed from that basic story, it went beyond its proper boundaries.

Each side presented expert witnesses. Our experts endorsed my limitation on the right of final cut. Cimino's experts, well-known directors, strongly disagreed. "Sacrosanct means sacrosanct," they argued—"no limits whatsoever."

On cross-examination, I asked their leading director-witness, "Well suppose we're making a picture about the Titanic." This was before Jim Cameron's great film. "And suppose the director decides to end the film before the ship hits the iceberg, so the film is only about people waving goodbye, walking on deck and attending parties in the grand salon. Is that okay?"

The director's answer: "Absolutely."

At this point, the arbitrator posed his own question. "Well, suppose we're making a martial arts movie, and the director cuts out all the scenes of fighting, so the film consists entirely of scenes of Chinese mountains and lakes. Is that the director's right, if he has final cut?"

"Absolutely."

And so it went, until the arbitrator and the lawyers retired to another room to view Cimino's new, "shortened" cut of *The Sicilian*. The picture included a scene of a Sicilian wedding, with dancing, drinking and merrymaking. As originally conceived, this was followed by the merrymakers walking peacefully home across the hills. Then, in Cimino's original, long cut, they were attacked by bandits and a fierce battle ensued. After the battle, we cut to a bloody hospital scene in which people from the wedding were seen wounded and dying, victims of the bandits' attack.

But, in Cimino's new overnight version, he had cut out the entire battle scene. So the film went directly, and, without explanation, from people having a wonderful time dancing and drinking at the wedding to the bloody scene of dead and dying people at the hospital from what was now an unknown cause.

I could see the arbitrator shaking his head. He had read the screenplay, so he could understand what had been cut out. An audience without that advantage would have been hopelessly confused.

In any event, after the screening of Cimino's new cut, the arbitrator was ready to announce his decision. Would he endorse my view that final cut must stay within the scope of the basic storyline, or Cimino's view that it was completely without limits, requiring Fox to release the film in Cimino's butchered new cut?

SUMMING UP: A PROFESSIONAL MEMOIR

The arbitrator did neither. He ruled squarely against Cimino and in favor of Fox and the producer. But he did it by finding that the version he had just viewed was not a <u>bona fide final cut</u>, but only a bad faith attempt by Cimino to force his views on my clients. Thus, Cimino's new cut could be ignored. The arbitrator ruled that the real "final cut" from Cimino was the two hour forty minute version he had originally delivered, which didn't comply with his contract. Thus, he ruled, Fox and the producers were entitled to cut down that longer version at their discretion and release their own cut, rather than Cimino's.

It was a huge win for Fox and the producers; but it had ducked the issue of the scope and extent of final cut. That issue remains undecided even today. When it arises, it will be embarrassing if both sides cite my seemingly conflicting arguments.

The third instance of my being accused of changing my position was quite different. It involved the world of boxing, rather than movies. For years I've represented Oscar De La Hoya. At the beginning, he was a champion fighter, pound for pound the best in the world. Oscar had brought an action in federal court seeking to terminate his contract with Top Rank, a major boxing promotion company owned by Bob Arum, then and now a famed promoter.

Our primary argument was based on California's "seven year rule," a statute providing that certain contracts were not enforceable after seven years. None of Oscar's individual contracts with Top Rank exceeded seven years; but, if you added them together, they did. That created the issue. What happens if, during the sixth year, the parties make a new contract for another five years? Is the new contract unenforceable? That was Oscar's situation. He was in the third year of his new extended contract, meaning that he'd been bound to Top Rank for a total of nine years. I argued that this violated the seven year rule and made the contract illegal.

Top Rank's famous and highly successful lawyer, Tom Girardi, argued that the new contract, for even more money, was perfectly valid, that nothing in the law prohibited parties to an expiring contract from negotiating a new deal.

I responded that the policy of the statute was to give an employee the opportunity to explore what the market had to offer and that, to give him the freedom to do that, there had to be "a moment of freedom" in which he was not bound by his old contract, before he could sign a new one. Oscar, I argued, had never had that "moment."

Federal Judge Matt Byrne, a splendid judge and a delightful man, agreed with my analysis and ruled that De La Hoya was free of his Top Rank contract. Oscar was thrilled. He went on to form his own company, Golden Boy Promotions, which became and remains a successful boxing promoter.

Years later, Judge Byrne died, far too young. He was given a funeral in Los Angeles' Cathedral attended by literally hundreds of lawyers, judges and other officials, who'd come to pay their respects. I was among them.

In any event, years later, I represented Dan Goossen, a veteran fight promoter, in an arbitration of a contract dispute with Andre Ward, an outstanding boxer, who sought to terminate his contract with Goossen, primarily based on the same seven year rule I'd argued in the De La Hoya case.

Like De La Hoya, Ward had signed a new contract with Goossen before his old Goossen contract expired, and, adding the two contracts together, Goossen had been Ward's promoter for almost nine years.

As you would expect, Ward's lawyer quickly handed the arbitrator Judge Byrne's written opinion in De La Hoya v. Top Rank, showing that I had represented De La Hoya and that I had successfully argued that, to make the new contract valid, there must be at least a "moment of freedom" during which the boxer or any employee is free from his old contract before he signs a new one, so that he has the opportunity to "test the market" unfettered by his old contract. Since Ward signed his new contract while still bound by his old one, my opponent argued "Mr. Fields' own rule requires that the two contracts be added together; and, if the total exceeds seven years, they are void. Therefore," he argued, "Ward is free of his Goossen contract, exactly as Mr. Fields was able to free De La Hoya from his Top Rank contract." It was a very effective argument.

This time, I had tried to find ways to distinguish Judge Byrne's decision in the De La Hoya case; but it just wouldn't work. Basically, my only choice was to argue that Judge Byrne (and I) had been wrong. "With respect," I argued, "Judge Byrne's rule, which I advocated at that time, would prevent the very common practice of renewing an employment contract before it expired, so as to ensure continuity in the relationship, rather than having to wait until the relationship was over before a new contract could be signed." I said that extending Judge Byrne's rule to every renewal of an employment contract that was signed before the old contract expired would render thousands and thousands of contracts on which businesses rely illegal and void. I said that, if you really think about it, no one really needs a "moment of freedom," because nothing stops an employee from "testing the market" a week, a month or even a year before the end of his contract to see what other employment would be available when his contract expires.

Ultimately, the arbitrator did not follow Judge Byrne's decision. He ruled that Ward continued to be bound by his extended contract with Goossen, and he even extended the contract term for the additional time that Ward had been unable or unwilling to fight in a Goossen promotion.

This time, the third time, I pretty much had to say "I was wrong before; but don't hold it against my present client. I'm right now." That, as you can imagine, is embarrassing.

SUMMING UP: A PROFESSIONAL MEMOIR

So, those cases—Vidal, Cimino and Goossen—were three in which I had to take a position that seemed—or, in the case of Goossen, actually was—the opposite of what I'd successfully argued before. Probably there's a fourth case out there waiting to torture me.

My representation of Oscar De La Hoya continued over the years through various bouts, cases and problems. Oscar is an extraordinary man and, before his retirement, was one of the greatest fighters of all time.

I, on the other hand, was a very <u>un</u>talented amateur boxer at an earlier time in my life. I had a pretty good left jab; but, for some reason, I couldn't throw an effective right hand punch—a serious disadvantage. For my birthday one year, Barbara arranged for me to visit Oscar at his training camp at Big Bear, high in the mountains. There, he would show me how to throw a right. And he did. He saw the problem in 10 seconds. All I had to do was turn my right hip in as I threw the punch. It worked—but much too late to save my boxing career.

Then, as a surprise, Oscar said, "Come on, let's go three rounds." So I got in the ring with this guy who'd been the World Champion in something like five different weight divisions. Fortunately, he stayed away, faked a punch or two and mostly laughed at my amateurish moves. After three rounds I was so exhausted, I thought I'd die in the ring. But it was an experience I'll long treasure. And I've got the pictures to show I went three rounds with the Champ. Yeah, right.

(See illustrations pages xii-xiii)

55

"Disney Wars"

For years, I considered Michael Eisner to be a highly intelligent and effective executive. Not only that, I considered Paramount's putting together the team of Barry Diller, Michael Eisner and Jeffrey Katzenberg as a masterstroke and that they were far and away the most talented "team" in Hollywood.

So, when I learned that Michael and Jeffrey were going to leave Paramount and join with Frank Wells, a brilliant Warner Bros. lawyer, in taking over Disney, I thought they were nuts; and I said so to Jeffrey. "You're leaving a great studio to go make Mickey Mouse cartoons. Tell me it's not so."

Jeffrey just smiled. "You'll see," he said.

And I did. Michael, Frank and Jeffrey completely reinvented Disney, turning it from a worn-out cartoon factory into a giant, multi-media powerhouse. I had always had great respect for Frank Wells, although, once he joined Disney, our relationship tended to be adversarial. The same was true of Eisner, only my relationship with him became even worse.

There were a number of examples. The first I recall involved Rupert Murdoch's brilliant idea for a worldwide news service, broadcast by satellite. Murdoch's Sky Network had a partnership with Disney to operate such a service in the UK It was called "BSkyB."

But costs of the new venture were mounting, and Disney was finding it hard to match Rupert's enthusiasm and determination. Finally, they announced their intention to withdraw from the partnership. Weeks of threats and negotiations followed; but Frank and Michael remained adamant. So did Rupert, whose interests I represented in the controversy.

Finally, we called a meeting at Rupert's home. Rupert and I were to meet Frank and Michael to see if there was any way to avoid litigation. I was convinced there was no way and that Disney would remain determined to walk away from BSkyB. With Rupert's approval, I had secretly prepared a lawsuit against Disney. I had also instructed a young associate to stand by at the courthouse for my call in the event that our meeting was fruitless, as I believed it would be.

After about an hour of conversation at Rupert's house, Frank and Michael announced (I thought rather arrogantly) that they'd said all they had to say—Disney was pulling out of the partnership. They rose to leave, and we said goodbye at Rupert's front door.

I immediately phoned my young associate who was standing by a public phone at the courthouse. "File the complaint," I said, "as quickly as you can." I then notified my friends in the media.

Only twenty minutes later, as Michael and Frank were driving back to Disney from the hills of Bel Air, they heard on the car radio that Disney had already been sued for breach of the partnership agreement.

It didn't take long for the case to settle. I can't disclose the terms, but my client was happy, and Disney was excluded from having any further interest in the partnership, its assets or its income. In my view, this was a serious mistake by Disney. Had they remained Rupert's partner, they would have participated in the fantastic growth his company enjoyed in the cable news business throughout the world. After that episode, my relationship with Disney was never quite the same.

That relationship grew worse when I represented George Lucas in negotiating his theme park deal with Eisner. At one point, I planned to bring a recording device to our meetings, to avoid disagreements over what was said.

It grew even more adversarial when I took a very tough position in negotiating a movie deal with Disney. I heard that Eisner was infuriated by my conduct and ordered me barred from the Disney lot. If so, it was a vindictive act that took us back to the days of Louis B. Mayer and Harry Cohn.

Eisner had previously barred Barry Hirsch from the lot. Barry is an excellent lawyer and a friend, and I started to organize a strike against Disney by the leading entertainment lawyers. I wanted all of us to refuse to have any dealings with Disney until Barry was readmitted. I argued that, otherwise, we'd all be afraid to take tough positions in negotiating with Disney for fear of Eisner's

SUMMING UP: A PROFESSIONAL MEMOIR

wrath. But it never came to that. Probably because of Jeffrey Katzenberg, Eisner relented and Barry was allowed back in before my "strike" took effect.

Now, I was the one being barred. I wondered if my friends would "strike" in my behalf. But, once again, it never came to that. Apparently, Jeffrey convinced Eisner to rescind his draconian order.

Later, however, when my client, David Geffen, was planning to sell his highly successful music business to Disney, Eisner demanded that David not use me as his lawyer in making the deal. David told him to go to hell. The result wasn't so bad. David sold his business to Universal for a great deal more money than he was going to get from Disney.

So to put it mildly, Michael Eisner and I were not pals. And that's the background to one of my favorite trials. For years, Jeffrey Katzenberg had worked for Disney with enormous success, particularly in developing Disney's highly successful animated feature films. During those years, Jeffrey worked for a relatively low salary. He'd bet his financial future on a unique bonus plan. Instead of cash or stock, that plan gave Jeffrey a share of the increase in Disney's net value; and that value had increased enormously, in significant part because of Jeffrey's outstanding work.

Frank Wells, who had been tragically killed in a helicopter crash, had been the lubricant that had enabled Eisner and Katzenberg to work together so successfully. With Frank gone, Eisner's behavior made Jeffrey determined to leave. The problem was that, in leaving Disney, Jeffrey was counting on the massive bonus that was due him, based on the fantastic increase in Disney's value over the years he had worked there. Eisner, on the other hand, was counting on not paying the bonus, claiming that any such bonus deal was forfeited by Jeffrey leaving the company at a point Eisner considered too early and, in the alternative, claiming that Jeffrey had voluntarily waived his bonus.

Now, with that strikingly hostile background, Jeffrey asked me to represent him in his fight with Disney over Eisner's refusal to pay him his bonus. I felt that Jeffrey could be due more than one hundred million. But to resolve the matter without a fight, Jeffrey was willing to take much less. Mike Ovitz, then an officer at Disney, wanted to settle the dispute for $50 million. I believe Jeffrey would have taken it. But Eisner remained adamant. He wouldn't pay Jeffrey a dime.

So, the litigation began and proceeded, with months of depositions and motions, until finally the day of trial arrived. The judge was Paul Breckenridge, the same excellent judge who had tried the *Beatlemania* case years before. The lawyers' first conference with Judge Breckenridge was also attended by the clients on each side. Eisner quickly told the Judge that his wife was "a Breckenridge," a tactic I thought would cut no ice with this straight-arrow judge.

The trial began a few days later, accompanied by massive publicity. I was aided by my partners Bonnie

Eskenazi and Brian Edwards. Lou Meisinger and Sandy Litvack represented Disney. The room was filled with reporters as the lawyers made their opening statements and the testimony began. Jeffrey testified to the making of the bonus promise and the highlights of what he'd accomplished for Disney over the years, such as *The Lion King*, *The Little Mermaid* and other monumental hits. Jeffrey and I had worked hard preparing for his cross-examination, and I thought he did very well.

Eisner's personal attorney testified. He'd been a member of Disney's committee that had reviewed Jeffrey's compensation. He claimed the committee decided Jeffrey was not to get any bonus if he left when he did. I handed him what had been identified as his own notes taken at the meeting. His note about what Jeffrey would get on leaving listed his salary and other benefits and, immediately after that, he'd written "bonus."

"Now, sir, when you listed Mr. Katzenberg's salary and then wrote 'bonus,' that was because Mr. Katzenberg was entitled to his bonus . . . right?"

"No. If he terminated early he'd lose his bonus."

"So, is it your testimony that, when you wrote the word 'bonus' right after his other benefits, what you meant was 'loses bonus'?"

"Yes."

I looked quickly at the Judge, who was scowling. I was sure he wasn't buying this lame explanation. So I decided to ask the kind of question I'd normally avoid.

"I see. So where you just wrote 'bonus' instead of 'loses bonus,' that's because there wasn't time to write the word 'loses'—is that right?"

"I don't recall. These were very quick notes. Something may have distracted me."

"What other words did you omit in your notes?"

"I don't recall any others."

"Was his losing the bonus a significant point to you?"

"Yes."

"But you can give us no explanation why you just wrote 'bonus' and left out the word 'loses'"?

"It's all I wrote."

"No more questions, Your Honor."

The next witness was Eisner himself. He had claimed that the contract didn't entitle Jeffrey to the bonus and, in addition, he'd told Jeffrey that it wasn't right for him to claim all that money from the company if he left early, and that Jeffrey readily agreed to forego the massive bonus for which he'd worked so many years with such success.

To me that seemed totally unbelievable; and we put on very substantial evidence that the contract entitled Jeffrey to the bonus and that he'd never waived it. But I felt that Judge Breckenridge needed to understand what was motivating Eisner to act as he did. There'd been a book about Eisner, and we knew that, in writing it, the author had conversations with Eisner that hadn't found their way into the book as published. But those conversations were still set out in the reporter's notes, which we had subpoenaed. My plan was to get those notes in evidence to show why Eisner was making these insupportable claims. After an extensive examination that I felt had severely weakened Eisner's case, I got to the final point.

"Mr. Eisner, you felt that Mr. Katzenberg was being overcompensated for what he'd done—isn't that right?"

"Not at all."

"Well didn't you say that 'you were the cheerleader and Mr. Katzenberg was just the tip of your pom-pom'—Isn't that right?"

"If I said that, I'm quite sure it was in humor."

"Well, you did say it . . . right?"

"In humor."

"Mr. Eisner, you hated Jeffrey Katzenberg, didn't you?"

"No, of course not."

"Didn't you tell the author of your book that you hated Mr. Katzenberg?"

"In one conversation I did say that."

"What you said was, 'I hate the little midget,' isn't that so?"

At this, Eisner rose up, leaned forward and pointed his finger at me. "Mr. Fields, you're getting into an area that is ill-advised." He followed this threat with a long, irrelevant and self-justifying speech.

Thinking that this non-responsive harangue probably offended the Judge, I listened patiently until Eisner finished. Then I went back to my question.

"Didn't you say on more than one occasion that you hated Mr. Katzenberg?"

My repeating the question seemed to generate even greater anger. Eisner leaned forward again to the point that he was almost standing. He launched into still another long, angry, and irrelevant speech that ended with another bizarre threat: "Mr. Fields, you are going down a direction that is not in your client's best interests."

In many years of trying cases, I had never seen that kind of arrogant behavior from a witness, and I was sure neither Judge Breckenridge, nor Lou Meisinger, nor anyone in the audience had ever seen it either. I felt the Judge was finally getting a clear picture of Michael Eisner and would realize that, out of sheer spite, he was determined to deny Jeffrey his huge, well-earned bonus. I decided to make that clear.

"Did you tell the author of your book, 'I don't care what Mr. Katzenberg thinks. I am not going to pay him any of the money.'?"

"I would say it again. In anger I said that."

That did it. I ended the examination.

The media certainly got it. They skewered Eisner that night and the next day. As one writer put it, "Michael Eisner is a very bright man. But he must never, ever again, get on a witness stand."

SUMMING UP: A PROFESSIONAL MEMOIR

The trial had been "bifurcated" into the trial on whether Disney owed Jeffrey his bonus, and if the answer was "yes," the trial on how much money Jeffrey would receive. The next day, Judge Breckenridge was ready to rule on the liability phase of the case. He announced his finding that Disney did owe Jeffrey the bonus we claimed, that Disney was in breach of that agreement and that he was ready to try the amount of damages.

At this point, Stanley Gold, a skilled attorney and member of the Disney Board, had seen enough. With Gold leading, the Board essentially took over and quickly settled the second phase of the case, agreeing to pay Jeffrey about six times what he had once been ready to accept from Mike Ovitz.

For years after the trial, Michael Eisner didn't speak to me. Recently, however, at a dinner party, he did say "Hello Bert." Eisner continued to run Disney for a time after the conclusion of the Katzenberg trial. But, it couldn't continue. Ultimately he was replaced. Did the trial cause his downfall? Not in itself. I think it was the beginning of a series of events that changed people's views of this enormously bright man, and that led to his departure. Along with Frank and Jeffrey, Michael had accomplished great things for Disney and its shareholders. But, it was time for something different. That "something" turned out to be Bob Iger, whom I've always liked and respected and who's done an extraordinary job.

I'm proud of getting Jeffrey the money he'd earned. To accomplish that, I had to show Michael Eisner's true feelings and motivation. But I had no desire to bring Michael down; and I take no pride in whatever part our trial may have played in that process.

56

Voir Dire

Often, the process of selecting a jury can be the most important phase of a trial. Even the strongest case can be lost if presented to a badly selected jury.

Over the centuries, some bizarre "rules" have arisen concerning what to seek and what to avoid in selecting jurors. Supposedly, Swedes and the English are cold, tough people hard to convince of an injury or to pay significant damages, while Jews and Italians are supposedly suckers for the plea of an injured plaintiff and will be inclined to make substantial awards.

I tell you up front—these generalizations are nonsense!

Before the trial in Katzenberg v. Disney, we tried the main elements of the case to a mock jury recruited by a firm that specializes in such things. Through a sound system and one-way glass partitions, we could watch and listen to the mock jurors before, during and after they conferred and reached a mock verdict.

As the jurors began to assemble and introduce themselves to each other, I pointed out two small, elderly Jewish men shaking hands and selecting seats next to each other. How did I know they were Jewish? One wore a yarmulke and both had Eastern European accents. One seemed to be a retired jeweler, the other a semi-retired clothing manufacturer. They quickly appeared to become friends.

I nudged my partners. "These are my guys," I said, "the first two picks on my jury. They're sympathetic and money in the bank for a plaintiff—and that's us."

Shortly after that I noticed a very large black woman, who looked angry as hell, seeming to scowl at everyone and everything.

"That's the number one juror we'd avoid. Wow! Before she's heard a word, you can tell she'll hate our case."

The jury was seated, there were brief instructions from an official, and we began a truncated presentation of the case for Katzenberg and Disney's defense. Katzenberg was seeking a huge amount of money based essentially on the deal made when Eisner, Wells and Katzenberg took over management of Disney.

We then overhead the mock jury's deliberations. One of the elderly Jewish merchants on whom I relied turned to his friend, but in a voice heard by the entire mock jury, said, "Look, in mine business, if I don't get it in writing plain as day, it don't count—forget it! This Katzenback is no different."

His new friend nodded and then spoke. "You got that right Sam. If he thought his bonus continued, he should have made that clear in writing. If he didn't, he's a schmuck and don't deserve the dough."

At this point, the large black lady I would have excluded from the jury with a peremptory challenge stood up and spoke out. "You two should be ashamed of yourselves. These three guys worked together for years before coming to Disney. Katzenberg believed he could rely on their original deal, and he worked night and day for all those years just to get the bonus they promised him. It would be not only unjust but downright cruel to say he can't get what he's entitled to because he trusted his two longtime friends!"

Wow, was I wrong! And what a mistake I would have made if this had been a real jury trial and I had relied on my stereotypical, surface opinions of the prospective jurors.

So what's the way to select a jury? You can hire a jury consulting firm, and they will even look into the background of potential jurors and sit with you in the courtroom, helping you with your selection.

I've used such firms. But generally I tend to rely on my gut reaction to the prospective jurors, quickly analyzing their responses to my questioning during the voir dire process (i.e., the questioning and selection of the jury).

What are the fundamental rules on which to rely? For me, there really are no hard and fast rules. It's mostly instinct, what most would call "the seat of my pants."

Of course, there is one thing to keep in mind—most prospective jurors just want to go home or back to work or anywhere other than a courtroom. Judges are aware of that, and most are extremely difficult to convince that a prospective juror should be excused.

In a jury trial a few years ago, another case against Disney for breach of contract, the Judge turned to the group of potential jurors, from which the actual jury would be selected. They were seated in the gallery of the courtroom, and, as they were picked to serve, they would take their places in the jury box.

The Judge first explained what the case was about and then began with some routine questions. "Is there anyone here who believes they can't fairly be a juror in this case?"

A man in the back raised his hand. "Yes sir," said the Judge, "what's the problem?"

"Well, your honor, I'm suing Disney for breach of contract—just like the plaintiff here."

The Judge frowned, "When did you file your lawsuit against Disney?"

"I filed it yesterday."

At this point, I was confident the man would be excused. I was wrong.

The Judge asked, "Well, do you believe you can put that aside and fairly decide this different case?"

"Oh, yes, Judge. I believe I can."

"Okay, you're on the jury. Take a seat."

And that wasn't all. Another man, closer to the front, raised his hand.

"What's your problem," asked the Judge.

"Well, Judge, the thing is I hate Disney!"

"You hate Disney? Why?"

"My church believes that Disney is evil, and I agree. We hate Disney!"

The Judge didn't wait even a second.

"Well sir, do you believe you could fairly decide this case?"

The man hesitated—then, "Yes, your honor. I believe I can."

"All right you're on the jury. Please take a seat in the jury box."

I couldn't believe it. I was delighted; but I knew it couldn't last.

The Disney lawyers, of course, exercised two of their peremptory challenges to eliminate the two jurors in question. But, that used up two challenges they could otherwise have used in selecting a jury they thought would be favorable to their case.

In the end, we won the case. I like to think it wasn't because the Judge put Disney at a disadvantage. But, who knows?

Some prospective jurors will use any excuse they can come up with to try to be eliminated from being selected for an actual jury. Almost any excuse you can think of has been used. Most do not work.

The most extreme instance I ever saw came in a case I tried a few years ago. In the course of the Judge's questioning the prospective jurors one by one, he turned to a young Asian man.

"Well sir, is there any reason why you can't serve as a juror in this case?"

The man made no response. He just stared vacantly at the Judge.

"Sir, I'm asking you a question. Is there any reason why you can't serve as a juror in the case?"

Again, the young man simply stared back at the Judge as if he hadn't heard a thing.

Now the Judge raised his voice. "Are you hearing impaired, sir?"

Still, the man continued to show no response and just stared at the Judge as if he hadn't heard a thing.

Finally, the Judge called us up to a conference at the bench. Both sides agreed that this juror, who seemed totally non-responsive, should be excused.

The Judge announced this to the jury pool; and, since the silent young man still showed no response, the Sheriff assigned to the courtroom was instructed to help him from the jury box and from the room.

Later, during the room break I saw a group of prospective jurors sitting on a bench in the hallway of the courtroom. The young Asian man who'd shown no visible reaction to the Judge's questions, was with them. He was laughing and animatedly talking with the others. He had to spend the rest of the day avoiding selection as a juror. But my money was on his doing it successfully.

57

"Waltzing Matilda"

I've always been fond of that Australian song. I may be wrong; but I think it's about the joy of a long hike along an open road.

I get that. For many years I was a walker—a long walker—usually on Sundays. I found no better way to recharge my batteries and prepare myself emotionally for the high pressure law practice that awaited me on Monday.

For years, Barbara and I literally walked across the city every Sunday. Our longest walk was from downtown, all the way out Wilshire Boulevard to the statute of St. Monica on the palisades overlooking the sea. Our shorter walks were from West Hollywood to Chinatown or from West Hollywood to the beach. We varied our route, sometimes taking Sunset, other times Olympic, Beverly or Pico Boulevards. At the end of our walks we'd have a Mexican, Chinese or seafood lunch with plenty of wine and take a taxi home.

There are things to see and absorb on a walk across the city that you'd never really "see" from a moving car. Heading east on Beverly, for example, we'd pass one ethnic enclave after another, each with its own distinctive street food and often its own storefront form of religion, like gospel words sung to Mariachi music.

Unless you've walked it, you'll never really understand how huge LA is and how the Westside is essentially not a part of an Eastside citizen's ordinary life or thoughts. Once, walking down 1st Street almost to downtown, we were stopped by a young Hispanic boy of 10 or 11. He was curious because we didn't seem to belong in the neighborhood. We told him we lived many miles away nearer the ocean and that we'd walked from there to visit his part of the city. He couldn't believe it. He pointed up a hill toward the west. He'd heard there was an ocean way out there, but, even though his whole life had been in Los Angeles, he'd never seen it. We assured him it was there and encouraged him to go find it. He shook our hands, and we walked on.

Once, when Barbara and I were walking along Wilshire just east of La Brea, a car pulled up to the curb just ahead of us. A guy opened the door nearest us, leaned out and said, "Are you Bert Fields?" I said I was, and he said, "You know, I read in the papers you walked across the city every Sunday, but I didn't believe it. God Damn!" He grinned. We grinned back. He closed the car door and drove away.

But our long walks aren't only in LA. In New York, we walk from Central Park to Battery Park and back. In Paris, we've often walked from our hotel near the Etoile to the Ile Saint-Louis, crossed the bridge, explored the Left Bank and walked back to our hotel. In London, we walked from our hotel in Chelsea to the Tower of London and back again, mostly along the Thames Embankment.

We're not confined to city walks. In the French countryside we walk for hours along the scenic routes laid out by a marvelous organization that connects almost every country town to its neighbor, with a series of varied but always beautiful trails.

And Barbara and I, together with our dear friend Harvey Leve, hiked across the Pyrenees from France to Spain, following the route used by Jews escaping from the Nazis in the mid-1940s.

There is something wonderfully calming and restorative in these long distance walks of ours, and walking for five hours with your wife makes it virtually impossible to leave any thought undisclosed and undiscussed. In any relationship, that's a good thing.

58

Happy Birthday

If you have a meal with Jeffrey Katzenberg, he'll always—and I mean <u>always</u>—get the check. His office calls ahead to make sure. We've had many meals together. Every time, I've tried to get the check—never with success—except one time.

We were to have lunch at The Grill in Beverly Hills. I arrived 15 minutes early in an attempt to get the check. As always, the maitre d'ess politely refused. Jeffrey had made his usual call in advance. Desperate, I came up with a brilliant lie. "This is a very special occasion," I said. "It's Mr. Katzenberg's birthday, and I simply have to get the check. We can't let him pay for his own birthday lunch."

It worked. She said that, just this once, under those special circumstances, she'd ignore Jeffrey's instructions and let me pay. I handed her my credit card and was shown to our booth.

Soon Jeffrey arrived, and we had a pleasant lunch—some business, some social. After we'd finished the main course, I heard a murmur go through the entire restaurant. Two waiters were approaching our table carrying a giant birthday cake with lighted candles. Jeffrey said, "What the hell is this?" Then the waiters broke into "Happy Birthday To You" as the entire restaurant watched.

It was pretty embarrassing; but I did get the check.

59

Writing Books

WHEN BARBARA SAW THE REFERENCE to a "professional memoir" on the cover page of my manuscript, she reminded me that I had a profession other than the law—I write books. It's true, I do.

Many years ago, when Mario Puzo read a brief I wrote in one of his legal battles, he remarked that I wrote well and suggested that I try writing something other than legal arguments. Well, I thought, if Mario thinks so, maybe I should. Over the next few months, I worked on the concept of a fictional lawyer, who ultimately became Harry Cain in my first book, a novel called *The Sunset Bomber*. Harry was a talented trial lawyer without peer in his professional life, but utterly hopeless in his personal life, regularly cheating on his loving wife, while working legal miracles in court. Most of the cases in the book were based on actual cases I had tried. I made up the sex.

This was relatively early in my own legal career; and I was concerned that potential clients would be reluctant to hire a lawyer who spent his time writing racy novels. So the book was published under the pseudonym "D. Kincaid."

Where did I get this particular name? The concept of an initial rather than a full first name was derived from

B. Traven, an author I greatly admired. But I have no recollection of how I came up with "Kincaid."

In any event, *The Sunset Bomber* sold fairly well; and I was determined to write a sequel. I began the new book; but, before it was completed, Lydia became ill with lung cancer. After a game fight for over a year, she died of the disease.

I had put aside the sequel during Lydia's illness; but, some months later, I returned to complete it, adding sections in which Harry Cain's wife dies in much the same way. Thus, *The Lawyer's Tale*, while relating new legal adventures of Harry Cain, also recounts the process of his wife's death and is, to some extent, a darker book than *The Sunset Bomber*.

On reading *The Lawyer's Tale*, my father said, "This is a good book, son, but when are you going to write something serious?" I guess, even after all those years, I still wanted his approval. So I set out to write "something serious." I've always been interested in English history. So I decided to explore the mystery of Edward IV's two sons, who were in the Tower of London awaiting the older boy's coronation when both of them mysteriously disappeared. After that, their uncle, Richard III, became King.

Did Richard have his nephews murdered? Certainly that was the story put out by the Tudors after Henry Tudor's forces defeated Richard's at the Battle of Bosworth Field in 1485. It's also the story written by Thomas More. But More wrote this under a Tudor King many decades after the event, so perhaps we can take his account with a grain of salt. It was an intriguing controversy; and I set out, with Barbara's aid and encouragement, to discover "the truth."

Well "the truth" about events that occurred 500 years ago is not so easy to establish. We searched all over England for years in search of the true facts. We learned, for example, that Richard was not the hunchback cripple lurching around the stage in Shakespeare's play. For one thing, he was a noted warrior who fought in many battles on horseback, wielding a sword and lance. Shakespeare's cripple could never have done that. We searched all over England for a suit of hunchbacked armor, which surely would have been saved if it had existed.

Evidently, after the Tudors took over, it was important for them to disparage Richard, and they covered England with a barrage of anti-Ricardian propaganda portraying Richard as an evil hunchback, twisted in both body and mind. Earlier portraits of Richard were even altered to add a hump. The problem was that sometimes the hump was added on the left shoulder and sometimes on the right.

We also tried to follow the clues as to what happened to the two princes in the Tower. Were they murdered and, if so, by whom? If not, were they smuggled out of the country—and, again, by whom? Why? And what became of them?

In any event, our research was finally completed, and the book was published under the title *Royal Blood: Richard III and the Mystery Of The Princes*. This time, I published it under my own name.

Okay Dad, that's the serious book, so are more sex novels okay? The fact is I really got more of a kick out of "history's mysteries." So I looked for another one. It didn't take long. For years, I'd been fascinated with the controversy over the authorship of the Shakespeare canon. Was it the fellow from Stratford, who never went beyond the 6th grade (if that) in a one-room rural school and apparently was never outside of England, or was it a highly educated and traveled nobleman who couldn't be seen to write plays for the public stage?

So I decided to undertake a study of "The Shakespeare Controversy." Again, it took years of research in various parts of England, and in such places as the British Library and the College of Arms.

As in the case of *Royal Blood*, I published the book under my own name. It's entitled *Players: The Mysterious Identity of William Shakespeare*. After its publication, I was invited to give talks on the subject and to attend various meetings and conventions of Shakespeare scholars, some of which turned into near violent confrontations between the "Stratfordians," who believed that the fellow from the small country town was the true author, and the "anti-Strats" who believed that the true author was someone else.

What was next? It's a secret. I essentially ghost-wrote a novel under someone else's name. It was great fun and it sold very well. But the secret will go to my grave.

Next I wrote *Destiny: A Novel Of Napoleon & Josephine*. And after *Destiny* came *Shylock: His Own Story*, a fictional account of Shakespeare's great character in *The Merchant of Venice*. It's dedicated to Dustin Hoffman, whose memorable performance as Shylock is what aroused my interest in the character.

The last book before this one was on Elizabeth I. It's called *Gloriana: Exploring the Reign of Elizabeth I*, the name given by Edward Spenser to the heroic queen in his poem based on Elizabeth. Here again, Barbara worked with me to run down all the facts and controversies that surrounded that great Queen, whom I consider the greatest monarch England ever had.

Elizabeth was in love with Robert Dudley, her "sweet Robin." But one problem: Dudley was already married to a rural heiress. One afternoon, however, the situation changed dramatically. Dudley's wife was found dead at the foot of a staircase, her neck broken. Naturally, Dudley and the Queen were suspected of her murder.

After considerable research, Barbara and I finally found what we were convinced was the actual staircase down which Dudley's wife fell. When most of its former location burned, the staircase had been moved to a rural farmhouse, where this beautiful and intricate staircase seemed completely out of place.

We noted, for example, that it was a "dog leg" staircase and that the final flight down which Dudley's wife fell was only five steps. No one was likely to die from a fall down only five steps.

Then we were able to find the coroner's report on her death. Under her bonnet, the coroner had found two wounds in her head, one of which was "two thumbs" deep. That would be an enormous and obviously mortal wound. Clearly, Dudley's wife was killed with the powerful downstroke of a very sharp and strong instrument—probably a heavy dagger or pike.

But who did this? Was it Dudley, who desperately wanted to marry Elizabeth? Or was it someone else who wanted Dudley blamed so he <u>couldn't</u> marry Elizabeth? Or was it some moronic thug who thought he was doing what the Queen wanted—much like the two knights who slaughtered Thomas Beckett in Canterbury Cathedral, believing they were doing what Henry II wanted? The mystery has never been solved. Suspicion of the Queen tended to dissipate; but Dudley remained a suspect for most of his life.

It took years, but *Gloriana* finally came out in 2017. My favorite portrait of the great Queen is on the cover.

Will I write more? Given more years, I certainly will. I love it, and I'm thinking about what to write next. But, at ninety, who knows?

60

JACK

ONE OF MY FAVORITE PEOPLE on the *Harvard Law Review* was Jack Kevorkian—not the "death doctor," but a brilliant and funny law student, whose real name was Aram.

This was during the Korean War, so, after law school, most of us went into the armed forces. In the Army, Jack was stationed in France and married a French girl. After the war, he opened a bilingual law practice in Paris, where he raised a lovely family—and never left.

After a time, it became an annual tradition for Jack to drive down to our mill in rural France. He'd always arrive with a good bottle of wine under each arm, ready to laugh and talk together for hours. As the years passed, these were evenings I came to treasure. Jack always had a refreshingly unique way of looking at life, literature, philosophy and everything else, as well as a delightful and infectious sense of humor.

Jack successfully handled some cases for us in France, always finding ingenious ways to accomplish our goals. When the government asserted a claim to our French property, Jack and I came up with a unique theory to defeat the claim. When the large law firm Jack had just left had a file that he contended was really ours, Jack simply walked into their offices, asked a clerk for the file and walked out with it. The file was one that should have been turned over to us, and its contents were of enormous assistance in resolving our problem.

Later, a Parisian dentist recommended by a friend "rented" our mill for eleven months at a nominal rent, supposedly to keep the walls warm in wintertime. The twelfth month was to be ours. But, when his time was up, the dentist refused to leave, citing a new French law that allowed tenants to stay indefinitely after the expiration of their leases, with the rent to continue subject to slight adjustments set by a government agency.

Jack recommended a French barrister to try the case— an Orthodox Jew who proved to be very effective. He and Jack came up with the argument that, although the new law didn't say so, it was designed to protect poor tenants in their main residences, not to allow a rich dentist with a home in Paris to create a second country estate in someone else's home. After fighting the case all the way to the highest court in France, Jack's theory prevailed, the dentist was finally evicted, and we were awarded actual and punitive damages.

Meanwhile, Jack's practice had grown, and he had become the "go to" American lawyer in Paris. But his interests went well beyond practicing law. He was active in supporting the new Armenian state, spoke and wrote effectively on behalf of many causes. Ultimately, he published an extraordinary book called *Confessions of a Francophile*, a collection of his essays on politics, philosophy, and simply life in Paris.

One morning when I was in Paris, Jack asked if I could join him for lunch with a client of his who had a problem in California. I never turned down a chance to see Jack and quickly agreed. With some difficulty, I found the place Jack mentioned. It was Les Diamantaires, an Armenian restaurant. There, at a table in the rear, was Jack and his client—William Saroyan. I had long been a Saroyan fan, having read—I think—everything he wrote. So I was thrilled.

They asked me to join them in a glass of a milky drink, that seemed to be an Armenian version of what the Greeks call Ouzo. It was delicious; and, as we began to talk, we had more. Saroyan outlined his problem. Without his permission, people in California were going to put on a play based on one of his stories. While we discussed his alternatives, more drinks came, and we drank them.

Ultimately, a marvelous lunch was served, but the drinking continued. So did the conversation, and, as time passed, we left Saroyan's law case and delved into Armenian life in America, political and philosophical issues, government, cooking and many other subjects.

Finally, I looked at my watch and was surprised to see that it was four o'clock. I began to make my exit. But Jack and "Bill" would have none of it. They insisted that we have dessert and, of course, more to drink! We did, and at five, hugged by Jack and Saroyan, I made it into the street and, somehow, to my hotel.

We succeeded in stopping production of the Saroyan-based play, and I got a nice note from "Bill." More importantly, I got an afternoon I'll never forget.

A few years later, Jack died in his beloved Paris. We had a memorial in New York, attended by his family, a multitude of friends and some of our law school classmates. I spoke and referred to lines from T.S. Eliot's *The Love Song of J. Alfred Prufrock*. I said that "Prufrock," despairing of a meaningless life, walked along the beach, where he "heard the mermaids singing each to each," adding sadly, "I do not think they will sing to me."

"Well," I said, "The mermaids sang to Jack Kevorkian—his whole life."

SUMMING UP: A PROFESSIONAL MEMOIR

61

Administrative Law?

I'M SURE the many administrative agencies of the U.S. Government do considerable good. My own experience would generally support that conclusion. But there are exceptions. One egregious exception occurred in the matter of Pom Wonderful before the Federal Trade Commission (FTC).

"Pom" was and is pure pomegranate juice. Its makers had spent millions of dollars on scientific research that generally demonstrated that pomegranate juice was promotive of good health, reducing arterial plaque and even potentially slowing the progression of prostate cancer. But their research, while impressive, lacked, in most instances, the support of "RCTs," Randomized Control Trials, which are not only randomized, but are also double blind, placebo-based experiments involving huge numbers of subjects.

The problem was that RCTs are enormously expensive, sometimes costing as much as $50 million or more. A company selling pure fruit juice simply can't afford to finance multiple RCTs in support of its various scientific studies. The makers of Pom had spent a fortune on solid scientific backing for the health benefits of their product. But to back every one of those studies with an RCT would have been financially impossible.

Against this background, the Federal Trade Commission claimed that the makers of Pom could not make any public statement asserting the health benefits of their fruit juice unless every such benefit was supported by RCTs. What that meant, as a practical matter, was they couldn't inform the public about the potential health benefits of Pom.

The Pom people pointed out that their product was pure fruit juice, not a drug, and that their health claims were supported by solid scientific studies, even if not by prohibitively expensive RCTs. It didn't matter to the FTC. The agency brought an administrative proceeding seeking damages and an injunction against the owners of Pom publicly asserting any health benefits of their product unless such claims were supported by RCTs.

This led to a lengthy "trial" in Washington, D.C. in which I represented the makers of Pom against the FTC. The trial was held in the courtroom at the FTC building before an Administrative Law Judge. In this case, the Judge was an intelligent, experienced and fair-minded jurist.

Each side called a panoply of expert witnesses, primarily doctors. The FTC's experts asserted that no health claims about Pom could properly be made unless they were supported by RCTs. The defense witnesses testified that the numerous scientific studies of Pom demonstrated its health benefits without the necessity of prohibitively expensive RCTs. After all, this was pure fruit juice, not a drug.

The FTC's doctors did not do well on cross-examination. To provide an example, I've set out excerpts from the actual cross-examination of two key FTC witnesses. Both were medical doctors with distinguished scientific and academic qualifications. One, Dr. Meir Stampfer of Harvard, was an expert principally in the area of internal medicine. The other, Dr. Arnold Melman, was a specialist in problems of sexual dysfunction. Both testified on direct examination by the FTC lawyers that it would be highly improper to make any public claim of the health benefits of pomegranate juice unless that claim was supported by RCTs involving thousands of subjects. In Dr. Melman's view, two such RCTs are required on any potential benefit before any such claim can be made.

The following are excerpts from the cross-examination of Dr. Stampfer.

"BY MR. FIELDS:

Q. Good morning, Dr. Stampfer.

A. Good morning. Well, good afternoon.

Q. I am Bert Fields, and I'm one of the lawyers for the Respondents in this case. I think we met before in the courtroom.

Let's begin where we ended. You said, I think, that Respondents' science doesn't support their claims because there's insufficient evidence of causality. Is that—is that correct?

A. Yes.

Q. Okay. And I think you said that to establish causality, you would have to prove the effect of their product beyond a reasonable doubt. Is that right?

A. Yes.

• • • •

Q. Okay. Now, the standard of proof that you've talked about today for efficacy claims is not one you consistently apply. Is that correct?

A. No. It is not correct.

Q. You apply it consistently?

A. Yes.

Q. Didn't you claim—make claims for the efficacy of moderate alcohol consumption in reducing the risk of coronary heart disease, diabetes, and cognitive impairment?

A. Individuals with—I don't believe that I have ever stated that a causal connection was established.

Q. Sir, did you—do you recall doing an interview on national radio, with a man named Norman Swan, and stating that—and by the way—I am going to refer to RX 5000. Do we have that? Do we have it for the screen?

If you will turn to page 2 of that interview, I think you will find that you said that moderate alcohol consumption lowers the risk of both cognitive impairment and heart disease. Am I correct in that?

A. Let me just look through this.

Q. Do you see where it says "Meir Stampfer" on the bottom of page 2? "Moderate alcohol consumption does appear to raise the risk of breast cancer a little bit, but it is statistically insignificant. It also lowers risk not only of cognitive impairment but also heart disease."

A. Yes.

Q. That's a classic—classic efficacy claim, isn't it, sir?

A. Yes. And I do have to say I must have misspoken in that interview by not using the terms exactly correct.

Q. Yes. And did you say the same kind of thing about coronary heart disease and moderate alcohol consumption in an interview with the *Modern Brewery Age*? Do you recall that?

A. I don't recall it, but it could well have happened.

Q. Well, let's take a look at RX 5001, which I think is a publication called *Modern Brewery Age*. Do we have that up on the screen?

· · · · ·

Q. Do you see, sir, where it says "Stampfer"—that refers to you, I take it—"said his research has shown"—your research has shown—"that moderate alcohol consumption can lead to a reduction in the incidence of coronary heart disease"? Correct?

A. Well, this was what the reporter reported.

Q. Pardon me?

A. There was no quotation of me. It was—

Q. Well, are you denying you said that, sir?

A. No, I'm not denying it. I'm merely pointing out what the document says.

Q. Okay, good. All right. And those claims for the efficacy of moderate alcohol consumption in reducing the risk of coronary heart disease and cognitive impairment, those were based upon observational studies, isn't that correct, at the time you made those statements?

A. Yes.

Q. Okay. And they were not randomized, double-blind, placebo-controlled trails, correct?

A. That's correct.

Q. To shorten things, I'm going to use the term "RCT trials." Do you understand that term?

A. RCT?

Q. Yeah. Some of you folks use that instead of what I just said, the randomized, double-blind, placebo-controlled studios, correct?

A. Yes.

Q. All right.

JUDGE CHAPPELL: "Some of you folks"?

MR. FIELDS: Well, I'm a little folksy, Your Honor. I'm from out on the Plains.

• • • •

Q. Now, it's correct that the causal link between moderate alcohol consumption and various diseases that you said had a reduced risk, that causal link hadn't been established. Isn't that correct?

A. That's correct.

• • • •

Q. Well, sir, you were talking to the public when you gave those interviews. Isn't that correct?

A. Yes.

Q. And are you now saying that moderate alcohol use does not lower the risk of cognitive impairment and coronary—vascular—cardiovascular disease?

A. What I'm saying is that that link is not—the causal link is not established.

Q. I understand. But even though the causal link was not established, you felt free to tell the public that moderate alcohol consumption did, in fact, lower the risk of these diseases, right?

A. In an interview setting, that was my statement, and it was a poor choice of words. And if I had more time and thought about it, I would have chosen a more accurate way to raise the—my opinion on this.

Q. Well, that's what I don't understand. Are you saying that, in fact, what you said in those interviews was untrue?

A. What I'm saying is that I used the wrong terminology, the wrong words. What I should have said was what I said earlier in the interview, that people with moderate alcohol consumption had lower cognitive decline, and I should not have used the term that moderate alcohol use lowers risk. That was a mistake on my part. I admit it.

• • • •

Q. Now, when you made those remarks about moderate alcohol consumption, Doctor, you were aware that moderate alcohol consumption is not totally safe. Isn't that correct?

A. It's—moderate alcohol consumption is not totally safe. That is correct.

• • • •

Q. And also, if it slips from moderate alcohol consumption to immoderate alcohol consumption, it can cause a lot of havoc and fatalities, right?

A. Absolutely.

Q. In fact, Doctor, you—you or your school received a substantial payment from Anheuser-Busch Beer Company. Isn't that correct?"

A. I received nothing.

Q. Did you understand my question? I said "you or your school."

A.   You or your school?

Q.   Yes.

A.   So, I'm answering the first part, is I received nothing, and the School of Public Health received a gift.

Q.   They received a very substantial amount of money from the beer company.

A.   150,000.

Q.   Yes. And you have also appeared and made presentations for the beer company, right?

A.   I spoke on the risks and benefits of moderate alcohol consumption, yes.

Q.   And those were presentations to the Anheuser-Busch Company, right?

A.   They were organized by Anheuser-Busch, yes.

Q.   Well—

A.   They were not presentations to the company. They—but the company organized them.

Q.   Okay. And they paid your expenses, the Anheuser-Busch people, right?

A.   Pardon?

Q.   They paid your expenses?

A.   Yes.

Q.   Okay. Now, you felt that when you made these statements about moderate alcohol consumption, the causal link between moderate alcohol consumption and these various diseases that you said had a reduced risk had not been firmly established. Isn't that correct?

A. Yes.

• • • •

Q. All right, sir. Now, is it correct that the same standard of proof that you've applied in making these statements about wine and beer apply to pomegranate juice?

A. The same standards, yes.

Q. Okay. So, it would be fair to say, without RCTs and without a causal link between proven beyond a reasonable doubt, that pomegranate juice may reduce the risk of certain diseases, correct?

A. Well, you used the—you used the word "may," and if you use the word "may," then it would be correct, because "may" implies that it's possible. But if you say "will," then it is not correct, because "will" implies that a causal link has been established.

Q. So, the—well, but you said that a causal link hadn't been established for moderate alcohol consumption, and yet you made a—on two occasions that I cited to you, you made the statement that it lowered the risk of all kinds of diseases, right?

A. I think I answered that question previously, that it was a poor choice of words, and I do not hold the view that a causal link between moderate alcohol consumption and reduced cognitive decline and reduced heart disease has been established.

SUMMING UP: A PROFESSIONAL MEMOIR

So, you have found a quotation that was made in an interview setting that was incorrect, just as you yourself have already misspoken a couple of times in extemporaneous speech, and this is what happens with extemporaneous speech.

Q. Yes. And so you feel that a more rigorous standard should be applied to pomegranate juice than you've applied to wine and beer?

A. Absolutely not.

Q. The same, correct?

A. The same standard."

That, of course, meant RCTs were not required, since he had publicly claimed the health benefits of wine and beer despite the absence of proof by any RCTs.

And here are some excerpts from the cross-examination of Dr. Arnold Melman, a specialist in "erectile dysfunction," who had testified on direct examination that no claims of benefit to males suffering from such dysfunction could properly be made unless that benefit had first been proven by two double blind, placebo based, randomized trials (i.e., RCTs).

"Q. Good afternoon, Doctor. Let's begin by reviewing some of the things you said were necessary to make a claim with reference to effecting erectile function. Do you know the term "RCT study"?

A. RTC?

Q. RCT.

A. I don't know what that is.

Q. Okay, Well it's a study term. It's a term commonly used by researchers to indicate a randomized, double-blind, placebo-based trial, and they call it for short "RCT." A number of experts in this case have used the term.

A. I don't know who "they" are. You'll have to tell me who "they" are.

Q. Yes. A number of experts in this case have used that term. You can assume that. But if you prefer, I'll say the whole thing each time.

A. I'd prefer that.

Q. Okay. So you have indicated in your testimony and in your report that the only kind of science that could justify claims to help erectile dysfunction are double-blind, placebo-based, randomized trials; right?

A. Yes.

• • • •

Q. You have said that in order to make a public claim for benefit to erectile function one must have a double-blind, placebo-based, randomized trial, and you've also said it has to be a trial done in two separate institutions at least; correct?

A. It should be, yes.

Q. Well, you said it has to be; isn't that correct?

SUMMING UP: A PROFESSIONAL MEMOIR

A.   Yes.

Q.   Okay. And so my question was, if Dr. Burnett—by the way, Dr. Burnett at Johns Hopkins is a very distinguished man in the field, isn't he?

A.   He is. He's a good friend of mine, so yes.

Q.   And if he did this at Johns Hopkins, he ran the double-blind, placebo-based, randomized test, and it came out positive, you would say that's still not enough to support making a public claim on behalf of this product; right?

A.   That's correct.

Q.   Okay. And you say that in addition, this has to be a very large group to make sense. It has to reach statistical significance. Isn't that what you said?

A.   Yes.

Q.   And you also say that to be competent and reliable evidence to support a public claim of benefit to erectile dysfunction the wives have to confirm what the husbands say.

A.   See, the tendency today in clinical trials looking at erectile dysfunction include not necessarily the wife but the sexual partner.

Q.   Yes. You have said that the—let's call it the sexual partner—must confirm what the male partner says in this test in order to justify making a public claim about helping—

A. Right.

Q. —erectile function.

A. That gives the most reliable information. That's correct.

Q. But you've said it's required, haven't you, sir?

A. Yes. I used the word "required" for drugs that are being submitted to Food and Drug Administration. If you want to take a lesser standard—I don't know what standard you're looking for. I'm talking about the use of drugs that are submitted to the Food and Drug Administration so they can be marketed in the United States.

JUDGE CHAPPELL: Hold on a second. I don't want to derail the cross-exam, but you're like two ships passing in the night.

Doctor, you keep talking about drugs. I'm not sure he's talking about drugs.

THE WITNESS: He is talking about drugs, Your Honor. This—

JUDGE CHAPPELL: So you're only prepared to talk about a drug the claim has made, not any other juice or spring water or anything else?

THE WITNESS: Your Honor, water is water. It has H_2O, a product. The active ingredient of the product is not water. Otherwise, they'd be selling Evian spring water. They're selling a product that is composed of drugs. In this case the drugs are polyphenol agents that have a specific biologic effect, or they claim that they do, so it's a product, even though they're calling it a juice, but it's a product with drugs in it.

JUDGE CHAPPELL: So let me make sure I understand you. In your opinion, pomegranate juice is a drug.

THE WITNESS: Correct.

JUDGE CHAPPELL: Thank you.

BY MR. FIELDS:

Q. I think that tells us a lot, Doctor.

• • • •

Q. You have—you have the opinion that before you make a claim of the ability to help erectile dysfunction, your product, you have to prove it; isn't that right?

A. Yes.

Q. And you have to prove it by going through these various steps that you've told us were required; right?

A. Yes.

Q. Okay. But, Doctor, you don't apply that standard consistently, do you?

A. I don't know what the implication of your question is.

Q. The implication is that you don't apply it consistently. Correct me if I'm wrong.

A. I'm correcting you. I'm correcting him. I don't know what he's talking about.

Q. Okay. We'll get to it. Are you the CEO and cofounder of a company called Ion Channel Innovations?

A. Yes, I am.

Q. That company makes a therapy for erectile dysfunction called hMaxi-K; is that correct?

A. That's correct.

Q. That's a form of gene transfer therapy for erectile dysfunction.

A. Yes.

Q. Potentially a competitive product with pomegranate juice; correct?

A. I don't know if it is or it isn't.

Q. By the way, isn't it correct that the standards in your mind for substantiating a claim for fruit juice are the same as for substantiating a claim for gene transfer therapy?

A. For what?

Q. Gene transfer therapy?

A. No, no. A claim for what?

Q. Oh. The claim to help erectile dysfunction.

A. It should be, yes.

Q. It should be the same. All right. Do you recall, sir, an interview you gave with somebody named Lizzy Ratner of *The New York Observer*, a paper of general circulation in New York?

A. No.

Q. All right. Let me read you statements and see if you recognize them.

• • • •

Q. Okay. And in that interview about hMaxi-K you told her that your product would not only help erectile dysfunction, but it also conceivably could benefit asthma, hypertension and diabetes.

A. Let me correct you, and that is that we do not have a product. There's no product. There's nothing being sold. This is in the testing phase. So there's no product.

• • • •

Q. And you think the word "product" is incorrect because it wasn't actually on the market; is that —

A. There's nothing on the market.

Q. I see.

A. No sales. This is in the testing process.

Q. Yes. But in the testing process you made these public statements about—

A. I didn't—what public statements?

Q. Well, how about that the men who tried hMaxi-K had spontaneous, normal erections? How about that they were like young men again? How about calling your product the fountain of youth? Did you call your product the fountain of youth, sir?

A. We did a phase I ED trial which was a nonplacebo-controlled phase I safety trial, and during the phase I safety trial, which was done on 20 men, several of the men got erections. This is just the response to a phase I trial. This trial—this product now has to go through phase II and III, phase III testing. hMaxi-K is not on the market. It's just gone through phase I testing.

Q. But despite that, despite the no RCTs, no double-blind, placebo-based, randomized tests, despite the fact that the wives were not interrogated, despite the fact—

A. Well, the wives were interrogated.

• • • •

Q. Sir, did you tell *The New York Observer* that the men that you had tested had spontaneous, normal erections?

A. Correct.

Q. Did you tell them that it was like they were young again?

A. Correct.

Q. Did you tell them that—did you tell her that you called your erectile dysfunction product the fountain of youth?

A. I said that would be the equivalent. Yes.

Q. Well, you called it the fountain of youth, didn't you?

A. I said it could be like that. That's correct.

• • • •

Q. Okay. Did you say that you were talking about modifying the aging process?

A. Yes. And that was based upon the result of an animal study which we published.

Q. An animal study—

A. Yes.

• • • •

Q. Sir, you made the claim that—

A. I didn't make a claim.

Q. You didn't make a claim.

A. No.

Q. Well, you said to the public that these gentlemen had spontaneous, normal erections, that they were like being young again, that you were talking about modifying the aging process, that it was the fountain of youth, and you don't call that making a public claim?

A. I didn't make a public claim.

Q. You didn't make a public claim.

A. No.

Q. I guess His Honor will have to decide. Sir, in fact you only had 11 men in the study you did; right?

A. No.

Q. That isn't true?

A. No, it's not true.

Q. How many men did you have?

A. Twenty.

• • • •

Q. Is it correct you've never done any testing of any kind on pomegranate juice?

A. Have *I* tested pomegranate juice? No.

• • • •

Q. The only research you've ever done on a food product was on alcohol, a substance called yohimbine; correct.

A. Yes.

Q. That was twenty years ago.

A. Right.

Q. You've never done a clinical trial on any food product; is that correct?

A. Well, by "food product" do you mean drugs? Drugs? I don't know what you—you'd have to define a food product for me.

Q. On your definition everything is a drug, but —

A. Well, that's true.

Q. — have you—you've never done any clinical work on something that ordinary people would call a food?

A. You mean like mushrooms and hemlock?

Q. Like mushrooms or like broccoli or carrots.

A. No.

Q. Thank you."

After a month of expert testimony from both sides, the Administrative Law Judge ruled squarely that RCTs were <u>not</u> required to support Pom's claims of health benefits, that those benefits could be publicly asserted if supported by scientific studies other than RCTs—just the kind of studies the makers of Pom had relied upon. Out of 600 different Pom ads, the Judge found that only 13 were insufficiently supported by scientific studies. Even this tiny fraction of ads was not found to be false; but only that they could be construed as making claims not yet supported by sufficient evidence. 587 ads escaped any adverse finding. Most importantly, RCTs were not needed for Pom's health-related ads, and the overwhelming majority of their health-related ads were just fine. It was a huge win for the makers of Pom. We had a victory dinner at the home of Pom's founders, because it was an immensely gratifying victory.

This was also the end of my involvement in the matter. My clients hired an administrative law specialist to deal with what could loosely be called the FTC's "appeal." But that would be a misuse of the word "appeal." There's a reason why, in the title of this chapter, I put a question mark after the words "Administrative Law." This was not an "appeal" as any lawyer would understand the term. It was the FTC simply ignoring the explicit factual findings of the judge who heard the case and the significant trial evidence that supported his decision and its reaching, whatever result these political appointees wanted, regardless of the evidence. The FTC simply ignored the factual findings of the experienced judge, who had heard all the witnesses and viewed all the evidence for over a month. The agency then issued an order that completely ignored his factual findings. Contrary to those explicit findings, the Commission simply ruled that the makers of Pom could not tell the public the proven health benefits of its pomegranate juice unless those statements were supported by not one, but two RCTs.

Obviously, the most optimistic revenues from sales of Pom couldn't afford to meet these requirements; and the public was, and continues to be, denied important specific information about the health benefits of that pure fruit juice—information backed by solid scientific studies—albeit not RCTs. And that's a disgrace.

So, when I speak of the FTC, as it was then constituted, I question whether the word "Law" in "Administrative Law" was applicable at all, as opposed to a word such as "policy" or "politics."

Did I regret all that time I lived in D.C., only to have the positive result of our "trial" completely ignored? Not really. I came to respect my excellent co-counsel, Kris Diaz and John Graubert, and the distinguished experts who testified to the potential health benefits of Pom.

And I came to love D.C. and particularly the Jefferson, a charming small hotel near the White House, where Barbara and I lived for all those weeks.

But, contrary to the findings of the Judge who heard all the evidence for over a month, the FTC's draconian order prevented my clients from informing the public of the specific health benefits of their pure fruit juice, and it certainly gave me an insight into why business owners sometimes complain about administrative agencies and how such an agency can abuse its power and create a horrible result, contrary to the evidence and the public interest. In reversing the Judge's ruling in the matter of Pom Wonderful, the FTC committed a classic such abuse.

62

Teaching

MY FATHER BELIEVED that every intelligent person had a duty to teach. He taught—at USC. I've taught—at Stanford for years, at Harvard for annual lectures and in guest lectures at various other universities.

At Stanford Law School, my partner Bonnie Eskenazi and I teach the course in what's called "Entertainment Law." But, the way we teach it, it's essentially a course on how to think hard about legal issues and find creative approaches to solving them—with an emphasis on the interesting issues that arise from the conflicting elements of the entertainment industry.

We've just finished teaching the course at Stanford for our seventh year now. Each year, the students seem brighter, and my personal enjoyment grows.

I wish I could thank Dad for aiming me in that direction.

63

SLY DEALINGS

THE PRACTICE OF LAW brought me two wives—not at the same time. Lydia came to me as a client, seeking a divorce from an American television star to marry an English movie star. One thing led to another, and she married me instead.

Five years after Lydia died, Barbara was referred to me as a client. She was and is a well-known art advisor. A PhD from Columbia, she even wrote the book on the subject.

One of her clients was Sylvester Stallone, the creator and star of the hugely successful *Rocky* films. Over the years Barbara helped Stallone establish a significant collection of paintings. Then, without any complaint or warning to Barbara, he sued her for advising him in connection with his purchase of a painting by William-Adolphe Bouguereau. After years of proudly featuring the Bouguereau behind a velvet rope in his home gallery, Stallone had apparently been told that the painting had been "slashed," although nothing like that was discernable by simply looking at the work. So Stallone, who has sued many people for many things, suddenly sued Barbara for "fraud." It was terrible for her, since the lawsuit got headlines in newspapers everywhere.

And, of course, Barbara had committed no "fraud." We consulted a distinguished expert who told us the painting had never been slashed or cut. After closely examining the painting under black light, the expert suggested that what Stallone's advisor had apparently seen were some fine lines caused by its having been rolled up many decades before. These lines were invisible to the naked eye but could be discerned by exposing the painting to a black light.

In any event, Stallone ultimately dropped his case against Barbara, and, I believe, traded his Bouguereau to its former owner for another painting. Later, Barbara and I married. I held no grudge against Stallone. The case was over, and I put it behind me. Evidently, Stallone had a very different attitude. When Mike Ovitz, then head of CAA, gave us a lovely engagement dinner, he got an angry letter from Stallone berating Mike for being nice to us.

Years later, I made things worse. Stallone had sued his own stepfather, a man who had raised him like a son. Stallone claimed that his stepfather had cheated him. Here was Stallone once again making a damaging public claim of "fraud." I was retained to defend his stepfather. The case was heard in Florida, and the court squarely ruled for my client and against Stallone.

Stallone's stepfather, a lovely gentleman, was in the imported cheese business. He was, of course, delighted with the court's decision; even though he continued to be saddened at being sued for fraud by the boy he'd raised. In any event, when the case was over, he sent me an entire wheel of Parmigiano-Reggiano about the size of a tire. It was superb.

I probably angered Stallone again by representing Peter Morton, the founder of the Hard Rock Cafes, in defeating an attempt by the owners of the Hard Rock Cafe in the East to stop Peter's opening of the Hard Rock Hotel and Casino in Las Vegas. Stallone was one of the owners of the Planet Hollywood chain that competed with the Hard Rock Cafes. Generally, what was good for the Hard Rock was not so good for Planet Hollywood. And, of course the Hard Rock Hotel and Casino in Vegas was a great idea and a huge success.

Over the years, Stallone has filed many lawsuits. I suppose some people back down or pay off when faced with the cost of defending these suits. My clients didn't. Probably, Stallone was surprised. My guess is that, after all these years, he's still full of anger at me, as well as Barbara.

Many of my clients had previously been adversaries. I opposed them and, later, they became clients. David Geffen, Ray Stark, Bob and Harvey Weinstein, Paramount, MGM and Universal are examples. I'm pretty sure that's never going to happen with Stallone.

64

A Chain of Events

MANY YEARS AGO, Bob Towne told me to expect a call from his new agent, a young man named Mike Ovitz.

Ovitz called, and we had lunch. He seemed bright and aggressive. He explained that he and a few others had started a new agency called "Creative Artists Agency" (CAA). He said, "I'll pay you a dollar a year never to sue me." And I never have.

Ultimately, Mike and CAA became a huge success. Over the years, I represented CAA and some of its key agents in various matters. Finally, Mike left the agency. But it remains a massive force in the entertainment business.

One day early in our relationship, Mike told me, "There's this kid who's dynamite. His name is Brad Grey. He's working for Bernie Brillstein, a well-known manager. You should represent him. Believe me, he's going places."

He certainly was. Brillstein's management business became Brillstein-Grey. Bernie retired, and under Brad's leadership, Brillstein-Grey became a hugely successful company that I represented in a number of matters.

For example, Brad was sued by a producer named Bo Zenga. During the discovery phase of the case,

Zenga evidently believed it would be a good tactic to avoid answering deposition questions by taking the Fifth Amendment. On question after question, he refused to answer on the ground that the answer might incriminate him. Evidently, he planned to tell his story for the first time at trial, catching us by surprise. It was frustrating; but I thought I had a way to make him pay for what I considered a sleazy tactic that shouldn't be allowed to succeed.

At trial, when Zenga took the stand prepared at last to testify, I objected. I argued that Zenga, like every American, had the right to avoid answering deposition questions based on the Fifth Amendment, but that, by doing so, he waived his right to testify to the same subject matters at trial—that a party to a lawsuit can't frustrate the discovery process by refusing to answer deposition questions and then spring the answers on his opponent for the first time at trial.

It was an unusual argument, but the Judge agreed. He sustained my objections to any testimony by Zenga on the subjects he'd refused to talk about in his deposition. In effect, this meant that Zenga couldn't testify to anything that could support his case. The result was a solid judgment for Brad, which was affirmed on appeal.

Later, Zenga sued Brad and me personally, claiming that, in the course of his case, we had authorized the wiretapping of his phone. We both denied it; and the case was thrown out before trial based on the statute of limitations. That judgment was also upheld on appeal.

By this time, Brad had become the CEO of Paramount Studios. Sadly, after serving in that demanding job for some years, Brad died of cancer.

Over the years, it had been quite a chain. Bob Towne led me to Mike Ovitz who led me to Brad Grey, who led me to Simpson/Bruckheimer. Don Simpson was a brilliant producer and half of the hugely successful production team of Simpson/Bruckheimer. One afternoon, as part of the process of casting a picture, Don was looking at film of a girl who might be cast as a burlesque queen. It happened to be a porn film in which the girl had appeared. The problem was that, without Don's knowledge, the porn film he was watching privately in his office was also playing on a TV monitor in a room just off the secretaries' pool. A secretary sued Simpson/Bruckheimer, claiming that she had unavoidably seen part of the porn film from her work station and that it had sickened her and subjected her to severe emotional distress.

I took the secretary's deposition and established that she had seen only ten to fifteen seconds of the film before the office manager shut the door to the room where the film was playing. At that point, I pulled a sheet of paper from my briefcase. I peered at her over my glasses and asked her where she rented her motion picture videos. With a look of surprise, she named a video store. I looked down at the sheet of paper as if studying it. Then I looked up and asked, "And you've rented quite a few adult films, haven't you?"

Sure that I was looking at a record of her purchases, she turned white and responded, "Not a lot of them, just one or two a month." That was the end of the case. Obviously, a woman who watched 12 to 24 porn films every year was not sickened or harmed in any way by accidently seeing ten to fifteen seconds of another such film. Her claim disappeared.

The paper I looked at in cross examining her? It was a report on a different subject in a different case. It was a bluff. It worked. I got lucky.

65

ANTHONY

At the beginning of my first case for Brad Grey, I was introduced to a private investigator named Anthony Pellicano. Over the years, I used Anthony in a number of significant cases. He was a superb investigator who, acting lawfully, helped me achieve excellent results.

Once, for example, Beatle George Harrison was receiving threatening letters from an anonymous source. Neither the English nor the American authorities seemed able to locate the sender of the scary letters. This was after the *Beatlemania* trial, and George turned to me for help. I turned to Anthony. About a week later, Anthony called to tell me he was in New York across the street from the guy who was sending George the letters. What did I want him to do?

It was extraordinary. The letters were stopped, George was thrilled, and I was stunned. How had Anthony done it? He would never tell me. But that was just one example. There were others. Anthony was an extraordinary investigator.

Another time, a woman claimed that a record company executive had made unwanted passes at her and that this resulted in her suffering severe emotional distress.

Anthony found that, at night, the woman was giving super-hot telephone sex talk to subscribers who paid her $20 per call. Confronted with her "night job," she dropped her case. Anthony had done it again.

Then problems arose. Apparently, Anthony was "cleaning out" the home of a recently deceased client when he discovered a hand grenade. He put the grenade in a drawer in his office and forgot all about it. Years later, the FBI arrived at Anthony's office with a search warrant. I'm not sure what they were actually looking for, but, in the course of their search, they found the hand grenade, as well as tapes of wiretapped telephone conversations.

Anthony was ultimately convicted of possessing the grenade, but also of a more serious crime—wiretapping. He received a stiff multi-year sentence.

Newspapers everywhere listed me, along with Brad Grey and Mike Ovitz, as potentially guilty of hiring Anthony to wiretap. *The New York Times* published a front page cartoon picturing Mike, Brad and me at the center of a sinister spiderweb. For two weeks, a suspicious trailer with two men in coats and ties was parked across the street from our home in Malibu. The FBI? Another time, two men strangely dressed in coats and ties were observed in a fishing boat just offshore from our home. The FBI again?

The fact is, I had used Anthony in a number of cases, and he had done a good job for me. But, if he was wiretapping, I didn't know it. Evidently, the U.S. Attorney reached that same conclusion. Unlike others, I was never charged with anything or designated a "target" of the investigation. I never even testified before the Grand Jury to whom Anthony's case was being presented.

Still, it was a scary time. A group of partners left our firm when the Pellicano story broke, believing that the case would bring the firm down. And I know of at least one instance in which the transactional lawyer for a powerful international bank recommended me to represent the bank in a major trial; but the bank's General Counsel vetoed the idea because of my "involvement" in the Pellicano case. The firm and I survived—even thrived. But it was a very troubling time.

I'm sorry for Anthony—by far the best detective I've known—and for Terry Christensen, a successful lawyer, who was convicted of authorizing Anthony to wiretap. They've gone through a very bad time. Anthony has just been released after years in prison, and I wish him well.

SUMMING UP: A PROFESSIONAL MEMOIR

66

"Civil Extortion"

MICHAEL FLATLEY was the wealthy owner and producer of two hugely successful troupes of Irish dancers, one called *Lord of the Dance* and the other *Riverdance*. When I first met him, Michael was single, but was engaged to be married.

He came to me because a Chicago lawyer was threatening him with a damaging media campaign accusing Michael of rape—a crime of which he was completely innocent. Months earlier, before his engagement, Michael had met an attractive girl at an event and said he'd give her a call. He'd called her a few days later and invited her to a night in Las Vegas, where one of his dance troupes was performing.

The girl accepted and, on her arrival in Vegas, she was picked up in a limo, taken to Michael's hotel and shown immediately to his two-bedroom suite. One bedroom was occupied by Michael's secretary/butler and the other by Michael. There was no question as to the room the girl was to occupy. She was told it was Michael's room, and, without protest, she saw her luggage placed there.

Later, Michael and she had dinner. Oddly, when Michael ordered a steak, she ordered only a slice of chocolate cake. The waiter, of course, noticed this odd behavior, which, in hindsight, we believed was deliberate on her part.

After dinner and a show, Michael and the girl retired to his room, where they had very consensual sex and slept together through the night.

The girl slept late and, when she awakened and went into the living room of the suite, Michael's secretary/butler was reading the newspaper, and Michael was working out on a treadmill. She greeted them both in a friendly way, then ate her breakfast, which had been ordered the night before, and went into Michael's bedroom to pack. As she prepared to leave the suite, she gave Michael a big hug in the presence of the secretary/butler, thanked Michael for the trip and said goodbye.

Months later, Michael got a letter from a Chicago lawyer for the girl claiming that he had raped her and listing some forty media outlets that would immediately be informed of that rape if Michael didn't pay them one million dollars.

That's when Michael came to see me. My advice was to take the offensive. Michael hadn't been engaged at the time of the incident and had no fear of it coming out that he'd had sex with the girl. He agreed, and, with the aid of Ricardo Cestero, an able young partner, I prepared a complaint against the girl and her lawyer. We sought damages for what I called "civil extortion," by which I meant that they had demanded money with the threat of exposing a criminal or embarrassing fact if Michael didn't pay. What the lawyer did was a crime; but to hold the lawyer and his client civilly liable for damages was a new concept.

We filed the complaint, and, hearing of our lawsuit, the girl apparently went into hiding. She just disappeared. The lawyer, however, was represented by insurance company counsel, who immediately moved to dismiss the complaint based on what's called the "Anti-SLAPP statute," which establishes an early procedure for dismissing claims based on statements protected by the First Amendment. The defense argued that not only was the lawyer's letter constitutionally protected speech, it was also within the so-called judicial privilege, since it involved a potential judicial proceeding. If he was right, we were out of court and could even owe the other side their attorney's fees.

I argued that the lawyer's letter to Michael was garden variety extortion, and that an extortionate letter was not protected by the First Amendment. As to the judicial privilege, I contended that the letter didn't threaten a lawsuit, which might have made it privileged. All it threatened, I said, was public exposure in the media; and that's not privileged. It's what I called "civil extortion."

After extensive written and oral argument, the Court denied the lawyer's motion. The case against him would proceed. Immediately, the insurance lawyers appealed. They made the same arguments to the Court of Appeals; but that Court affirmed the decision of the trial court, denying the motion to dismiss our complaint.

Next, the Chicago lawyer petitioned the California Supreme Court to hear the case. Like the U.S. Supreme Court, California's highest court takes on only a small percentage of the cases that apply for a Supreme Court hearing. In the Flatley case, however, the Supreme Court granted a hearing. This was an ominous sign. It could mean that the Supreme Court was dissatisfied with the ruling of the Court of Appeals in favor of Michael. Naturally, I was worried.

Both sides submitted new briefs to the Supreme Court; and, finally, the day arrived for oral argument in the impressive courtroom of the Supreme Court in San Francisco. It quickly became apparent that the Court wasn't necessarily dissatisfied with the ruling of the Court of Appeals. They were just very interested in what seemed to them a completely novel question. What, if anything, was "civil extortion," and could a lawyer's extortionate letter still be privileged or otherwise protected by state law or by the U.S. Constitution?

The Justices asked numerous questions. One female Justice asked, "What if my boyfriend gets angry and throws a rock through my window? What if I say, 'if you don't pay to fix that window, I'm reporting you to the police.' Is that extortion?"

I had to answer, "Yes, it would be." But I added that you'd be okay if you threatened to sue him for breaking the window. You can threaten civil litigation if you're not paid. But you can't threaten exposure to the police or the media unless you're paid. You can even say that, if you sue him, the lawsuit will bring him lots of bad publicity. That's a closer case; but it's still privileged. It's not extortion. But the appellant here didn't do that. He simply threatened to expose my client <u>to the media</u> if my client didn't pay a million dollars. That's civil extortion. And it's not protected by the First Amendment or any other law.

When the Justices posed tough questions to counsel for the Chicago lawyer, her answer was amusing. "Okay," she said, "so my client doesn't have a way with words." But, she argued, even if he didn't phrase his letter carefully, the substance of it was that Mr. Flatley was going to be sued.

The Supreme Court didn't buy it. They affirmed the decision of the Court of Appeals upholding our complaint. You can find the Supreme Court's opinion in the Official Supreme Court Reports. It's been cited in over 120 subsequent judicial opinions, most of which refer to the new tort of "civil extortion" and to the "Flatley Rule." The insurance company's law firm withdrew from representing the Chicago lawyer, and we ultimately obtained a large judgment against him. The press reported that Michael Flatley was totally vindicated. He was thrilled. We never found the girl who ate the chocolate cake.

67

Extraordinary People

HARVEY WEINSTEIN was—and is—an extraordinary man. Along with his brother Bob, he changed the American motion picture business, taking what we used to call "art films" that played in single, rundown theatres in New York, San Francisco and Los Angeles and, with super-skilled promotion, making them into major American hits. These included such outstanding films as *The King's Speech*, *Pulp Fiction*, *The English Patient*, *Good Will Hunting*, *Shakespeare in Love*, *Fahrenheit 9/11* and many others.

Harvey and Bob built Miramax, named after their parents, Miriam and Max. After selling the company to Disney, they formed The Weinstein Company, which generated more hits with fairly low production costs, creating a valuable film library and enabling Harvey to launch a successful television business.

More than 20 years ago, I had a case against Miramax for Sybil Robson over a film she'd financed. After some preliminary sparring, I took Harvey's deposition. Soon thereafter, he agreed to a very sizeable settlement. Sybil was thrilled, and Harvey was angry. What did he do? Characteristically, he asked me to represent Miramax. And that started a long and fascinating relationship. For years, I represented first Miramax and then The Weinstein Company in numerous lawsuits and negotiations. It was always interesting and mostly fun. Generally, I represented the company in matters that arose in California. In New York cases, they were generally represented by David Boies.

I first met David about a bitter lawsuit between Brad Grey and the comedian, Gary Shandling. This was before Brad became the head of Paramount. At the time, he was the head of Brillstein-Grey, a hugely successful management company. Brad had been Shandling's manager and partner in some successful television ventures which had been split between them in a prior settlement deal. That led to a subsequent claim by Shandling that Brad had cheated him. I considered the claim misguided; but the issues were complex and Shandling's lawyers evidently believed his claims and pressed forward with the litigation.

Shortly before the case was to be tried, David Boies called. He was going to try the case for Shandling and was in town for a few days. He suggested that we talk. We met late the next afternoon and hit it off at once. Pretty soon, I had my secretary bring in a bottle of iced Chardonnay and two glasses.

As we drank the wine, we discussed many things, finally getting to Shandling v. Grey. We fenced for a while—always with courtesy and humor—and, while we did, we somehow finished the bottle—and settled the case.

To this day, David believes he got the better end of the deal. He even wrote a book saying so. Although I say it with admiration, he's all wet—Grey got by far the best of the deal. I suppose the fact that each of us believes he prevailed is the sign of a good settlement.

In any event, David and I have remained friends and have worked together on many situations for the Weinsteins. But Bob and Harvey didn't always see eye to eye. We decided that if any conflict arose between the brothers, I'd represent Bob, and David would represent Harvey. Still, David and I worked together—for the company—and when problems arose, we solved them.

Then, in 2017, it all came crashing down. Harvey's penchant for bizarre sexual encounters with an extraordinary number of women was exposed. Harvey denied it all; but woman after woman asserted that he groped them, tried to grope them or tried to talk them into a groping. And they claimed that these numerous encounters were accompanied by Harvey's pleading, promising, urging and, in some instances, masturbating.

In short, Harvey was ruined. He was fired by TWC and quickly became the poster boy for the "Me Too" campaign against sexual harassment. Were all the allegations true? It certainly seemed that many of Harvey's accusers were telling the truth. But, I suspect that some of them saw a chance at free publicity or were just angry or anxious to aid the crusade against sexual harassment.

In any event, with the hideous and widespread publicity about Harvey, the company was hit very hard in many critical ways. Bob tried valiantly to keep it together. But ultimately, it slid into bankruptcy, owing me $2 million of which I'll probably never see a dime. Do I miss the golden days of Harvey and Bob and all those marvelous films and their challenging legal problems? I do. Do I still remain a fan of Bob and wish him the best? I definitely do. Looking back, do I wish I hadn't put in all that time and effort without getting paid? Not really. It was an exciting ride.

But what about Harvey? Yes, he demonstrated enormous talent and drive. But no one can ignore his widespread instances of bizarre sexual harassment, and shouldn't he at least have grasped the possibility—indeed the likelihood—that his conduct would come out and would severely damage, if not destroy him as well as the company he and Bob had built? Probably. But could anyone have anticipated the tidal wave of public attacks on sexual predators in film, in government—almost everywhere? After all, many men had gotten away with sexual misbehavior for decades—probably centuries. Some, like Donald Trump, were accused of such conduct, but went on to attain high office.

So, what's the future for Harvey? People tend to forgive a confirmed and reformed malefactor who seeks and receives what at least appears to be successful treatment or even a term in prison. Will Harvey emerge again—perhaps in some new way, some new career? It seems unlikely; but stranger things have happened, and Harvey is a most unusual man.

David Boies is a superb lawyer. He got some bad press for helping Harvey and also for representing a lady who claimed to have invented a unique blood test, the validity of which was attacked, creating enormous trouble for her and her company. The media criticism of David was undeserved. But bad press sometimes "goes with the territory."

David was representing his clients, and, as always, doing so ethically and with skill. Even the most unpopular client is entitled to a defense—as vigorous a defense as his attorney can truthfully muster. That's what David provided—as he always has and always will.

68

"De-Clienting"

Mohamed Al-Fayed wasn't the only client from whom I parted ways. There were quite a few.

For years, I represented Fox and related companies in all kinds of cases. I started representing the studio when Marvin Davis owned it; and when he sold it to Rupert Murdoch, the relationship continued. The BSkyB case I described was just one example of a case on behalf of Fox or a Murdoch company. There were many such cases, and it was a good relationship. Then it ended.

At the time, I had another case against Disney. Nikki Finke, then the star reporter for the *New York Post*, wrote an article helpful to my client and very critical of Disney management. Nikki was about to be promoted to a top editorial position at the *Post*, which was owned by Murdoch's News Corp, the company that also owned Fox. Nikki's article enraged Disney; and Disney threatened to pull all of its advertising from the *Post* if she wasn't immediately fired.

Surprisingly, News Corp caved in to Disney's arrogant demand. Instead of promoting Nikki, they fired her—totally without cause. I was enraged; and, in that state, I wrote a letter to Rupert, Peter Chernin and other top

Fox executives. I said things like, "How the mighty have fallen" and called them "toadying weenies" for caving in to Disney's bullying demand and firing Nikki.

I wrote the letter never expecting to represent Fox again; and I never have. I like and respect Rupert Murdoch, whose companies I've since opposed. But when I wrote that angry letter, I knew the relationship was over. Would I do it again? You bet.

Some years later, I was lead counsel in major litigation against Rupert's company with respect to the financial aspects of satellite ownership. After Rupert's lawyers brought on a complex motion to dismiss our case, which did not succeed, the matter was settled, generating massive sums for my client.

Notwithstanding the important principles and vast amounts of money at stake, Rupert remained a courteous gentleman throughout the proceedings.

Years ago, I withdrew from representing Madonna and Michael Jackson, although it wasn't really the fault of either of them. I had represented Madonna's company in a number of matters. Then, she was cast as Eva Peron in the film version of *Evita*, the huge Broadway hit. Madonna flew to Buenos Aires for a part of the shoot. But, once there, she encountered mass protests that threatened to become violent. The shouted claim was that she was a "Peronista," a supporter of the infamous former dictator.

I got a call from Madonna's manager frantically telling me that she was terrified by the angry mob gathered outside her hotel. She actually feared for her life; and neither her manager nor her hotel had any solution. Could I think of anything?

I knew one man who could possibly help. I called my longtime client and friend, Gustavo Cisneros. Although Venezuelan, Gustavo had superb contacts throughout Latin America. He said he would immediately do what he could.

In twenty minutes, Gustavo called back to say that Madonna should remain in her room. The problem would quickly be solved. In another twenty minutes, the President of Argentina was standing beside Madonna on the balcony of her hotel room, telling the crowd that she was not a "Peronista," but a wonderful actress just playing a role, and that all of Argentina should welcome and embrace her.

The crowd's anger subsided and turned to cheers. Gustavo's personally enlisting the aid of Argentina's President had saved Madonna's peace of mind and possibly even her safety. I told Gustavo how grateful I was for his help; and I told Madonna's manager to have her call Gustavo and at least send him flowers.

A few days later, I contemplated billing Madonna for what had been accomplished. They had turned to me in desperation. I had contacted my friend Gustavo; and, through Gustavo's swift intervention, what had seemed a life-threatening situation was turned into a celebration of Madonna's visit.

A sizeable fee seemed appropriate. $100,000? $200,000? Possibly—certainly not unreasonable under the circumstances. "No," I thought. I'll just bill her for my time making and receiving the phone calls. So I sent Madonna's business manager a bill for $2,500.

But, of course, "no good deed goes unpunished." I got a stern letter back from her business manager. He insisted that I itemize and justify my $2,500 bill, after which he would determine how much of it, if any, was justified. I wrote back telling him that Madonna should forget the bill, but should also forget my phone number and never seek my services again.

More than a year later, Madonna's manager did seek my services. Madonna was in a battle with Warner Records and wanted my help. My anger had long ago faded, and I realized that she probably didn't even know what her business manager had done in the *Evita* situation. So I said "yes." After we won a hotly-contested hearing in Delaware, the case was settled on very favorable terms for Madonna, so this particular "firing" of a client had a happy ending.

Not so with Donald Trump. As I previously discussed, I fired him for disgusting misconduct.

I've fired clients other than these—some famous, like Michael Jackson, Mohamed Al-Fayed and Van Morrison, some not. Maybe I need client management therapy. Once when I was handling a case for Columbia Pictures, I learned that Columbia had done something to another client of mine that I considered extremely unfair. Again, my anger took over. I withdrew from representing the studio. Jon Dolgen, a friend, who was then one of Columbia's top officers, called and asked, "Who's your career counselor, Icarus?"

Maybe he was right.

69

THE POWER LIST

YEARS AGO, *The Hollywood Reporter* published an annual list of what it called the 100 most powerful people in the entertainment business—its "Power List." The listed people were ranked from 1 to 100, and their photos were shown along with a very brief statement of why they were on the list.

Each year, the *Reporter* would call to get my opinion as to where certain people belonged on the "Power List." On one such occasion, I said, "You know who's really powerful in this community? It's Chuck of Chuck's Parking Service. You leave one of those huge parties with 200 guests. It's windy and raining, and all these powerful people are clamoring for their cars at the same time. Right then, who's the most powerful guy in town? It's Chuck. He handles every big party. He can have your car first or you can be number two hundred. Now that's real, raw power."

I was half kidding. But they did it. They included Chuck in that year's "Power List". I've forgotten what number Chuck was, but he found out how he came to be included; and, for years after that, whose car was the first one brought out when the big party ended? That's right.

Ours.

70

GREED

Jim Cameron is a great director, and I'm proud to be his lawyer. Two of Jim's films, *Titanic* and *Avatar*, are among the the highest-grossing films in the history of the motion picture business. Even before that, Jim directed *The Terminator* and *Aliens*, which were also highly successful.

I knew *Titanic* was going to be a huge hit when, on a trip to China, I visited two different schools, and the girls in both already had *Titanic* posters featuring Leonardo DiCaprio on their walls, even though the picture hadn't even been released yet in China.

When Jim was in the middle of shooting *Titanic*, the film was seriously over budget, primarily because of the tremendous, unforeseen costs of constructing the replica of the huge ship, something that was in no way Jim's fault. Nevertheless, Jim, being an honorable guy, went to a Fox executive and offered to make up for the cost overruns by giving up his entire "back-end deal," i.e., his percentage of the film's gross receipts.

The Fox executive's response is a moment that will live in the annals of film lore. He said, "Jim, that's not good enough." He insisted that Jim significantly reduce his upfront cash fee as well. Understandably, this angered Jim, who had no legal or even moral obligation to give up anything. So he essentially told the Fox executive to "get lost." And that seemed to be the end of it.

But, as a director would say, "cut" to many months later, when the release of *Titanic* was bringing in billions and making Jim's "back-end deal" worth a fortune. At this point, I got a call from a different Fox executive, who said that, since Jim had agreed to give up his back-end deal, they were sending over a contract amendment to document that agreement. "Not so," I said. "Jim <u>offered</u> to give up his back-end deal, but you guys rejected his offer—told him it wasn't enough. Remember, from law school (he was a lawyer), if you reject an offer or make a counteroffer, the offer is terminated. Well, Jim's generous offer was rejected—and terminated."

He remembered, and that was the last we heard of the claim. Thus, "greed goeth before a fall." Yes, I know it's "pride" that "goeth," but "greed" seems to fit.

In any event, the studio doesn't have anything to complain about. *Titanic* made Fox over a billion dollars. Then, Jim went on to break his own record and make the studio even more money with *Avatar*.

71

Marketing?

ONE DAY RECENTLY, a member of the Management Committee of our firm asked me if I would speak to the firm's associates about the things they should do to get new clients.

I said I'd be the wrong guy to give that talk, since, looking back on my entire career, I couldn't think of a single thing I'd ever done in order to get clients. Mostly, one client would refer another, and that person would refer still someone else. Sometimes, people I'd opposed in bitter fights or difficult negotiations became good clients.

Do I have a secret for building a successful law practice? Winning cases certainly helps. But, other than that I have no idea what works.

72

Trust Matters

SOME TIME AGO, Shelly Sterling called me about a potential problem concerning the trust that held most of the assets of Shelly and her husband Donald, a lawyer, highly successful real estate developer, and "owner," with Shelly, of numerous "Sterling" buildings throughout Southern California; as well as the Los Angeles Clippers professional basketball team. The two trustees were Shelly and Donald.

As I got into the matter with my partner, Pierce O'Donnell, and we discussed it with Shelly, we realized two things. One was that Donald was acting in a bizarre fashion, insisting, for example, that no tenant be allowed to occupy space in the prime six-story "Sterling" building at the corner of Wilshire Boulevard and Beverly Drive in the heart of Beverly Hills. This entire prime office building was empty except for a Sterling family office on the top floor. The second thing we realized was that, despite its somewhat unsuccessful record, the Clippers were a very valuable asset that was not reaching its full potential and that the team should be sold.

Multi-billionaire Steve Ballmer indicated that he'd pay more than $2 billion for the Clippers. It was a great price, and Shelly was determined to accept it. The problem was that Donald adamantly refused to sell the team; and, as a co-trustee, he could block any sale. But Donald was behaving more and more erratically; and, at our suggestion, Shelly persuaded him to be examined by two highly qualified psychiatrists. They each confirmed that Donald was no longer mentally able to serve as a trustee of this highly valuable and complex family trust. Reluctantly, Shelly agreed with our idea of seeking his removal as a trustee, leaving her in control of the trust and thus able to sell the team. She loved Donald and didn't want to hurt him. But she really had no choice.

We filed a proceeding to remove Donald as a trustee, and that led to a vigorously contested proceeding in the California Superior Court. The Clippers and the Sterlings were big news and the courtroom was overflowing with reporters.

The two psychiatrists testified to administering well-accepted tests to Donald and to the results clearly indicating his lack of capacity to serve as trustee of this large and complex trust.

Donald's lawyers had retained their own psychiatrist, a practitioner from Las Vegas, who testified, seemingly without scientific support, that Donald was not impaired at all and could function ably as a trustee. Pierce masterfully cross-examined this doctor, utterly destroying his opinion and his value as a witness.

I cross-examined Donald. His first few answers were not answers at all, but just sarcastic non-responsive jibes at me personally. At first, there were titters from the crowd of reporters. But that was fine with me. I thought, if I just let him continue, the Judge will soon get the true picture of Donald and so will the media. As the examination went on, they certainly did. Donald's responses became bizarre and, sometimes, provably false. He plainly demonstrated in that single cross-examination why he could not remain a trustee.

When Donald left the stand, Shelly, who still loved him and felt sorry for him, rose and walked over to comfort him. Donald pushed her away shouting, "Get away from me, you pig!" His brutal insult was heard by the Judge and those in the first rows of the courtroom. Surprisingly, the Judge rapped for order and announced from the bench, "For those of you who didn't hear it, Mr. Sterling just called his wife a pig." That was a judicial "first."

We then put on a valuation expert who testified that the Clippers franchise was worth $1.5 to $1.8 billion, significantly less than Steve Ballmer had indicated that he'd pay.

After some additional testimony, the Judge took the case under submission. At this point, Steve Ballmer could still have backed away from his statement that he'd pay over $2 billion. Since he'd heard testimony that the team was worth significantly less, that would not have been a surprise. To his credit, however, Ballmer made it clear that he'd told Shelly $2.1 billion and he was sticking with that number.

SUMMING UP: A PROFESSIONAL MEMOIR

It was late in the day. We were confident we'd won. So was Ballmer, whose excellent lawyer, Adam Streisand, had been a valuable ally throughout the proceeding. What concerned us was the potential delay that would result from Donald's appealing the Court's decision and the likelihood that Donald could get an order preventing any sale pending that appellate decision.

To avoid that, we had worked out a plan. Adam Streisand and Bob Baradaran, a brilliant partner in our firm, had prepared in advance all the documentation essential to the sale of the team. Those documents were signed and ready to be put into effect the moment the judge signed his order.

We wanted to take no chance of a slipup. The next morning, as soon as the courtroom opened, Adam Streisand was there, ready to tell us the moment the judge made his decision and signed and entered his order.

Finally, the order came. As we expected, it was squarely for Shelly. Donald was found unfit to remain as a trustee and was removed. As sole trustee, Shelly was free to sell the team. Adam immediately called our office. Within seconds, the documents conveying the team to Ballmer were put into effect, and a wire transfer of $2.1 billion went from Ballmer's account to the account of the Sterling Trust.

Long before our opponents even learned of the Court's decision, the sale was completed and a very pleased Steve Ballmer owned the Clippers.

It was a happy ending for Shelly, a lovely and gracious lady, who'd stood by Donald through some very trying situations and, remarkably, is still standing by him—although she's continued to be the sole trustee of a much more valuable trust.

73

"Old Glory"

Every day, I fly the American flag from the deck of our home overlooking the sea in Malibu. This country has given me and my family extraordinary things. My father got off a boat when he was five years old, accompanied by his mother and four siblings. They spoke no English and had no money. Evidently, they'd walked across Europe to get the boat.

Even with that start, Dad made it to Johns Hopkins, became an eye surgeon and teacher. I got to Harvard and enjoyed a rewarding career and life. My son, a Stanford PhD, was a senior official in the Treasury Department, as well as a partner in Blackstone. He's now retired and lives in Hawaii. There is no country in the world in which such miraculous changes could have occurred in such a relatively short time.

My father was much too old to serve in the Second World War; but he volunteered, giving up a lucrative medical practice he never fully recovered. He believed he owed this to America. During the Korean War, I turned down the chance for a teaching deferment to do the same thing Dad had done. I enlisted. I felt I owed it to America—maybe even more than he had.

We don't ever talk about it, but my family and I are indebted to this country for everything—our education, our success, our lives. Even recognizing its faults, it is unique in the rights, freedoms, protections and opportunities it affords its citizens—that it afforded me and my family.

So, every day, if, walking down the beach in Malibu, you pass our house, you'll see the American flag flying proudly—even defiantly.

74

SUMMING UP

I'VE TRIED TO SHARE some of the cases and events of my professional life that come to mind. There were many more cases and many more events. It's been a wonderful ride. Some tragedy, yes; but many years of love, happiness and satisfaction.

As I approach the end, it's with a smile. Would I like it to go on forever? Sure. But I've got no complaint. I was dealt a winning hand and played it as well as I could.

It's enough.

Acknowledgements

There would be no book without the skill and dedication of the publisher Bobby Woods, the efforts of Roberta Dunner, and the patience of my dear wife, Barbara.

About the Author

Bertram Fields was born in Los Angeles. A practicing lawyer, he graduated *magna cum laude* from Harvard Law School, where he was an editor of the *Harvard Law Review*. After serving as a First Lieutenant in the U.S. Air Force during the Korean War, he began the general practice of law. Since then, he has tried many landmark cases in the entertainment, sports and communications industries and has been the subject of numerous personal profiles in magazines and newspapers. He is currently a partner at the firm Greenberg Glusker Fields Claman & Machtinger LLP. He also teaches at Stanford Law School and lectures annually at Harvard.

Mr. Fields is the author, under a pseudonym, of two novels, *The Sunset Bomber*, published by Simon and Schuster, and *The Lawyer's Tale*, published by Random House.

Under his own name, he has written *Royal Blood: Richard III and the Mystery of the Princes*, a biographical work on Richard III and *Players: The Mysterious Identity of William Shakespeare*, an analysis of the Shakespeare authorship question. Both books were published by HarperCollins.

His following books, *Destiny: A Novel Of Napoleon & Josephine*, *Shylock: His Own Story*, and *Gloriana: Exploring The Reign Of Elizabeth I* are currently published by Marmont Lane Books.

Mr. Fields lives in Malibu, California with his wife, Barbara Guggenheim, a nationally known art consultant.

INDEX

ABC, *131, 228-230*
Adjani, Isabelle, *183, 184-186*
Al-Fayed, Mohamed, *164-165, 315, 318*
Aliens, 321
American Cancer Society, *202*
Amistad, 130
Anheuser-Busch, *278-279*
Arum, Robert ("Bob"), *233*
Ashby, Hal, *202*
Aspinall, Neil, *106, 107, 108*
Around the World in 80 Days, 38
Avatar, 321, 322

Bach, Richard, *76-81*
Ballmer, Steve, *324, 326, 327*
Bancroft, Anne, *57-58, iv*
Baradaran, Bob, *327*
Beatlemania, 106-111, 242
Beatles, The, *106-111, 183, 186*
Beatty, Warren, *148, 201-202, 204, 228-230, xv*
Begelman, David, *140-146*
Berg, Jeff, *108*
Bergman, Ingrid, *51*
Bertolucci, Bernardo, *183*
Best of Everything, The, 18
Blazing Saddles, 60
Boies, David, *311-312, 313-314*
Brando, Marlon, *104-105, 194*
Breckenridge, Paul, *108, 110, 111, 242, 244, 246, 247*
Brillstein, Bernie, *298*
Brillstein-Grey, *298, 311*

Broad, Eli, *166*
Brooks, Mel, *57-61, iv*
Brown, Richard ("Rick"), *35*
BSkyB, *239, 315*
Byrne, William Matthew ("Matt"), *234, 235-236*

Caan, James ("Jimmy"), *71, 74, 172, 174*
Cameron, James ("Jim"), *321-322*
Cassavetes, John, *118*
CBS, *67, 134*
Cestero, Ricardo, *306*
Chase-Riboud, Barbara, *130, 131*
Chernin, Peter, *315*
Chinatown, 187
Christensen, Terry, *304*
Chuck's Parking Service, *320*
Cimino, Michael, *230-233*
Cisneros, Gustavo, *317*
Clavell, James, *213-215*
Clinton, Bill, *147*
Cohn, Harry, *97, 240*
Cohn, Roy, *41-43*
Columbia Pictures, *140, 217, 224, 226, 318-319*
Columbo, 169, 174
Confessions of a Francophile, 269
Copland, Aaron, *17*
Copyright Society of the USA, *28*
Creative Artists Agency (CAA), *203, 208, 296, 298*
Crowley, Arthur, *51-55*
Cruise, Tom, *176, xviii*

Daily Variety, *122*
Davis, Marvin, *133, 134, 214*
Diana, Princess, *164, 165*
De La Hoya, Oscar, *233-235, 237, xii-xiii*
Death of a Salesman, *129*
Depardieu, Gerard, *183-184*
Destiny: A Novel of Napoleon & Josephine, *164, 333*
Diller, Barry, *133-135, 238*
Diaz, Kris, *292*
DiCaprio, Leonardo, *321*
Disney (Studios), *57, 238-248, 249, 253, 310, 315-316*
Dolgen, Jonathan ("Jon"), *207, 319*
Donen, Stanley, *122-123*
Dorskind, Al, *168*
Dragnet, *67, 93, 95, 167, viii-ix*
Dudley, Robert, *265-266*

Earthquake, *192*
Edwards, Blake, *141, 142, 145, 146*
Edwards, Brian, *243*
Eisner, Michael, *238-248*
Ehrlich, Jake, *150-151*
Erlichman, John, *17*
Elephant Man, The, *60-61*
Elizabeth I, *265-266, 333*
Ely, Walter, *41, 42, 43*
English Patient, The, *310*
Eskenazi, Bonnie, *243, 294*
Evans, Robert ("Bob"), *187-191*
Evita, *316, 318*

Fahrenheit 9/11, *310*
Falk, Peter, *71, 118-120, 122, 167, 169-171, 174, xiv*

Fayed, Dodi, *164, 165*
Federal Trade Commission (FTC), *271, 272, 273, 291, 292, 293*
Feldman, Phil, *127, 128*
Fields, Jim, *20, 329*
Fields, Lydia, *15, 20, 44, 55, 58, 75, 98-100, 196, 198, 201-205, 206, 262, 294, iv, v*
Fiend Who Walked the West, The, *188*
Finke, Nikki, *315, 316*
Fisher, Eddie, *40*
Flatley, Michael, *305-309*
Foley, Roger, *112-114*
Foreman, Percy, *152-153*
First Artists Corporation, *127*
Fox (Studios), see *20th Century Fox*
Fox Network, *134*
France, Anatole, *56*
Friday Night Lights, *16*

Gandhi, *226*
Gandolfini, James, *173-174*
Gang, Martin, *27-28*
Gang Tyre & Brown, *27*
Garr, Teri, *224*
Garrison, James ("Jim"), *216-219*
Garrison, Michael ("Mike"), *46-50*
Geffen, David, *207, 241, 297*
Gelbart, Larry, *224*
Girardi, Thomas ("Tom"), *234*
Gloriana: Exploring the Reign of Elizabeth I, *265, 266, 333*
Godfather, The, *192, 193*
Gold, Stanley, *247*
Goldwyn, Sam, *97*
Good Will Hunting, *310*
Goossen, Dan, *257-237*

337

Graubert, John, 292
Greenberg, Glusker, Fields, Claman
 & Machtinger, 333
Grey, Brad, 298-300, 302, 303,
 311-312
Groman, Arthur, 36, 37
Guggenheim Fields, Barbara, 20,
 164, 183, 208, 237, 256-258, 261,
 263, 265, 293, 295-297, 332, xix
Gustafson, Deil, 115-117

Haldeman, H.R. ("Bob"), 17
Hammer, Armand, 83
Hamilton Air Force Base, 18
Harrison, George, 106-108,
 111, 302
Hart, Gary, 147-149
Harvard Law Review, 18, 27, 267, 333
Hardwicke, Sir Cedric, 56-57
Harney, David, 87, 91, 92
Harvard Law School, 17-18, 185, 333
Hayworth, Rita, 136-137
Hirsch, Barry, 240-241
Hirsch, Claudia, 87-92
Hirsch, Clement, 87-92
Hoffman, Dustin, 127-196, 142,
 202, 204-205, 223- 226, 265,
 xv, xviii
Hoffman, Lisa, 224
Hollywood Reporter, The, 122, 320
Holmes, Larry, 112, 113
Hunt, Vernon, 87, 89

Iger, Robert ("Bob"), 247
International Herald Tribune, 176

International Creative Management
 (ICM), 108
Ion Channel Innovations, 287
Ishtar, 204

Jackson, Michael, 207-212,
 316, 318
Janavs, Dzintra, 181, 182
Jaws, 103
Jonathan Livingston Seagull, 76-81
Johnson, Lyndon Baines, 153
"Juggler of Our Lady, The", 56

Kal Kan, 87
Katzenberg, Jeffrey, 57, 237,
 241-248, 259-260
Katzenberg v. Disney, 249-251
Kerkorian, Kirk, 140, 141, 145
Kevorkian, Aram ("Jack"), 267-270
Kern, Jerome, 28
Kincaid, D., 231
Kingsley, Ben, 226
King's Speech, The, 310
Khan, Yasmin, 136
Kohl, Helmut, x

Lansing, Sherry, 202-203, iii
Lange, Jessica, 224, 226
Lawyer's Tale, The, 263, 333
Leibig, Tony, 185-186
Lelouch, Claude, 183
Lennon, John, 108, 110
Leve, Harvey, 257
Lindstrom, Dr. Peter, 51
Lion King, The, 243

Little Mermaid, The, 243
Litvack, Sanford ("Sandy"), 243
Lord of the Dance, 305
Los Angeles Clippers, 324-325, 326, 327
Los Angeles County Museum of Art (LACMA), 35-37
Lucas, Campbell, 77-81, 195, 196, 200
Lucas, George, 235
Lynch, Allen, 51, 52, 54

MacDonald, Jeanette, 28
MacLeish, Archibald, 17
Madonna, 151, 316-318
Mancuso, Frank, 189, 190
Marshall, Robert ("Bob"), 109
M*A*S*H, 69
May, Elaine, 118-123, 204, xiv
Mayer, Louis B. ("L.B."), 28-29, 97, 240
MCA, 167
McCarthy, Senator Joseph ("Joe"), 41
McCartney, Paul, 108
Meisinger, Louis ("Lou"), 217, 218, 243, 246
Melman, Dr. Arnold, 273, 281-291
Mengers, Sue, 142-143
Merrick, David, 84-86
Meyer, Ron, 208, 209
MGM, 28-29, 139-144, 297
Midler, Bette, 185
Miller, Arthur, 129
Mikey and Nicky, 118

Miracle Worker, The, 58
Miramax, 310, 311
Modern Brewery Age, 275
Morgan, Henry, 94
Morrison, Van, 318
Morton, Peter, 154-155, 296
Murdoch, Rupert, 134, 238-240, 315, 316
Murray, Bill, 224

NBC, 134, 169, 170
New York Observer, The, 286, 288
New York Post, 315, xvi
New York Times, The, 303
Niarchos, Stavros, 37
Nichols, Mike, 118
Nicholson, Jack, 187, 191, 229
Noble House, 213-215
Norton, Ken, 112, 113

Occidental Petroleum, 82-83
O'Donnell, Pierce, 130-132, 324, 325
Ono, Yoko, 110
Ovitz, Michael ("Mike"), 203-204, 208, 209, 224, 242, 247, 296, 300, 303

Pacht, Mendel Jerome ("Jerry"), 178
Paramount Studios, 76-81, 118, 119-122, 133, 187-191, 217, 228-230, 238, 297, 300, 311
Pellicano, Anthony, 302-304
Pepsi Cola Company, 137
Piranha, 215

Piranha II, 215
Players: The Mysterious Identity of William Shakespeare, 264, 333
Pollack, Sydney, 224-226
Pom Wonderful, 271-293
Price, Frank, 224
Profile Bread, 125-126
Pulp Fiction, 310
Puzo, Mario, 105, 180, 181, 192-200, 260, vi-vii

RAF Station Brize Norton, 18
Rain Man, 226
Ralston, Vera Hruba, 98-100
Reds, 228-231
Reichle, Julie, 124-126
Reiner, Ira, 122
Republic Pictures, 98
Richard III, 151, 152, 262-263, 333
Riverdance, 305
Robinson, Edward G., 35-37, ii
Robinson, Gladys, 35-37
Robson, Sybil, 310
Rocky, 295
Rogers, Wayne, 69-75, 202, iii
Rohner, Frank, 67-68, 69-70, 171
Rossellini, Roberto, 51
Roth, Lester, 166
Rothman, Frank, 22, 26, 37, 140, 141-145, 217, 218
Royal Blood: Richard III and the Mystery of the Princes 263, 264, 333
Rudin, Milton ("Mickey"), 27
Russian Tea Room, The, 225

Salkind, Alexander, 194-200
Saroyan, William, 269-270
Scent of Mystery, 39
Schisgal, Murray, 223
Schlosser, Herbert ("Herb"), 170-171
Schulman, John, 199-200
Scientology, 176-177
Shandling, Garry, 311
Shakespeare, William, 151, 263, 264, 265, 333
Shakespeare in Love, 310
Sheinberg, Sidney ("Sid"), 103, 170-171
Shylock: His Own Story, 264, 333
Sicilian, The, 179, 227, 230-233
Silberberg, Mendel, 35, 37
Simpson, Don, 300
Simpson/Bruckheimer, 300
Somoza Debayle, Anastasio, 157, 158
Sopranos, The, 173, 174
Spelling, Aaron, 171, 172
Spengler, Pierre, 200
Spielberg, Steven, 103, 295-297
Spinks, Leon, 112-114
Stagg Foods, 87, 88
Stallone, Sylvester, 295-297
Stampfer, Dr. Meir, 273-281
Stanford Law School, 18, 166, 294, 333
Stark, Ray, 171-172, 297
Starr, Ringo, 107
Sterling, Donald, 324-328, xxii-xxiii
Sterling, Shelly, 324-328

Streisand, Adam, *327*
Sulaiman, Jose, *112*
Sun Also Rises, The, *188*
Sunset Bomber, The, *261, 262, 333*
Superman, *105, 194, 198*
Swarts, Louis ("Louie"), *28-30*

Tai Pan, *213-215*
Tannenbaum, David, *27, 28. 31, 32, 34, 35, 37, 38, 93*
Taylor, Elizabeth, *38, 40, 211*
Time, *184-186*
Time Inc., *184*
Titanic, *321-322*
Toback, James, *144*
Todd, Mike, *38, 39, 40*
Todd, Jr., Mike, *38-40*
Tootsie, *223-226*
Top Rank, *233-234, 235*
Towne, Robert ("Bob"), *187-191, 298*
Tramont, Jean-Claude, *142, 143, 145*
Tropicana Hotel, *115-117, 192*
Trotter, John ("Jack"), *88, 91, 92*
Trump, Donald, *220-222, 313, xi*
20th Century Fox ("Fox"), *133-134, 217, 230, 232-233, 315-316, 321-322*
Two for the Seesaw, *58*
Two Jakes, The, *187-191*

UCLA, *16, 17*
UCLA Hospital, *203*
Universal Studios, *103, 169-170, 180, 292, 227, 241, 297*

Vidal, Gore, *179-192, 227*

Walt Disney Studios, The, *see Disney*
Wapner, Joe (Judge), *82, 83*
Ward, Andre, *235-236*
Warner, Jack, *95, 97*
Warner Bros., *95, 96, 97, 194, 199, 238*
Warner Music, *151, 318*
Wasserman, Lew, *167-169*
Wayne, John, *87*
Webb, Jack, *67-68, 93-97, 125, 167-169, viii-ix*
Weinstein, Bob, *215, 297, 210, 312-313*
Weinstein, Harvey, *147, 272, 310, 312-313*
Weinstein Company, The (TWC), *310, 311*
Wells, Frank, *238-240, 241*
Wild, Wild West, The, *46*
Woods, Bobby, *332*
World Boxing Council (WBC), *112-114*
Writers Guild (WGA), *179-182, 192, 227, 230*

Yates, Herbert ("Herb"), *98-100*
Young & Rubicam (Y&R), *184-186*
Young Frankenstein, *60*

Zeffirelli, Franco, *183*
Zenga, Bo, *298-299*

MARMONT LANE BOOKS WOULD LIKE TO THANK ELLEN BASKIN, TOM ANDRE, ANDREW GOLOMB, ROBERTA DUNNER, CHARLIE HAYGOOD, JIM MCHUGH, AND CYNTHIA BELL FOR THEIR ASSISTANCE IN THE MAKING OF THIS BOOK.

Marmont Lane
BOOKS

MARMONTLANE.COM